POLYANDRY IN ANCIENT INDIA

Polyandry in Ancient India

SARVA DAMAN SINGH

MOTILAL BANARSIDASS PUBLISHERS PRIVATE LIMITED • DELHI

First Published: 1978
Reprint: Delhi, 1988

ISBN: 81-208-0487-2

MOTILAL BANARSIDASS

41 U.A. Bungalow Road, Jawahar Nagar, Delhi 110 007
8 Mahalaxmi Chamber, Warden Road, Mumbai 400 026
120 Royapettah High Road, Mylapore, Chennai 600 004
Sanas Plaza, Subhash Nagar, Pune 411 002
16 St. Mark's Road, Bangalore 560 001
8 Camac Street, Calcutta 700 017
Ashok Rajpath, Patna 800 004
Chowk, Varanasi 221 001

PRINTED IN INDIA

BY JAINENDRA PRAKASH JAIN AT SHRI JAINENDRA PRESS,
A-45 NARAINA INDUSTRIAL AREA, PHASE I, NEW DELHI 110 028
AND PUBLISHED BY NARENDRA PRAKASH JAIN FOR
MOTILAL BANARSIDASS PUBLISHERS PRIVATE LIMITED,
BUNGALOW ROAD, DELHI 110 007

For Kumud

who symbolizes for me

the solace of solitude,

and the silence of love

Sarva Daman

Contents

Acknowledgements

It is a pleasant duty to express my indebtedness to all those who helped me write and publish the present book. I am grateful to Professor A. L. Basham for reading the *Introduction* and the first chapter; to Professor D. P. Singhal for his unceasing interest and encouragement; to Professor B. N. Puri for placing his personal library at my disposal; to Mr. L. R. Shukla and Dr. D. P. Dikshit, former students of mine now lecturers in Lucknow degree colleges, for all kinds of help lovingly given.

To Anwar Nadeem, Manju and Raj Daman, I am indebted for their affectionate participation in the trying process of the book's production. To my wife Kumud, who helped and healed with love, care and solicitude, typed half the book, read proofs and did much more, words of acknowledgement might sound somewhat dumb, if not perfunctory!

Mr. Gopal Narain Bhargava has laid me under a debt of gratitude by printing the book with great expedition and meticulous attention to accuracy as well as technical excellence.

Department of History,
University of Queensland,
St. Lucia, 4067,
Brisbane, Australia.

SARVA DAMAN SINGH

Abbreviations

AB.	*Aitareya Brāhmaṇa.*
ABORI.	*Annals of the Bhandarkar Oriental Research Institute.*
AL.	*Altindisches Leben.*
Āp. Dh. S.	*Āpastamba Dharma Sūtra.*
ASI.	*Archaeological Survey of India.*
AV.	*Atharva Veda.*
Āv. Cū.	*Āvaśyaka Cūrṇi.*
CHI.	*Cambridge History of India.*
ERE.	*Encyclopaedia of Religion and Ethics.*
GS.	*Gṛhya Sūtra.*
HOS.	*Harvard Oriental Series.*
IHQ.	*Indian Historical Quarterly.*
Ind. Ant.	*Indian Antiquary.*
JAOS.	*Journal of the American Oriental Society.*
JDL.	*Journal of the Department of Letters,* Calcutta University.
JRAI.	*Journal of the Royal Anthropological Institute.*
JRAS.	*Journal of the Royal Asiatic Society.*
JUPHS.	*Journal of the U. P. Historical Society.*
KS.	*Kāṭhaka Saṁhitā.*
LSI.	*Linguistic Survey of India.*
Mbh.	*Mahābhārata.*
MS.	*Maitrāyaṇī Saṁhitā.*
Nāyā.	*Nāyādhammakahāo.*
Nisī. Cū.	*Niśītha Cūrṇi.*
RV.	*Ṛgveda.*

ŚB.	*Śatapatha Brāhmaṇa.*
SBE.	*Sacred Books of the East.*
SLAI.	Meyer's *Sexual Life in Ancient India.*
Sm. C.	*Smṛticandrikā.*
SV.	*Sāma Veda.*
TA.	*Taittirīya Āraṇyaka.*
Taitt. B.	*Taittirīya Brāhmaṇa.*
TS.	*Taittirīya Saṁhitā.*
VS.	*Vājasaneyi Saṁhitā.*
ZDMG.	*Zeitschrift der deutschen morgenländischen Gesellschaft.*

Table of Chronology

c. 2500–1500 B.C.	Harappan Civilization, in and beyond the Indus valley.
c. 1600–1000 B.C.	Composition of the Hymns of the *Ṛgveda* and the earlier parts of the later *Saṁhitās.*
c. 1000–900 B.C.	Mahābhārata War.[1]
c. 1000–600 B.C.	Later *Vedas, Brāhmaṇas* and the early *Upaniṣads.*
c. 800–500 B.C.	The *Nirukta.*
c. 700–400 B.C.	The Principal *Śrauta-sūtras,* and some of the *Gṛhya-sūtras* (Āśvalāyana, Āpastamba, etc.).
c. 600–300 B.C.	*Dharmasūtras* of Āpastamba, Gautama, Baudhāyana, Vasiṣṭha, and the *Gṛhya-sutras* of Pāraskara, Baudhāyana and some others.
c. 600–400 B.C.	The Epics in existence as popular poems before they were finally revised. They contain a tradition harking back to the Vedic days.[2]
c. 563–483 B.C.	The Buddha.

[1] Cf. Raychaudhuri, H.C., *Political History of Ancient India,* Fifth Edn., Calcutta, 1950, pp. 7-8.

[2] Cf. Singh, S. D., *Ancient Indian Warfare with Special Reference to the Vedic Period,* Leiden, 1965, *Introduction* and p. 5. Basham (ed.), *A Cultural History of India,* Oxford, 1975, p. XIII, places the "beginning of composition of *Mahābhārata*" around 800 B. C.

c. 500–300 B.C.	The compilation of the *Nikāyas* and the *Vinaya* more or less complete. Aśoka's Bhabru Edict cites passages from the *Sutta Piṭaka*.
c. 400 B.C.–400 A.D.	Compilation of the *Mahābhārata* completed.
c. 300 B.C.–100 A.D.	Kauṭilya's *Arthaśāstra*.[1]
c. 300 B.C.–200 A.D.	*Jātakas*.
c. 300 B.C.–600 A.D.	*Nāyādhammakahāo*.
c. 200 B.C.–200 A.D.	*Manusmṛti*.
c. Ist Century B.C.	Final Composition of the *Rāmāyaṇa*.[2]
c. 100 A.D.–300 A.D.	*Yājñavalkya Smṛti*.
c. 100 A.D.–300 A.D.	*Viṣṇu Dharmasūtra*.
c. 100 A.D.–400 A.D.	*Nārada Smṛti*.
c. 200 A.D.–400 A.D.	*Bṛhaspati Smṛti*.
c. 300 A.D.–600 A.D.	Some of the extant *Purāṇas*, such as *Vāyu*, *Viṣṇu*, *Kūrma*, *Mārkaṇḍeya* and *Matsya*.[3]
c. 4th Century A.D.	*Kāmasūtra* of Vātsyāyana.
c. 400 A.D.–600 A.D.	*Kātyāyana Smṛti*.
c. 448 A.D.	Hūṇas in the Oxus valley.[4]
c. 505 A.D.–587 A.D.	Varāhamihira, author of the *Bṛhat Saṁhitā*.
c. 515 A.D.	Accession of the Hūṇa chief Mihirakula.
c. 600 A.D.–650 A.D.	*Āvaśyaka Cūrṇi*.
627 A.D.	Hiuen-Tsang started on his journey to India.

[1] Cf. Kane, *History of Dharmaśāstra*, Vol. II, Part I, Poona, 1974, p.XI. Basham, *loc. cit.*, places it in its original form before 300 B.C.

[2] The first and seventh books may be somewhat later. Cf. Basham, *loc. cit.*

[3] *Ibid.*, p. XIV, places these early *Purāṇas* between 300 and 400 A. D. The dates given above are based on the *Chronological Table* given by Kane, *loc. cit.*, pp. XI, XII.

[4] Cf. Majumdar, R. C., and others, *An Advanced History of India*, London, 1948, p. 1008.

630 A.D.–644 A.D.	Travelled around in India.
645 A.D.	Hiuen-Tsang left India.
c. 600 A.D.–900 A.D.	Most of the other *Smṛtis*, and some of the *Purāṇas*.
c. 650 A.D.–750 A.D.	*Tantravārtika* of Kumārila.
Between 1000 A.D. and 1027 A.D.	Alberūnī in India.
c. 1200 A.D.–1225 A.D.	*Smṛticandrikā*.[1]

[1] Cf. Kane, *loc. cit.* The dates of the *Dharmaśāstra* literature given in our table are based on his work.

Introduction

The union of *puruṣa* and *prakṛti* quickens the world into being; the metaphorical mating of the sky and the earth (*dyāvāpṛthivī*)[1] proclaims the principle of universal parenthood. The union of the male and the female multiplies life in its myriad forms; the love of man and woman raises progeny that brings the past into the present and perpetuates the race. Erotic impulses brook neither defiance nor indefinite deferment of fulfilment; and the coming together of man and woman fructifies in the family, which has been a feature of almost all levels of cultural development notwithstanding its many variations of form.

Little wonder, then, if we hear that society is rooted in the family; that marriage is the foundation of social existence. Universality of celibacy would be tantamount to racial suicide; hence the Hindu disapproval of the unmarried state for women, and of lifelong celibacy for most men. To be mothers were women created; to be fathers men.[2] Marriage is a bodily rite, *śarīra-saṁskāra,* which every man and woman should perform.

The student and the householder, the hermit and the ascetic, all arise out of the *gṛhasthāśrama,* the order of the householder.[3]

[1] Cf. *RV.*, IV. 56; VI.70; VII.53; X.59.8-10. *RV.*, VI., 70.6 has:....*ūrjaṁ no dyauśca pṛthivī ca pinvatāṁ pitā mātā viśvavidā sudaṁsasā.*

[2] Cf. *Manu,* IX. 96, *prajānārthaṁ striyaḥ sṛṣṭāḥ santānārthaṁ ca mānavāḥ....*

[3] *Ibid.,* VI. 87, *brahmacārī gṛhasthaśca vānaprastho yatistathā/ete gṛhasthaprabhavāś-catvāraḥ pṛthagāśramāḥ //*

In conformity with the *Veda* and the *Smṛti,* the householder is upheld as the best of them all; for it is he who supports the other three.[1] As the ocean shelters the rivers big and small, the householder protects the men of all the orders.[2] As all living beings subsist on air, so all the orders subsist on the wherewithals provided by the householder.[3] Doubtless, the duties of the householder are not for one of 'weak organs'; for they must be sedulously shouldered by a person seeking happiness here, and bliss beyond.[4]

The arch-priest of brahmanical morality, Manu, is not alone in this deliberate attempt at magnifying the role of the householder; Gautama is alike emphatic in his laudation of the family, the mainstay of the race;[5] and, indeed, calls *gṛhastha* the only *āśrama.*[6] We can understand why. The family assures the legitimate expression and fruition of libido, side by side with the fulfilment of social obligations.[7] The *dharmaśāstra* sees in the *gṛhasthāśrama* the main prop of the order of the universe, and of human society. The *arthaśāstra* sees in it the foundation of material culture. The sacred and the secular alike extol the family.

Thus, the family looms large in the story of human evolution; but we cannot pretend even to a semblance of certitude in tracing

[1] *Ibid.*, VI. 89, *sarveṣāmapi caiteṣām vedasmṛti vidhānataḥ | gṛhastha ucyate śreṣṭhaḥ sa trīnetān bibharti hi ||*

[2] *Ibid.*, VI. 90, *yathā nadinadāḥ sarve sāgare yānti saṁsthitiṁ | tathaivāśramiṇaḥ sarve gṛhasthe yānti saṁsthitiṁ ||*

[3] *Ibid.*, III. 77, *yathā vāyuṁ samāśritya sarve jīvanti jantavaḥ | tathā gṛhasthamāśritya vartante sarva āśramāḥ ||* Cf. Also III. 78, *yasmāt trayopyāśramiṇo jñānenānnena cānvahaṁ | gṛhasthenaiva dhāryante tasmājjyeṣṭhāśramo gṛhī ||*

[4] *Ibid.*, III. 79, *sa saṁdhāryaḥ prayatnena svargamakṣayamicchatā | sukhaṁ cehecchatā nityaṁ yo'dhāryo durbalendriyaḥ ||*

[5] *Gautama,* III. 35, *teṣāṁ gṛhastho yoniraprajanatvāditareṣāṁ.*

[6] *Ibid.*, III. 36. *ekāśramyaṁ tvācāryāḥ pratyakṣa-vidhānādgārhasthyasya.*

[7] *Manu,* IX. 28, *apatyaṁ dharmakāryāṇi śuśrūṣā ratiruttamā | dārādhīnastathā svargaḥ pitṝṇāmātmanaśca ha ||*

its origins from the mists of yore. The inevitable cradle of humanity's growth, it is a dynamic institution in interminable dialogue and adjustment with its changing environment. It varies considerably in form not only from one era to another and from one culture to another, but also within eras and within cultures. Forms of family may change or disappear within a culture, yielding place to new ones, constituting an important part of social change. Indian social thinkers are fully conscious that laws must change in temper with the times[1]; that *deśa* (place) and *kāla* (time) condition the character of *dharma*.[2] Happiness is the goal of all human endeavour; and many roads may lead to the elusive millennium. Should we therefore frown upon human institutions that may not form part of our current mores or 'folkways'? It is not condescension that they merit, but informed appreciation with reference to the geographical and environmental factors that brought them into being.

"The combination of mating with parenthood constitutes marriage in higher animals including man."[3] Indeed, all cultures institutionalise this relationship between men and women who copulate in an acceptable way. The word "marriage" conveys the sense of that relationship. Marriage is something more serious than the pleasure of two or more people in each other's company. It is an institution that assures the multiplication of the race, and forms a vital part of the intimate texture of society. It is an adjustment between the biological purposes of nature and the sociological designs of man. It defies definition in its unageing variety, for no definition could cover all its forms throughout the

[1] Cf. *Manu*, I. 85, *anye kṛtayuge dharmāstretāyāṁ dvāpare' pare | anye kaliyuge nṛṇāṁ yugahrāsānurūpataḥ ||*

[2] *Ibid.*, I. 118.

[3] Malinowski, B., *Sex, Culture and Myth*, London, 1963, p.3.

history of civilization.[1]

> Wedlock has gone through very many phases, and has by no means evolved along lines of harmonious and advancing development. Wedlock is a mode of associated life. It is as variable as circumstances, interests and characters make it within the conditions. No rules or laws can control it. They only affect the conditions against which the individuals react.[2]

There have been eras and forms of society in which domination by the male was not quite so certain as some would have us believe. It is significant that the Zulu dictionary defines man as an animal trained by women. Families have been both matriarchal and patriarchal. Both matrifiliation and patrifiliation occur in almost all societies. Some might stress one more than the other; while some might spare themselves definite dogmas of emphasis or equality, leaving it to the individuals to decide which side of the family they would associate with.

The evolution of species visualized by Huxley and Darwin stirred the contemporary anthropologists to investigate the origins of human institutions such as the family, marriage and property.

[1] Cf. Sumner, *Folkways*, pp. 348-49. He points out that the word "marriage" is often enough loosely used to denote wedding, nuptials or matrimony, of which only the last would be an institution.

[2] *Ibid.*, p. 349. Cf. Risley, H., *The People of India*, IInd Edn., Delhi, 1969, p. 214: "All sorts of connubial permutations and combinations have been in vogue in different times and places throughout the world. They have resulted not from any innate deprvity on the part of those who practised them, but from the action of some overmastering social force which disturbed the balance of the sexes and brought about matrimonial connections which we now regard as more or less abnormal."

J. J. Bachofen[1] posited a distant past, when men and women cohabited without constraints of any kind. Promiscuity yielded place to group marriage, in which a group of brothers and sisters lived communally, which in turn led to matriarchy. With what anthropological data he could muster, aided by ancient mythology, Bachofen suggested that feminine revolt against unregulation led to the matrimonial relationship dominated by women. The myth of the Amazons illustrated the establishment of gynocracy; women headed the family; children took their names from their maternal family; and inheritance descended through lines of female succession. Bachofen explained mother right as a consequence of the economic and political supremacy of women in the early stages of primitive society. He could find little evidence to support the suggestion that patriliny was sometimes succeeded by matriliny; but many patrilineal societies contained clear traces of earlier matrilineal cultures. Early "nomadic" existence militated against the development of any deep association between the father and child, whereas a close association between the mother and child was a matter of physical necessity. But the superior might of man told in time and matriarchy was brushed aside by patriarchy.

A Scottish contemporary, J. F. McLennan[2] also advocated the theory of mother right, but on other grounds. It is inconceivable, according to McLennan, that anything but the want of paternal certainty could have long prevented the acknowledgement of kinship through males. He theorized that there was a stage in the progress of men in which a woman was not usually appropriated to a particular man as his wife.[3]

1 Bachofen, J. J., *Das Mutterrecht: Eine Untersuchung über die Gynaikikritie der alten Welt nach ihrer religiosen und rechtlichen Natur*, Stuttgart, 1861.

2 McLennan, J. F., *Primitive Marriage, An Inquiry into the Origin of the Form of Capture in Marriage Ceremonies* (originally published in Edinburgh, 1865), edited by Riviere, P., Chicago, 1970.

3 *Ibid.*, pp. 66-67.

> All the evidence we have goes to show that men were from the beginning gregarious..... We hear nothing in the most ancient times of individuals except as being members of groups. The history of property is the history of the development of proprietary rights *inside* groups, which were at first the only owners, and of all other personal rights—even including the right in offspring—it may be said that their history is that of the gradual assertion of the claims of individuals against the traditional rights of groups.[1]

And "as among other gregarious animals, the unions of the sexes were probably in the earliest times, loose, transitory, and in some degree promiscuous."[2] Promiscuity promoted harmony through lack of jealousy in the groups, which held their women in common. The struggle for food and security affected the balance of the sexes; healthy male children commanded more careful rearing in preference to females, some of whom were considered quite expendable. Thus began the social phenomenon of female infanticide.[3] The males were in a majority in the primitive groups. The origin of exogamy must be referred to that want of balance. And the origin of polyandry, too, must be referred to the same cause.[4]

The children attached to their mothers belonged to the "horde". But when the system of kinship through women was established, "every group stood resolved into a number of small brotherhoods, each composed of sons of the same mother. And within these, the feeling of close kinship would simplify the constitution of the polyandrous arrangement."[5]

[1] *Ibid.*, p. 67.
[2] *Ibid.*
[3] *Ibid.*, p. 68. McLennan also visualizes wars for women, cf. p. 69.
[4] *Ibid.*, p. 68.
[5] *Ibid.*, p. 70.

Polyandry was, McLennan asserted, a modification of and an advance from promiscuity. He referred to tradition found "everywhere" harking back to a time when marriage was unknown, and to some legislator who brought it into being.[1] The *Mahābhārata*[2] refers to an age of sexual unregulation, before Śvetaketu laid down the law that wives and husbands should remain faithful to each other. The Chinese likewise reminisce that "in the beginning men differed in nothing from other animals in their way of life. As they wandered up and down in the woods, and women were in common, it happened that children never knew their fathers, but only their mothers." The emperor Fou-hi prohibited this promiscuous intercourse of the sexes and instituted marriage.[3]

The ancient Egyptians owed the institution of marriage to Menes,[4] and the Greeks to Kekrops. The Greeks had initially no idea of a stable conjugal union. They indulged in permissive promiscuity, and the offspring of these irregular connections bore the mother's name. Kekrops convinced the Athenians that this kind of abuse was not conducive to their well-being, and formulated the laws and rules of marriage.[5] The remote Laplanders' songs refer to Njavvis and Attjis, who instituted marriage and bound their wives by sacred oaths.[6]

[1] *Ibid.*, pp. 71-72.
[2] *Mbh.* I. 113,8-19.
[3] Cf. Goguet, A.Y., *The Origin of Laws, Arts and Sciences,* 3 vols., Edinburgh, 1761, Vol. III, pp. 311, 313.
[4] *Ibid.*, Vol. I, p. 22.
[5] *Ibid.*, Vol. II, p. 19.
[6] Düben, G. von, *Om Lappland och Lapparne,* Stockholm, 1873, p. 330. Westermarck, *The History of Human Marriage,* III edn., London, 1901, p. 9, says that "popular imagination prefers the clear and concrete; it does not recognize any abstract laws that rule the universe. Nothing exists without a cause, but this cause is not sought in an agglomeration of external or internal forces; it is taken to be simple or palpable, a personal being, a god or a king. Is it not natural, then, that marriage, which plays such an important part in the life

In the rudest form of polyandry the wife did not reside with her husbands, who were unrelated to one another, but with her mother or brothers. Her children belonged to her mother's house, where they were born. The next stage saw the wife living in a house of her own, where she cohabited with her husbands according to fixed rules. Despite her partial detachment from her family, her children retained the maternal connection as heirs to the family property. The succeeding stage, the least "rude" of them all, saw the wife going to live with her husbands in their family. Her children were born there; and it was to their fathers' family that they now belonged. "This could only happen when the husbands were all of one blood, and had common rights of property—in short, when they were brothers."[1] The polyandry of the Nairs and the Tibetans represented, respectively, the lower and higher forms of polyandrous evolution.[2]

W. Robertson Smith agreed with McLennan's hypothesis on the basis of his researches on kinship and marriage in early Arabia, and asserted that "male kinship had been preceded by kinship through women only",[3] and that polyandry was a definite stage in the evolution of marriage. It finally led to monogamy with acknowledged individual paternity and male kinship. These concepts arose out of the higher form of polyandry which McLennan identified with the Tibetan. In a marriage of this type the "law of male descent readily establishes itself before the rise of the idea that the child belongs to one father".[4] The brothers with one wife were jointly regarded as the fathers of their children; but as

---

of the individual, as well as in that of the people, should be ascribed to a wise and powerful ruler, or to direct divine intervention?"

[1] McLennan, *op. cit.*, p. 78.

[2] *Ibid.*, p. 79.

[3] Smith, W. Robertson. *Kinship and Marriage in Early Arabia*, New edn., London. 1903, preface. p. xi.

[4] *Ibid.*, p. 146.

time passed, the eldest brother arrogated to himself the headship of the family. He then desired to monopolise his wife and children, and in order to do so, found individual wives for his younger brothers as well. Thus monogamy came to the fore, with its concomitants, individual fatherhood, paternal descent and male kinship.[1]

Morgan[2] showed that women among North American Indians were in no way inferior to men, and enjoyed undoubted advantages in certain respects. They had a matrilocal marriage in the past, as they had even now. Matriarchy followed a stage of general promiscuity and preceded male ascendancy in Morgan's hypothetical reconstruction of an evolutionary sequence.

The triumph of patriarchy over matriarchy marked, according to Engels and Briffault, the beginning of female exploitation by the male. This thesis was propounded by F. Engels in his famous book: *The Origin of the Family, Private Property and the State,* first published in 1884. Briffault believed that the maternal instinct was the original cradle of all tender emotions; and therefore responsible for all human organization.[3] He credited women with the discovery of totemism, witchcraft and religion. In discussing the influence of maternity upon the central role of women, he clearly saw "the relation of innate endowment to social institutions in the shaping of human nature".[4]

[1] *Ibid.,* p. 147. "That the Arabs passed through a stage of polyandry, of the type in which a woman had several members of one kin as her husbands, meets all the conditions of a legitimate hypothesis." Cf. also pp. 164-165, where Robertson Smith says that "Tibetan polyandry must have existed side by side with Nair polyandry". He seems to doubt McLennan's belief that the less "rude" forms grew out of the "ruder" variety.

[2] Morgan, L. H., *Ancient Society, or Researches in the Lives of Human Progress from Savagery, through Barbarism to Civilization,* New York, 1877.

[3] Cf. Briffault, R., *The Mothers,* 3 vols., London, 1927.

[4] Malinowski, B., *Sex, Culture and Myth,* London, 1963, p. 125.

It is now generally conceded that an inflexible, uniform pattern of evolution cannot be hypothesized for the baffling diversity of all human experiences; and that the maternal line of descent does not always warrant the facile assumption of female supremacy, even though history is not innocent of that experience. Plutarch expressly states that women were the sole owners of property in ancient Sparta; and the ancient Indian tradition contains intriguing allusions to *strī-rājya* or realms ruled by women. The greater importance of women in early antiquity is also clearly reflected in the leading deities of humanity in its infancy, who were all feminine. Fromm[1] explains that maternal love is all-protective and unconditional, and therefore the most important. Paternal affection depends on demands, principles and laws. It is conditional on the fulfilment of filial obligations, and is unequally distributed. An all-giving maternal deity assumed preponderance in the context of common nomadic living, in which material wealth and property played a limited minimal role. The rise of property with problems of defence and transmission led to the patriarchal family, and to the inevitable supersession of the female deity by the male.

That the kinship structure rather than biological birth determines descent, becomes clearer with the increasing volume of anthropological evidence. In a number of societies the pater or husband establishes his authority over all the children borne by his wife, even though he is not the genitor.[2] But this discovery does not obliterate the still existing phenomenon of matrilineal descent.[3]

[1] Fromm, E., *The Art of Loving*, New York, 1963.

[2] Cf. Murstein, B.I., *Love, Sex and Marriage through the Ages*, New York, 1974, pp. 10-11.

[3] The maternal family system still exists among the tribes of the Iroquoi's Confederation and other American Indians, and also among certain African, Asian

The Finnish sociologist, E. Westermarck[1] spearheaded a strong attack on the theory of initial promiscuity. He pointed out that prostitutes tended to be relatively infertile. The promiscuous would vanish for the same reason, owing to underreproduction. "Evolution thus gallantly sprang to the defense of the 'moral'."[2] But many species of animals living in total promiscuity have not become extinct on that account. It is probably mechanical overindulgence on the part of prostitutes, drained of all sentiment or emotion, that leads to a partial diminution of fecundity. We must also consider the contraceptive precautions adopted by prostitutes through the ages. And we do not detect any symptoms of the polyandrous societies edging towards extinction owing to underreproduction.

It is partial promiscuity, not total, that we may visualize for early antiquity; for somewhat stable relationships between two or more individuals are bound to arise in any situation in response to personal attractions and inclinations. Man has in fact always coexisted with a measure of promiscuity, sometimes latent, if not blatant; apologetic, if not aggressive.

W. H. R. Rivers called attention to the close association of communal property and sexual communism.[3] The Scythians,

---

and Polynesian groups, such as the Kamchadales, the Chammoros, the Balondas, the Dyaks, the Garos, the Khasis, the Trobriand Islanders, the Tahitians, the Tongans, and the Hovas of Madagascar. Cf. Fielding, William J., *Strange Customs of Courtship and Marriage*, London, 1961, p. 174. The list is by no means exhaustive. The Trobriand Islanders are, according to Malinowski, utterly ignorant of physiological paternity. The process of generation is regarded as a matter between the spirit world and the female organism.

1 Westermarck, E., *The History of Human Marriage*, 3 vols., London, 1921.

2 Murstein, *loc. cit.*, p.11.

3 Rivers, W. H. R , *Social Organization*, New York, 1924, p. 115.

according to Strabo,[1] "possessed all things in common, and specially their wives and children, who were cared for by the whole community". The ancient Britons also practised community of wives and children, and, indeed, had "all things in common."[2]

Sexual communism may coexist side by side with individual marriage in our own times, as we find among the Bororo of Brazil and the Masai of East Africa.[3] It is almost universal among the Chukchee of northeastern Siberia.[4] We may also refer to the experiments in communal living in modern Europe and America, and also in Israel.

The protagonists of matriarchal precedence in the sequence of evolution have been provided food for fresh thought by G. P. Murdock's meticulous study of 250 societies.[5] Varying modes of descent were discovered at different levels of culture; and there were examples of patriarchy preceding matriarchy.

Westermarck[6] was the greatest champion of the eternality of marriage and monogamy. He argued that early man must have lived in monogamous families like the gorilla and

1 Strabo, *Geography*, vii. 3.9. This communism of women and children reminded Strabo of the social ideal of Plato. Cf. *Republic*, V; also Herodotus, *History*, IV. 104; I. 216; IV. 172.

2 Xiphilinus, *Epitome of Dio Cassius, Hist. Rom.*, lxii, 6; cf. also Caesar, *De bello Gallico*, V. 14.

3 Fielding, *op. cit.*, p. 226. The older men among the Bororo are regularly married and live in their respective huts. The bachelors, however, have a special residence of their own, where they jointly own the girls they capture or buy from the village. The Masai practise extensive wife-lending. Cf. *Encyclopaedia Britannica*, 1974.

4 Fielding, *loc. cit.*, p. 227.

5 Murdock G. P., *Social Structure*, New York, 1949.

6 Westermarck, *op. cit.*

the chimpanzee. Larger groups grew out of monogamous beginnings. He pointed out that in many species the male and the female stayed together after mating until the birth of their offspring. The human infant is incapable of taking care of himself for a period of at least ten years or so; which makes it imperative for the parents to stay together longer than animals. Instinct is accountable for this natural tendency; parents do not desert their young except under duress; the principle of natural selection operates in favour of monogamy.[1]

The sexual jealousy of the male is a common trait between man and many other species. It must have been a telling factor supporting pair marriage. Westermarck further reasoned that the primitive tribes' preoccupation with premarital chastity was an instinctive corollary of the pairing instinct, which protected the pubescent for future pairing. He also stressed the usefulness of monogamy in ensuring a mate for every individual in response to equal numbers of men and women.

Westermarck's thesis is seriously challenged by the clear-cut data of Murdock, who tells us that 70% of his societies countenanced premarital sexuality.[2] Malinowski[3] points out that "in some communities pre-nuptial intercourse is not meant to lead to marriage, and among the Masai, Bhuiya and Kumbi of India, two pre-nuptial lovers are not supposed to marry. Among the Trobriand Islanders sexual freedom is considerable." He also draws attention to some societies in which the wife is obliged to submit to the embraces of other men at the very beginning of marriage.

1 I don't know how Westermarck would explain the painful phenomena of rampant divorce and broken homes; and of children borne by single mothers.

2 Murdock, *op. cit.*

3 Malinowski, *Sex, Culture and Myth*, p. 5.

> Such customs express the superstitious awe with which sexual intercourse, and above all defloration, is regarded by primitive peoples. As such they should be considered side by side with the numerous instances in which girls are artificially deprived of their virginity, without the intercourse of any man; with pre-nuptial defloration by strangers; with temporary prostitution of a religious character, and with sexual intercourse as a puberty rite.[1]

In medieval Europe, too, the bride had coitus with someone other than her husband, in the form of *jus primae noctis*, the right of the lord to the bride of one of his subjects.[2]

Murdock's data are also fatal to the argument of one-to-one ratio between the sexes, since they prove that this ratio fails to prevent the formation of polygynous societies. 193 of his societies were characterized by polygyny, as against only 43 by monogamy. Indeed, these statistics negate the assumption that monogamy is a consequence of biological evolution. Human beings are not endowed with any inherently monogamous propensity; but have instead a natural desire for diversity in their sexuality. Some societies are therefore permissive in matters of sex, while some others relax the restraints on extra-marital congress on special occasions; and yet others allow petting and flirtation at their parties.

Westermarck's reference to the primates in support of his conclusions recoiled on him, when fuller evidence revealed that the chimpanzee, the gorilla and the baboon were not at all monogamous. Despite the fact that the females might have a favourite male, they frequently enjoyed sex wherever available,

[1] *Ibid.*, p. 8. Cf. also Rivers, *The Todas*, p. 503.
[2] Cf. *Encyclopaedia Britannica*, 1974, vol. XVI, p. 600.

without even blushing at incest.[1] Briffault mocked Westermarck's vain wish to find Christian morality among the apes.[2]

Desmond Morris[3] lends support to the notion of a pairing instinct among human beings. He pictures early man as a puny creature in a hostile environment, who could effectively use his meagre prowess and primitive weapons only in a hunting band. If the strongest men in a band monopolized all the women, the indispensable aid of the somewhat weaker men would not be readily available in the incessant struggle for survival. Hence each man had to have his woman; and the bands favouring pairing would have the best chance of survival. But the "behavioural" scientists have failed to find any pairing instinct in the case of man, "whose complex central nervous system requires little aid from fixed instinctual responses".[4] In undertaking acts of protest, such as self-immolation and fasts unto death, man disregards the instinct for survival whenever he so decides. And the widespread incidence of premarital sexuality gives the lie to the suggestion that premarital chastity is linked with the elusive instinct of pairing.

Malinowski, however, agreed with Westermarck's contention that "even in its biological aspect..marriage is rooted in the family rather than the family in marriage".[5] He emphasized a difference in kind between man and other animals:

[1] Cf. Murstein, *op.cit.*, p. 12.

[2] Cf. Majumdar, D. N., *Races and Cultures of India*, Fourth edn., Bombay, 1973, p. 165: "Many today take Westermarck's hypothesis of monogamy as wish fulfilment though superimposed on an anthropological edifice; others hold that the theory of family and monogamous marriage derives its sanction from "the myth of middle class morality and perfection, the vulnerability of which was demonstrated during the first world war.... "

[3] Morris, D., *The Naked Ape*, London, 1968.

[4] Murstein, *op. cit.*, p. 12.

[5] Malinowski, *op. cit.*, p. 3.

> In man rut is absent, and sex holds him in permanent readiness and tension. Cultural regulations, the various taboos and barriers step in and fetter him, where natural endowment has left him freer than the beast. They safeguard the family by the prohibition of incest, the clan by rules of exogamy, and the bonds of marriage by the ban on adultery and what might be called the principle of legitimacy.[1]

This biological distinction between men and animals was called in question by Hamilton, Kempt, Sokolowsky, Bingham, Hartman and Miller, who could not discover any period of rut among the primates and many other species.[2] Malinowski[3] maintained that man carried over the family from the stage of animal barbarity to culture; and discounted the possibility of preceding promiscuity on the ground that gregarious proclivities did not furnish the foundations of human organization. But if the very biological basis of such theorizing is dubious if not erroneous, the ship of Westermarck's moral monogamy truly totters on its keel.

H. J. S. Maine[4] was a notable advocate of patriarchy, which was, according to him, almost as old as man. The basis for this conclusion was his belief that the concept of private property could not be harmonized with that of matriarchy. But it was Sigmund Freud[5] who propounded a patriarchal theory with all the frills of a lively imagination. He posited primal hordes in

[1] *Ibid.*, p. 128.
[2] Cf. Majumdar, D. N., *op. cit.*, p. 165.
[3] Malinowski, *Sex and Repression in Savage Society*, London, 1927.
[4] Maine, H. J. S., *Ancient Law*, London, 1861.
[5] Freud. S. *Totem and Taboo*, in A. A. Brill (ed.) *The Basic Writings of Sigmund Freud*, New York, 1938, pp. 807-930; *Moses and Monotheism*, New York, 1955.

early antiquity, each led by a predominant father who kept all the sexually attractive women to himself, to the dismay and deprivation of his sexually mature sons. The sons, however, united, slew and ate their father. The cannibalistic act harked back to the belief that eating a powerful animal or adversary conferred upon the eaters the heroic qualities of the victim. Thus the exercise of eating their father achieved the sons' identification with him. Though they hated their father for his power and possession of the women, they yet loved and looked up to him for his strength and quality of courage. This ambivalence of sentiment led to a consciousness of guilt, which was aggravated by the threat of open competition for the possession of women, and also by the inability of any of the brothers to replace the father. The brothers then developed the taboo of incest, preventing access to mothers and sisters,[1] in a bid to preserve their new-found unity. This taboo might have been helped by the homosexual relationships formed during the period of subjection to the almighty father.

The consciousness of guilt led the sons to look for women outside their immediate surroundings; and that became the basis of the law of exogamy. They also set up a totemic system, under which the father was replaced by an animal. And they prohibited the slaughter of this animal as a gesture of symbolic atonement. The belief gained ground that the animal would, if well looked after, bestow benefits on the group in the form of abundant game and crops. It was during this period that gynocracy came into its own, in the absence of any preeminent male authority. But the unsatiated craving for the father slowly but surely led to the anthropomorphic transfiguration of the totems. Both male and female deities bloomed into being. The appearance of female deities was somewhat tenuously explained

[1] Which suggests that there was no such restriction before.

by Freud as a partial recompense for the gradual transformation of the matriarchy into a patriarchy. "No longer high on the totem pole", the animals were now sacrificed to the gods. A number of gods initially owed a vaguely tentative allegiance to a paternal supergod, who became the sole God with the passage of time, commanding universal allegiance of all earthly inhabitants.

New patriarchs arose, though they were not quite like their awesome predecessor. They observed taboos against murder and incest; and the stronger amongst them grew into chieftains and kings. The patriarchy was transformed into the state, and the primal father was the final victor in a figurative sense, because ultimate power again rested in the "father" of the state.[1]

Freud's theory was the product of his own environment, inspired by the structure of the contemporary European family. It did not accord with all observed societies, which, however, could be explained away by the assertion that their evolution was not yet complete. But Kroeber called it illogical, because the search for brides outside the family should have led to the dispersion of the family instead of uniting it.[2] Franz Boas wondered whether ethnic phenomena represented the simple expression of psychological laws. Totemism displayed deep diversity in different parts of the world; and how could the same psychological source account for such significant variety?[3]

Malinowski asked whether culture was present when the slaying took place. How was the guilt transmitted without benefit of a racial unconscious, if it preceded culture ? He found himself at his wit's end to believe that a group of normal young

[1] E.g., many Indian texts propound a paternal concept of kingship.

[2] Cf. Hays, H. R., *From Ape to Angel. An Informal History of Social Anthropology*, New York, 1960; Murstein, *op. cit.*, p.14.

[3] *Ibid.*

men would suffer years of sexual deprivation before gathering courage to kill their father.

> It is easy to perceive that the primitive horde has been equipped with all the bias, maladjustments and ill tempers of a middle class European family and then let loose in a prehistoric jungle to run riot in a most attractive but fantastic hypothesis.[1]

Fairly early in human history, copulation was subjected to cultural control by banning it between persons "related to one another by a real, assumed, or artificial bond of kinship."[2] The prohibition of sexual intercourse between a man and his mother, sister, daughter and other specified kin is a world-wide phenomenon.[3] Exceptional circumstances at times and places led to departures from the rule. The Egyptian pharaohs married their sisters; and, like them, the Hawaiian and Inca rulers, too, hit upon the device of sibling marriage for preserving the sacrosanct character of the royal line. And the Azande of Africa allowed father-daughter marriage for a high chief.[4]

Some old Iranian and Greek writings, however, suggest the currency of brother-sister as well as father-daughter incest among commoners in ancient Iran.[5] The Indian tradition, likewise,

[1] Hays, *loc. cit.*, p. 224.

[2] Murdock, *Social Structure*, p. 261.

[3] There are all kinds of variations around the world. For example, a man may be permitted or even required to marry his first cousin if she is the daughter of his mother's brother, but may not even touch her if she is the daughter of his father's brother.

[4] Cf. Murstein, *op. cit.*, p. 19.

[5] Cf. Slotkin, J. S., "On a Possible Lack of Incest Regulations in Old Iran", *American Anthropologist*, 1947, 49, pp. 612-615. Also West, E. W., (tr.), *Pahlavi Texts,* Part II. *The Dadistān-ī Dīnīk and the Epistles of Mānūskīhar, SBE,* vol. XVIII, Oxford, 1882, pp. 389 ff.

has clear reminiscences of ancient incest.[1] And Egyptian marriage records have also yielded evidence to show that brother-sister marriage was by no means rare among the Egyptian commoners under Roman rule.[2]

Nevertheless, the ubiquity of the incest taboo has long attracted observers, authors and theorists, who have sought to explain it in a variety of ways. Incest prohibitions may have been dictated by the evolutionary pressures on early man. The avoidance of copulation between siblings and between father and daughter may have kept births in the family within the limits of its economic productivity. The genetic disadvantages of inbreeding to slow-maturing animals bearing single offspring presumably discouraged it; for the harmful effects could sometimes be dramatically demonstrated within one generation.[3] Primitive man was not indeed utterly incapable of prescientific percipience.

Free sexual competition within the family would also tend to undermine its unity.[4] Erotic impulses were therefore frustrated within the family, so that they could be directed outside for the sake of socialization. As the maturing children sought sex elsewhere, the political and social benefits accruing to the family from a growing nexus of crisscrossing affiliations accelerated the process of socialization.

[1] See below, pp. 39-42, 79-80.

[2] Middleton, R., "Brother-sister and Father-daughter Marriage in Ancient Egypt", *American Sociological Review*, 1962, 27, pp. 603-611.

[3] Cf. Adams, M. S., and Neel, J. V., "Children of Incest", *Pediatrics*, 1967, 40, pp. 55-62; cf. also Schull, W. J. and Neel, J. V., *The Effects of Inbreeding on Japanese Children*, New York, 1965; also Murstein, *op. cit.*, p. 22.

[4] In some marriage systems, however, a woman may share her husband with a daughter by an earlier marriage; or a man may share his wife with a son by a different mother.

Thus, the rules of incest and exogamy forced men and women to look beyond the domestic family for the satisfaction of their sexual needs. Claude Lévi-Strauss[1] holds that they did not represent suppression of desire so much as the need to make the individual respect the rule of reciprocity, one of the vital factors of social organization. The prohibition of incest in relation to reciprocity enabled men to part with their women; for they received someone else's daughters and sisters in return for their own. Time and experience vindicated the value of reciprocity, which led to the institution of marriage. The concept of incest, according to Lévi-Strauss, marked the beginning of human culture. But exogamy, not the incest taboo, led to bonds with other groups through marriage rather than copulation, a private activity. Reciprocity could be achieved through various other ways. Despite a fair measure of truth and sense in what he says, Lévi-Strauss fails to provide a total explanation for the strength and severity of attitudes relating to incest.[2]

[1] Lévi-Strauss, Claude, "Reciprocity, the Essence of Social Life", in R.L. Coser (ed.), *The Family : Its Structure and Functions*, New York, 1964, pp. 36-48. Also see his *The Elementary Structures of Kinship (Les Structures élémentaires de la Parenté)*, Revised edn., translated from the French by Bell, J. H., Sturmer, J. R. von, and Needham, R., Editor, Boston, 1969.

[2] Also see Fortune, R. F., "Incest", in R.L. Coser (ed)., *The Family: Its Structure and Functions*, pp. 70-74. The theory of an instinctual horror of incest does not bear scrutiny. Cf. Hobhouse, L. T., Wheeler, G. C., and Ginsberg, M., *The Material Culture and Social Institutions of the Simpler Peoples*, London, 1917. There is no simple, instinctive revulsion against incest; on the contrary, there is a strong element of actual allure. The suggestion that familiarity and habituation extinguish interest, does not at all account for the incest taboo; the theory of "aversion to similarity" is unsubstantiated. The psychoanalysts posit a near-universal desire for incest to explain a near-universal taboo. But the universality of the incestuous wish is called in question by some scholars. Malinowski, questioning Freud's picture of the universality of the "Oedipus complex", suggests that the sibling tie is stronger in its temptation than the parent-child attraction in Trobriand culture. Slater's

That we cannot posit a single sequence or pattern of identical development for all mankind, is the most important lesson learnt from the foregoing discussion. Every theory of the origin of the family is beset with difficulties of one kind and another. Human institutions develop in accordance with endless contingencies, as unpredictable as the quirks of human caprice. Therefore, the journey from the known to the unknown is fraught with the perils of uncertainty and speculation.

That the "primitive" societies of today preserve the earliest forms of the family, is a definitely dubious assumption. "Primitive" is a loaded word, significant only in relation to the level of modern technology, and not quite applicable to the complex kinship protocol of some of these "primitive" peoples, far more detailed and developed than that of "civilized" societies.

The world has been familiar with marriage since recorded history began. We are on the firm ground of facts when we study the forms of marriage actually found in human society; or for

---

"life-expectancy" theory explains incest in terms of the old age, sexual incapacity, or death of parents by the time their children become sexually mature. He fails to account for the taboo against brother-sister marriage. Certainly not all prehistoric parents were too old to perform when their children became old enough to enjoy sex. Cf. Slater, M. K., "Ecological Factors in the Origin of Incest", *American Anthropologist,* 1959, 61, pp. 1042-1059. The fanciful theory of "learned avoidance" postulates frustrating sex experience short of coitus between brother and sister in the pre-puberty period, leading to aversion. The only thing that "learned avoidance" should really mean is that the children in the family are taught and trained not to have sex within the family. Cf. Fox, J. R., "Sibling Incest", *British Journal of Sociology,* 1962, 13, pp. 128-150. Incest taboos are very complex phenomena rooted in deep human impulses and experiences, including apparently ambivalent primary motivations. Just what these are, what they stem from, and how variable they are, remains a question yet to be fully answered.

which there is unmistakable evidence in the past. Group marriage, polyandry, polygyny and monogamy have all been practised before, as they are now, often coexisting in close propinquity. No form is necessarily higher than the other, as the meaning or value of any expression of sexuality is determined by the social context within which it occurs.

Scholars, such as W. H. R. Rivers, S. C. Das, A. Aiyappan, K. P. Chattopadhyay, Kathleen Gough, Fürer-Haimendorf, D. G. Mandelbaum, Prince Peter, K. M. Panikkar and D. N. Majumdar, studied polyandry in modern India with reference to specific areas or peoples; but the investigation of its past history in the Indian context remains a desideratum. Modern institutions contain clear vestiges of the past; and the past of polyandry in ancient India is the main concern of the present book. What is the literary evidence for its prevalence in the past ? Was it practised only by non-Āryans, or was it common to both Āryans and non-Āryans ? What was the social attitude to polyandry reflected in literature ? How did the institution increasingly succumb to monogamy or polygyny, in which man acquired the right to have more than one wife; but woman was deprived of the right to have more than one husband ? All these changes in attitudes and institutions form fascinating subjects of historical enquiry. We therefore propose to fill a gap in historical research with reference to an institution as interesting as it is ancient, as significant as it is slighted, or sought to be swept under the carpet.

Most of the earlier scholarly statements splendidly illustrate the turning of the proverbial blind eye to polyandry in ancient India. Macdonell and Keith assert that "polyandry is not Vedic. There is no passage containing any clear reference to such a custom."[1]

[1] *Vedic Index*, vol. I, pp. 115-116. Cf. Keith in *CHI*, vol. I, pp. 79, 88; Hopkins, *JAOS*, XIII, pp. 354-355; *CHI*, vol. I, p. 230; Westermarck, *The History of Human Marriage*, 3rd edn., London, 1921, vol. III, p. 143.

Meyer is also equally emphatic in his opinion that "polyandry is nowhere found in the Veda",[1] and mocks at the notion of "the development of marriage by way of promiscuity and other horrors, into monogamy".[2] Winternitz[3] states that he cannot believe that the *Chāndogya Upaniṣad* refers to polyandry. Professor B. S. Upadhyaya[4], however, concedes that the *Ṛgveda* "does refer to a stage however remote from the Ṛgvedic age, when the practice actually obtained, but had become defunct in the period under our survey." Kane[5] cannot find a single Vedic passage clearly referring to the practice of polyandry. Typical of this attitude is the statement of Altekar who says that the custom is "practically unknown to Hindu society".[6] I. B. Horner would have us believe that "the custom did not obtain at the time of the rise of Budddhism".[7] And Mildreth Pinkham[8] cannot make up her mind in relation to the Hindu scriptures. Shakambari Jayal's book on the status of women in the epics devotes a small paragraph to the polyandry of Draupadī, an isolated "single case".[9]

[1] Meyer, *Sexual Life in Ancient India*, London, 1930, vol. I, p. 115, n. 2.

[2] *Ibid.*, p. 116, n.

[3] Winternitz, *Die Frau in den indischen Religionen*, vol. I, p. 51. Cf. *Chāndogya Up.*, IV. 4.2.

[4] Upadhyaya, B. S., *Women in the Ṛgveda*, 3rd edn., Delhi, 1974, p. 124.

[5] Kane, P. V., *History of Dharmaśāstra*, vol. II, Pt. I, 2nd edn., Poona, 1974, p. 554. He echoes the authors of the *Vedic Index*, whom he cites in support. He wants us to believe that "in those ancient times polyandry was unheard of". Cf. *ibid.*

[6] Altekar, A. S., *The Position of Women in Hindu Civilization*, 2nd edn., Delhi, 1973, p. 112.

[7] Horner, I. B., *Women under Primitive Buddhism*, London, 1930, p. 40.

[8] Pinkham, Mildreth Worth, *Woman in the Sacred Scriptures of Hinduism*, New York, 1941, pp. 34, 155.

[9] Jayal, S., *The Status of Women in the Epics*, Delhi, 1966, pp. 95-96. A perfunctory appendix on polyandry, contained in a page or so, calls the custom quite unfamiliar to the Vedic society. Cf. pp. 314-316.

S. C. Sarkar[1] is indeed a rare scholar, who comes to the conclusion that polyandry was known to the *Vedas*. But some of his sweeping statements call for a cautious review. Sociologists, such as Iravati Karve[2], K. M. Kapadia[3] and D. P. Vora[4] also attest the existence of polyandry in ancient India. P. Thomas's work[5] on Indian women through the ages is overambitious in its scope and inadequately documented; and makes only passing allusions to polyandry.

Indeed, the classic instance of the polyandrous Kaṇhā (Draupadī) who "lusted yet for more, and with a hump-backed dwarf played the whore", is, explanatory excuses apart, by no means solitary. The practice of polyandry, known alike to the gods and men, harks back to the age of the *Ṛgveda*. The *Vedas*, the *Sūtras* and the *Smṛtis*, the *Mahābhārata* and the *Rāmāyaṇa*, the Buddhist texts as well as the Jaina, Kauṭilya and the *Kāmasūtra* all attest its existence in early India. And the evidence of literature is reinforced by the later iconography and art, and by the presence of polyandrous pockets from Tibet in the north right down to Ceylon in the south. Doubtless, polyandry was widely prevalent in the ancient world in one form and another; and its traces still exist in the life and literatures of many lands. Later day morality sought to ignore or to explain away its past presence; but should we, too, view it with a hypocritical horror at a time when both in the east and west many mores of the traditional society are in the melting pot of moral scepticism and reasoned rejection ?[6]

1 Sarkar, S. C., *Some Aspects of the Earliest Social History of India* (Pre-Buddhist Ages), London, 1928.
2 Karve, Iravati, *Kinship Organization in India*, 2nd edn., Bombay, 1965.
3 Kapadia, K. M., *Marriage and Family in India*, 3rd edn., Bombay, 1966.
4 Vora, D. P., *Evolution of Morals in the Epics*, Bombay, 1959.
5 Thomas, P., *Indian Women through the Ages*, London, 1964.
6 My interest in the subject dates back to 1971, when I presented a paper on "Polyandry in Ancient India" to the International Congress of Orientalists held in Canberra.

We must look at polyandry as an institution not at all to be ashamed of, if only some people practise it,[1] and most don't. The needs of a given human and natural situation evoke specific social institutions, and purveyors of value judgements would do well to leave history and its study to those who would substitute understanding for judgement as tendentious as it may be egregious.

We shall carefully analyse all the ancient Indian evidence on the subject, and attempt to explain the practice of polyandry with reference to the environmental imperatives that produced it. If our study helps enlarge, in whatever measure, our horizons of empathy and understanding, without obsession with the ever-shifting mores of the moment, we shall deem our labours duly rewarded.

[1] In an address to the *Indian Science Congress* of January, 1940, D. N. Majumdar pointed out that polyandry was practised by nearly forty million people all over the world. Reported in *The Madras Mail,* January 5, 1940, under the title "Marriage Customs of cis-Himalayan Tribes".

CHAPTER ONE

What is Polyandry?

The Greek word *polyandria* derived from *polyandros* is the parent of the English term "polyandry", made up of "poly+ andr-, anĕr+ia–y", referring to the "condition of [a woman] having many men". Its antonym "polygyny", composed of *poly* and *gynia*, signifies "the condition of [a man] having many women". Neither of the two words contains any etymological connotation of marriage. "Polygamy", usually understood in the sense of a man marrying more than one woman, comes from *poly* and *gamia* meaning "many marriages", and should, properly speaking, cover both polyandry and polygyny.

McLennan took polyandry to signify the marriage of one woman to more than one man. In a letter addressed to Charles Darwin he wrote:

> ....It gives men *wives.* Till men have wives they may have tastes, but they have no obligations in matters of sex. You may be sure polygyny in the earlier stage never had the sanction of *group opinion.* They would all envy and grieve at the good of their polygynous neighbour. Polygyny, then, did not at first give men wives. Wifedom begins with polyandry which is a contract.[1]

Lubbock (Lord Avebury) found it "far from easy to dis-

[1] McLennan. *Studies in Ancient History,* New York, 1896, pp. 50-51.

tinguish between communal marriage and true polyandry".[1] Spencer considered polyandry "as one of the kinds of marital relations emerging from the primitive unregulated state; and one which has survived where competing kinds, not favoured by the conditions, have failed to extinguish it".[2] And Briffault[3] regarded it as a remnant of group marriage.

Those who regarded polyandry as a consequence of harsh living conditions, included Sumner,[4] Keller,[5] Vinogradoff[6] and Westermarck.[7] In an article on "Marriage" in the *Encyclopaedia Sexualis*,[8] Westermarck expressed his opposition to McLennan's notion of polyandrous evolution in the following words :

> To explain polyandry is to trace it to its causes and when this is done, it is found that certain circumstances lead

[1] Lubbock, Sir J., *The Origin of Civilization and the Primitive Condition of Man*, 5th edn., New York, 1892, p. 145.

[2] Spencer, *The Principles of Sociology*, 3 vols., 3rd edn., New York, 1921, vol I, pp. 656-657.

[3] Briffault, *The Mothers*, London, 1927, vol. I, pp. 628-629.

[4] Sumner, *Folkways*, 1940, p. 351: "Polyandry is due to a hard struggle for existence or to a policy of not dividing property. A Spartan who had a land allotment was forced to marry. His younger brothers lived with him and sometimes were also husbands to his wife. Wives were also lent out of friendship or in order to get vigorous offspring." Cf. Xenophon, *Lacedamon*, I. 7.8; Plutarch, *Lycurgus*, 15.

[5] Sumner and Keller, *The Science of Society*, 4 vols., New Haven, 1927, vol III, pp. 1857-1863.

[6] Vinogradoff, Sir P. *Outlines of Historical Jurisprudence*, vol. I, New York, 1920, pp. 199-200.

[7] Westermarck, E., *The History of Human Marriage*, vol. III, pp. 187-191. Cf. Linton, Ralph, *The Study of Man*, New York, 1936, pp. 182-183: "Any social worker will testify that even in our society hard times often result in what is essentially a polyandrous arrangement, although the secondary husband is usually known as a boarder."

[8] *Encyclopaedia Sexualis*, 1935.

> to unions in which the husbands are brothers and other circumstances to unions in which they are not so; but I see no reason whatsoever to assume that the former kind of union has developed out of the latter. It would indeed be rather surprising if a people so cultivated as the Nayars had preserved the primitive form while lower castes living in the same neighbourhood had grown out of it and changed their polyandry into fraternal.

And in *The History of Human Marriage*[1] Westermarck listed the principal causes conducive to polyandry, supported by concrete illustrations from various parts of the world. The first of these causes is the disequilibrium in the ratio of the sexes. There may be more men than women in a given society for a variety of reasons. Affluence is said to breed more females, and austerity males. Female infanticide may disturb the sex ratio, as does the selling of women outside the community. A sizeable immigration of male bachelors may also result in a scarcity of women, which may be accentuated by female deaths in child-bearing, or by the practice of polygyny among some peoples.

The second cause is economic. An inhospitable and poor terrain may necessitate curbs on the growth of population. Where fragmentation of small properties would lead to economic perdition, the need to keep the family property undivided would make polyandry a panacea. It would reinforce the bond of fraternity and ensure the pooling of property and manpower for purposes of production. A. R. Radcliffe-Brown[2] actually explains adelphic polyandry in terms of the unity and solidarity of the sibling group. But as in Tibet and elsewhere, we may also have to

[1] Westermarck, *loc. cit.*, ch. XXX.

[2] Radcliffe-Brown, A. R., "The Study of Kinship Systems", *JRAI*, vol. LXXXI, 1941.

reckon with the phenomenon of non-adelphic polyandry involving fathers and sons, and uncles and nephews.[1]

When the wealthy practise polyandry, that is because they want to keep their wealth undivided, and their influence unimpaired. When the bride-price in some areas is too high for a single individual to afford, many men pool their resources to purchase a common wife.[2] Household expenses in some pastoral cultures may be more easily defrayed by pooling the heads of cattle amongst a given number of owners, made possible by their collective marriage to one woman. The Toda polyandry, however, provides a conspicuous exception to this proposition.[3]

The prolonged absence of men from their homes, necessitated by the demands of their profession or livelihood, may also

1 Prince Peter, *A Study of Polyandry*, The Hague, 1963, pp. 53, 557-559. Cf. also Sumner, *Folkways*, p. 367, where we are told of a custom widely prevailing in many parts of Russia and the contiguous Slavonic regions until the 19th century. The father married his son, as a boy, to a mature young woman, whom he then made his own concubine. By the time the boy grew up into a mature male, his wife was already advanced in life and the mother of several children. He then did what his father had done before him. This custom also existed in Bulgaria. It was not polyandry, but could the father be called a cicisbeo?

2 Prince Peter, *loc. cit.*, p. 62, refers to the instance of "near-polyandry" in modern France, where Polish coal-miners working in the north clubbed together to have a woman in common. They all made equal contributions to support her, and were provided an evening meal and a night's entertainment at the woman's quarters, each according to his turn. There was no marriage; yet the affinity of such an orderly arrangement with the character of polyandry would be undeniable.

3 Cf. *ibid.*, p. 560, where Peter points out that the Todas have "an unusual type of polyandry, apparently divorced from what is elsewhere always the essential correlate of the institution, namely, the non-division of the inherited family property. Toda brothers share one wife in common, but their buffaloes are at the same time individually owned, as is also any other form of property that they may have."

lead to polyandry in some societies to ensure protection and support for their wives by their kinsmen. More often than not, the polyandry arising out of these circumstances is fraternal in character. But in case of the Nayars, men of the martial class, the consequent polyandry was non-fraternal. The hereditary profession of arms obligating the males of a whole race to military service from the days of youth to the decline of manhood "was a system of policy utterly incompatible with the marriage state".[1] The military preoccupation of the Nayars took an inevitable toll of their manhood and created a constant disparity in the male-female ratio of their population. As Majumdar remarks, this "should have led to polygyny rather than monogamy, but as matriarchal residence was incompatible with polygyny, the Nair reaction was definitely against it."[2]

The desire to have children despite his physical inadequacy may induce a man to call in another person to sire his children. This person may be a kinsman, but in most cases he is not; and the consequence is non-adelphic polyandry. If the wife has freedom to choose her husbands, she may bring in a more potent partner to make up for the deficiency of her present husband. Thus the desire for offspring or for improved sexual relations may alike lead to polyandry. The female wish for a greater measure of happiness, prestige and security may in some cases provide the main motivation.

The sixth edition of *Notes and Queries on Anthropology* defines polyandry as the institution or custom "by which a woman is permitted to have more than one husband at the same time."[3] It also defines cicisbeism as a more or less permanent union of a

[1] Majumdar, D. N., *The Matrix of Indian Culture,* Lucknow, 1947, p. 7.

[2] *Ibid.,* pp. 6-7.

[3] *Notes and Queries on Anthropology,* Royal Anthropological Institute, 6th edn. 1951, reprinted 1954, p. 71.

woman with one or more men without giving them the full status of consort.[1] Thus there is no ritual of marriage in cicisbeism.

What, then, do we understand by marriage? The *Notes and Queries* define marriage as "a union between a man and a woman such that children born to the woman are recognized legitimate offspring of both parents." This definition implies that marriage is a union between one man and one woman, and that it establishes the legitimacy of children[2]. Westermarck was fully conscious of the pitfalls of definitive formulation when he described marriage as "a more or less durable connection between male and female, lasting beyond the mere act of propagation till after the birth of the offspring." Quite understandably, then, the *Notes and Queries*' definition of marriage has been called in serious question. The meaning of marriage must therefore be clearly grasped before we proceed with our study of polyandry in ancient India.

Fischer[3] agrees that the purpose of marriage lies in the principle of legitimacy. He argues that the concept of polygamy should be applied to situations in which the polygamous spouse goes through a succession of marriage rites with different partners. In adelphic polyandry, "the woman does not contract different successive marriages. There is no reason for this since the social position of her children is guaranteed completely by the fact that she is married." Her marriage, with which her community is

[1] *Ibid.*, p. 118.

[2] Cf. Malinowski, B., "Parenthood, The Basis of Social Structure", in R.L. Coser (ed.), *The Family: Its Structure and Functions*, New York, 1964, p. 10, n. 2: ". . . .plural marriages such as polygyny and polyandry, are always based on an individual legal contract between one man and one woman, though these contracts may be repeated."

[3] Cf. Fischer, H. Th., "Polyandry," *International Archives for Ethnography*, vol. XLVI, Leiden, 1952

concerned, makes her husband the social father of her children. Fischer coins a new term, "polykoity", from the Greek *polukoiteoo* derived from *koite*, "bed", to describe all plural relations between the sexes, whether between a woman and many men, or between a man and many women. Polykoity thus includes both polyandry and cicisbeism; and polyandry is a form of polykoity "tolerated and recognized by the community".[1] Polyandry "is met with almost exclusively as a form of polykoity", i.e., without polygamy or multiple marriages, which would be pointless because a woman's marriage to one of her husbands would suffice to ensure the legitimacy of her progeny. Polyandry must include cicisbeism to prove its existence.[2]

Fischer's criteria cannot be easily applied to situations where the role of social father is assigned to different husbands, as among the Todas. Furthermore, the *pursütpimi* ceremony among the Todas may confer paternity on a man who may not be one of the woman's married husbands.[3] And how would Fischer explain the phenomenon of corporate polyandry among the Iravas,[4] who at once vest several individuals with the paternal role ?

E. R. Leach[5] agrees that marriage must be adequately defined before we attest the existence of polyandry in any society. A definition only in terms of legitimacy is inadequate, as several distinguishable classes of rights are discernible in the institutions

[1] *Ibid.*, p. 106.

[2] Cf. also Piddington, R., *An Introduction to Social Anthropology*, p. 115: "It is probable that many if not all alleged examples of fraternal polyandry are in fact forms of cicisbeism."

[3] Prince Peter, *op. cit.*, p. 510.

[4] Cf. Tambiah, S. J., "Polyandry in Ceylon with Special Reference to the Laggala Region", in Fürer-Haimendorf (ed.), *Caste and Kin in Nepal, India and Ceylon*, Bombay, 1966, p. 265.

[5] Leach, E. R., "Polyandry, Inheritance and the Definition of Marriage", *Man*, vol. 55, no. 199, 1955.

commonly classed as marriage. The legal and social concomitants of marriage are not always and everywhere identical; and a comprehensive definition of marriage must include several subtypes of the institution. To quote Leach:

> On the one hand we have a formal and legal arrangement, by which, so far as Ceylon is concerned, a woman can only be married to one man at a time......On the other hand we have another institution of 'marriage', which is entered into quite informally but which nevertheless, by virtue of its public recognition, serves to provide the children with claims upon the patrimonial property of the men with whom the woman cohabits and publicly resides.......... If we accept this second institution as a form of 'marriage', then polyandry in Ceylon is a form of polygamy. If we confine the term 'marriage' to the first institution, polyandry in Ceylon is a form of polykoity.[1]

Kathleen Gough[2] disputes the definition of marriage as "a union between a man and woman",[3] but accepts its function of legitimizing progeny. Marriage, as she sees it, constitutes "a relationship between a woman and one or more other persons, which provides that a child born to the woman under circumstances not prohibited by the rules of the relationship is accorded full birth-status rights common to normal members of his society or social stratum."[4]

[1] *Ibid.*

[2] Gough, Kathleen, E., "The Nayars and the Definition of Marriage", *Journal of the Royal Anthropological Institute*, vol. 89, pt. I, 1959.

[3] *Notes and Queries on Anthropology*, 1954.

[4] Gough, K. E., *loc. cit.*

As we have pointed out before,[1] any attempt at defining marriage is a self-defeating exercise, if unanimous acceptance is what we are looking for. We agree that mere access to "another man's wife" should not be classed as polyandry. But if an arrangement involving a woman and many men becomes synonymous with or indistinguishable from what may be commonly connoted by marriage in terms of stability, recognition, birth-status and property rights of children in a given section of any society, it does not matter that the formal ceremonial ritual was not gone through in case of all men. Stable relationships characterized by well-defined sexual rights, joint economic interests and hearths and homes, enjoying the same status and recognition in public opinion as accorded to any other form of marriage, make any distinction between polyandry and so-called cicisbeism somewhat pedantic and unnecessary. We must also beware of the danger of forcing modern definitions of marriage on the past. Voltaire was not wrong when he accused scholars of playing tricks on the dead. The 18th century Italian cicisbeo was a European phenomenon, and did not have his carbon-copies in other continents. His analogy cannot be validly applied to institutions far removed in time and space and wholly legitimized by stability and social sanction. Some modern definitions of marriage serve only to circumscribe its true dimensions; and attempts at watertight classifications ignore the inclusive rather than exclusive situations of the past as well the present. For example, as D. N. Majumdar points out, polyandry of the cis-Himalayan tribes exists along with monogamy, polygyny and even group-marriage when several brothers "marry several wives without the exclusive right of any one brother to any one wife".[2]

Kauṭilya was no doubt right when he said that no kind

[1] See above, Introduction, pp. 3-4.

[2] Majumdar, D. N., *Races and Cultures of India*, p. 164.

of marriage was prohibited, provided that it pleased all those that were concerned with it.[1] The Sanskrit word for marriage, *vivāha*,[2] simply means "leading away" or "taking a wife", and the traditional Hindu classification of marriages includes such forms as the *gāndharva*, the *rākṣasa* and the *paiśāca,* that do not involve any ceremonial ritual.[3] Unequivocal social sanction with corresponding obligations is thus more important than mere ritual, the cause of protracted academic quibbles amongst students of polyandry. We have been repeatedly reminded that polyandry is a product or concomitant of harsh living conditions in an unfriendly and penurious environment.[4] Doubtless, then,

[1] *Kauṭilya*, III. 2.13, *sarveṣām prītyāropaṇamapratiṣiddham*. Cf. Shamasastry, R., (tr.), *Kauṭilya's Arthaśāstra*, Fifth edn., Mysore, 1956, p. 172; also Kangle, *The Kauṭilīya Arthaśāstra*, Part I, p. 99.

[2] Cf. Monier Williams, *Skt-English Dictionary, s. v.*

[3] Cf. *Kauṭilya*, III. 2.6, *mithaḥ samavāyād gāndharvaḥ;* 8, *prasahyādānād rākṣasaḥ;* 9, *suptamattādānāt paiśācaḥ.* Also, *Manu*, III. 21, 32, 33, 34. *Gāndharva* is a secret association between lovers; *rākṣasa* is the forcible seizure of a maiden; and *paiśāca* is the seizure of a sleeping or intoxicated maiden.

[4] See above, text and footnotes 4, 5, 6 and 7 on p. 28. Prince Peter examines various reasons regarded as responsible for polyandry, and says that "historical tradition is a good one, a sex ratio favouring men is a bad one, sociological reasons are indifferent explanations, but economic ones are perhaps the most satisfactory of them all. Among others, individual reasons given, the desire that brothers should not quarrel appears to weigh heavily with the people themselves; this is sometimes expressed in the form of not wanting many sisters-in-law, so that the menfolk will not become involved in their differences." Cf. Peter, *op. cit.,* p. 568.

He then proposes an anthropological theory of polyandry: "Polyandry is a latent male homosexual and near-incestuous form of the marital institution, correlated with excessive economic and social pressure on the nuclear family of peoples living in a difficult natural or social environment, provided no cultural norm is opposed to it; it persists through historical tradition, or as the result of a reactionary 'national' defence mechanism." *Ibid.,* p. 569. The psycho-analytic component of this formulation is somewhat baffling, if not incomprehensible. For a reasoned criticism of his theory see Tambiah, *op. cit.,* pp. 305-307.

the life of early man was by no means easy; food was scarce and hard to come by; and a grim struggle for survival weighed ever so heavily on his unresting hands. That polyandry in antiquity was much more common than it is now, is a conclusion reinforced by its continually receding frontiers.[1] That it was known to the Āryan and the non-Āryan, the rich and the poor alike in ancient India, is clearly borne out by the evidence presented in the pages that follow.

[1] The reformed Hindu Code recognizes only monogamy as a lawful form of marriage. Polygyny and polyandry now have no legal basis.

CHAPTER TWO

Polyandry in the Vedic Period

The *Ṛgveda* depicts the Āryans as a dynamic race full of verve and vigour, hope and adventure. The echoes of their hymnal songs are as audible across the ages as the dour din of their battle-drums. They fight as inveterately as they love and proliferate; and pray for power and progeny, long life and good health; for profusion of food and drinks; for victory and the extermination of their foes. Their hymns brimming with theatrical thunder and loud declamation proclaim the reality of life despite its transience, and portray its ruling passions in all their febrile or ecstatic intensity. They do not strut on the stage of life without a sense of its promise and enjoyment untainted by the shadow of pessimism. An onrushing people in the throes of migration, rocked by opposition as well as rancorous internecine feuds, need men in order to win. And the men need women in order to multiply. Thus migratory hardships lead to institutions and relationships often at variance with what we may regard as right or wrong at a later date.

The *Ṛgveda* is fully cognizant of marriage as attested in the expression, "the wife is the home".[1] Indeed, marriage leads to a life of piety and rectitude;[2] and to procreation, a divine function, instanced by the union of *dyāvā-pṛthivī*, the heaven and the earth,

[1] *RV.*, III.53.4., *jāyedastaṁ.*

[2] *Ibid.*, X.85.24. *ṛtasya yonau sukṛtasya loke . . .*

styled as *pūrvaje pitarā*[1] or the primeval parents. The *Āvestā* in Iran also knows marriage, and tells us that the oblations offered by a maiden or a bachelor are unacceptable alike to the gods and ancestors.[2]

Thus we do not find promiscuity in the *Ṛgveda*, even though we have unmistakable evidence of considerable sexual freedom amongst the Āryans. There are clear references to an epoch when sexual relations between brother and sister, father and daughter, were neither impermissible nor unheard of. The famous dialogue between Yama and Yamī (X.10) visualizes the union of brother and sister despite the remonstrance of Yama, who refuses to oblige his sister. Yamī's words emphasize the antiquity and desirability of brother-sister marriage; but those of Yama mark the prohibitive morality of a new age. To cite Yamī:

> Yea, this the immortals seek of thee with longing,
> progeny of the sole existing mortal.
> Then let thy soul and mine be knit together, and as
> a loving husband take thy consort.[3]
> ......
> Even in the womb god Tvaṣṭar, vivifier, shaping
> all forms, creator, made us consorts.
> None violates his holy ordinances: that we are his
> the heavens and earth acknowledge.[4]
> ......
> I, Yamī, am possessed by love of Yama, that I may

1 *Ibid.*, VII.53.2; X.65.8, *pitarā pūrvajā*; cf. also I.159.2. They are called *mātarā* in I.159.3; and *janitrī* in I.185.6. *AB.*, IV.27.5 speaks of their marriage.

2 *Ashi Yashta*, C, X.54.

3 *RV.*, X.10.3, *uśanti ghā te amṛtāsa etadekasya cit tyajasaṁ martyasya / ni te mano manasi dhāyyasme janyuḥ patistanva 'mā viviśyāḥ /.*

4 *Ibid.*, 5, *garbhe nu nau janitā dampatī kardevastvaṣṭā savitā viśvarūpaḥ / nakirasya pra minanti vratāni veda nāvasya pṛthivī uta dyauḥ /.*

> rest on the same couch beside him.
> I as a wife would yield me to my husband. Like
> car-wheels let us speed to meet each other.[1]
> ......
> ...In heaven and earth the kindred pair commingle.[2]

Yama replies:

> Thy friend loves not the friendship which considers
> her who is near in kindred as a stranger.
> Sons of the mighty Asura, the heroes, supporters of
> the heavens, see far around them.[3]
> ......
> Shall we do now what we ne'er did aforetime? We who
> spake righteously now talk impurely?[4]
> ......
> Who knows that earliest day whereof thou speakest?
> Who hath beheld it? Who can here declare it?
> Great is the law of Varuṇa and Mitra. What, wanton,
> wilt thou say to men to tempt them?[5]
> ......
> They stand not still, they never close their eyelids,
> those sentinels of gods who wander round us.
> Not me—go quickly, wanton, with another, and
> hasten like a chariot wheel to meet him.[6]
> ......

[1] *Ibid.*, 7, *yamaṣya mā yamyaṁ kāma āgan tsamāne yonau sahaśeyyāya | jāyeva patye tanvaṁ riricyāṁ vi cidvṛheva rathyeva cakrā |*

[2] *Ibid.*, 9,... *divā pṛthivyā mithunā sabandhū* ...

[3] *Ibid.*, 2, *na te sakhā sakhyaṁ vaṣṭyetat salakṣmā yadviṣurūpā bhavāti | mahasputrāso asurasya vīrā divo dhartāra urviyā pari khyan |*

[4] *Ibid.*, 4, *na yat purā cakṛmā kaddha nūnamṛtā vadanto anṛtaṁ rapema... |*

[5] *Ibid.*, 6, *ko aṣya veda prathamasyānhaḥ ka īṁ dadarśa ka iha pra vocata | bṛhanmitrasya varuṇasya dhāma kadu brava āhano vīcyā nṛn |*

[6] *Ibid.*, 8, *na tiṣṭhanti na ni miṣantyete devānāṁ spaśa iha ye caranti | anyena madāhano yāhi tūyaṁ tena vi vṛha rathyeva cakrā |*

> Sure there will come succeeding times when brothers
> and sisters will do acts unmeet for kinsfolk.
> Not me, O fair one,— seek another husband, and
> make thine arm a pillow for thy consort.[1]
> ......
> I will not fold mine arms about thy body: they call
> it sin when one comes near his sister.
> Not me,—prepare thy pleasures with another : thy
> brother seeks not this from thee, O fair one.[2]

Yamī speaks of the sanctity of custom upholding the marriage of twins, and accuses Yama of violating a holy ordinance. The latter seeks refuge in the evolving concepts of incest taboos and exogamy. He is afraid of "public opinion", of the laws of Mitra and Varuṇa; of the unwinking eyes of gods' sentinels. The fear of detection and censure is the greatest deterrent. Hence the outburst of Yamī :

> Is he a brother when no lord is left her ? Is she a
> sister when destruction cometh ?
> Forced by my love these many words I utter. Come
> near, and hold me in thy close embraces.[3]
> ......
> Alas! thou art indeed a weakling, Yama, we find in
> thee no trace of heart or spirit.
> As round the tree the woodbine clings, another will
> cling about thee girt as with a girdle.[4]

[1] *Ibid.*, 10, *ā ghā tā gacchānuttarā yugāni yatra jāmayaḥ kṛṇavannajāmi / upa barbṛhi vṛṣabhāya bāhumanyamicchasva subhage patiṁ mat /*

[2] *Ibid.*, 12, *na vā u te tanvā tanvaṁ saṁ papṛcyāṁ pāpamāhuryaḥ svasāraṁ nigacchāt / anyena mat pramudaḥ kalpayasva na te bhrātā subhage vaṣṭyetat /*

[3] *Ibid.*, 11, *kiṁ bhrātāsadyadanāthaṁ bhavati kimu svasā yannirṛtirnigacchāt / kāmamūtā bahve tadrapāmi tanvā me tanvaṁ saṁ pipṛgdhi /*

[4] *Ibid.*, 13. *bato batāsi yama naiva te mano hṛdayaṁ cāvidāma / anyā kila tvāṁ kakṣyeva yuktaṁ pari ṣvajāte libujeva vṛkṣaṁ /*

We have quoted extensively from *RV.*, X.10 to bring out the growth of exogamous practices in Āryan society. The spirited assertion of a woman's right made by Yamī to unite in the fullness of desire with whomsoever she likes, is as candidly reiterated in the later texts, and is doubtless symptomatic of a society where women enjoy social and sexual freedom. There are other examples of incest in the *Ṛgveda*, between father and daughter, mother and son. The Ṛgvedic poet can with impunity imagine such relationships between the Vedic deities. We hear of the love and union of Prajāpati and his daughter;[1] of Pūṣan wooing his mother;[2] of Sūrya following Uṣā, aglow with the light of her lover,[3] as a young man chases a maiden.[4] A beloved here, Uṣā is called the mother of Sūrya elsewhere.[5] One hymn makes her the daughter,[6] and another the sweetheart,[7] of heaven. All these passages cannot be dismissed as fanciful descriptions of deified nature, as, indeed, poetic fancy cannot be unrelated to the mores of its given society. That no impropriety is felt to be committed, let alone blasphemy, in conjuring up these incestuous relationships, shows that a mode of behaviour acceptable to the gods must have had its basis in known human parallels.[8]

[1] *Ibid.*, X.61.5-9; *AB.*, III.33; cf. *ŚB.*, II.1.2.8.

[2] *RV.*, VI.55.5, *māturdidhiṣu.* He is also called his sister's lover in *ibid.*, VI.55.4, *pūṣaṇaṁ. . . .svasuryo jāra ucyate.*

[3] *Ibid.*, I.92.11.,. . .*yoṣā jārasya cakṣasā vibhāti.*

[4] *Ibid.*, I. 115.2, *sūryo devīmuṣasaṁ rocamānāṁ maryo na yoṣāmabhyeti paścāt.*

[5] *Ibid.*, I.113.1, 2; VII.78.3. She is the wife of Sūrya in VII.75.5, *sūryasya yoṣā*, and in IV.5.13, *patnīḥ sūro.*

[6] *RV.*, I.30.22, *duhitardivaḥ.*

[7] *Ibid.*, I.46.1, *priyā divaḥ.*

[8] V. M. Apte assures us that "the so-called incestuous intercourse between father and daughter in the story of Prajāpati (X.61.5-7), and between brother and sister in the dialogue between Yama and Yamī (X.10) can be satisfactorily explained(in the opinion of the present writer)on a mythological or astronomical basis". Cf. *The Vedic Age*, p. 394. Such explanations are necessitated only by later morality.

The ancient Iranians, closely related to the Ṛgvedic Āryans, regarded the union of brother and sister, parent and child as sacred, under the name of *khvêtuk-das*,[1] to which we have had occasion to refer before.[2] Its antiquity must have contributed to the sanctity of the custom amongst the Āvestan people.

The *Ṛgveda*, however, represents an age of transition, when the rules of incest and exogamy definitely come to the fore. But despite assertions to the contrary,[3] the *Ṛgveda* does attest the existence of polyandry in Āryan India. It is known alike to the gods and men, who would be mystified by the negative constructions put upon their candour by the moralists of succeeding ages. We must go to our evidence in an honest spirit, and take it for what it signifies, without allowing our current attitudes to colour our vision of the past.

We begin our investigation with the twin Aśvins and their bewitching bride Sūryā, the daughter of Savitā. If the number of hymns addressed to them serves as an indication, the Aśvins are the most important Ṛgvedic gods after Indra, Agni and Soma. Called the "sons of Dyaus",[4] they are "horsemen" as their

[1] Cf. *SBE*, vol. 18, Oxford, 1882, pp. 389 ff. A later Hindu law-giver, Bṛhaspati tells us that a king should not disturb popular practices even though they may be improper, and cites several usages, such as the Pārasīka custom of "marrying one's mother". *tathā mātṛvivāhopi pārasīkeṣu dṛśyate.* Bṛhaspati quoted in *Smṛtica.* 1.10, *Smṛtimu.* (varṇāśrama p. 130). Vide Jolly's *Recht und Sitte*, English translation, p. 102.

[2] See above, *Introduction*, p. 19. Incestuous relationships are also attested among the old Irish, cf. Strabo, IV.5.4.

[3] See above, *Introduction*, pp. 23-24. Cf. Apte, *loc. cit.*, p. 394: "Polyandry is not referred to anywhere in the *Ṛigveda.*" Ram Gopal tells us that it was "abhorrent to Indo-Aryans even to think of polyandry". Cf. his *India of Vedic Kalpasūtras*, Delhi, 1959, p. 443. Professor A. L. Basham, *The Wonder that was India.*, p. 174, however, holds that the practice was not wholly unknown.

[4] *RV.*, I.117. 12 ... *divo napātā*..., which seems to be the equivalent of Lettic *dēwa deli,* and Lithuanian *dēwo sunelei.*

very name Aśvinau signifies. They personify the luminous glow of early dawn, heralding the transition from darkness to light. They are young, handsome and ever so brilliant, and ride a resplendent chariot made for them by the Ṛbhus according to the *Ṛgveda*.[1] It is indeed an astonishing vehicle with three wheels, and alike triple in some other parts of its construction.[2] Exceedingly fond of honey,[3] the Aśvins are as sweet in their sympathetic succour to the sick and the distressed;[4] and have their counterparts in the Lettic God's sons and the Greek Dioskouroi in Indo-European mythology. The *Ṛgveda* describes how the Aśvins win the hand of the refulgent Sūryā, the sun-god's daughter. They are repeatedly referred to as wooing Sūryā or competing in a divine chariot race for her hand;[5] or as driving her triumphantly home[6]. The beaming bride, "the youthful daughter of the sun, delighting in you (Aśvins), ascends there your chariot, heroes".[7] Elsewhere, "she also came for friendship, maid of noble birth, [and] elected you as *husbands*, you to be her lords".[8] The meaning is unambiguous; the Aśvins are at once her "husbands" or *patis*, the divine practitioners of adelphic polyandry. We find it impossible to agree with the suggestion that they are the "groomsmen"[9] of Soma, who is also the husband of Sūryā in another context. The original Ṛgvedic passage from the well-known marriage hymn has no word that could be

[1] *RV.*, X,39.12. Cf. my *Ancient Indian Warfare with Special Reference to the Vedic Period*, Leiden, 1965, particularly the chapters on *Chariots* and *The Horse and Cavalry*.

[2] *RV.*, I. 34.2, 9; I.47.2; I.118.1,2; I.157.3; VII.71.4; X.41.1.

[3] *RV.*, I.117.6, etc.

[4] Cf. *Ibid.*, I. 116.4, 15; 117.7,14,17, etc.

[5] *Ibid.*, X.39.11, *yamaśvinā suhavā rudravartanī puroratham kṛṇuthaḥ patnyā saha.*

[6] *Ibid.*; I.116.17; 117.13; 118.5; 119.5.

[7] *Ibid.*, I.118.5, *ā vāṁ rathaṁ yuvatistiṣṭhadatra juṣṭhvī narā duhitā sūryasya.*

[8] *Ibid.*, I. 119.5, *ā vāṁ patitvaṁ sakhyāya jagmuṣī yoṣāvṛṇīta jenyā yuvāṁ patī.*

[9] *Ibid.*, X.85.9, *somo vadhūyurabhavadaśvināstāmubhā varā*...Cf. Upadhyaya, B. S., *Women in Ṛgveda*, p. 121.

rendered as "groomsmen". It only tells us that the Aśvins chose (*varā*) Sūryā, which is also stated in the preceding passage. The word *varā* comes from the root *vṛ*, which means "to choose", in the present context, for marriage. Soma is an additional husband, in the sense that he is called the first husband of every maiden a little later in the same hymn.[1] The suggestion that Sūryā is the light of the sun transferred to the moon or Soma through the evening twilight identifiable with the Aśvins, is ingenious, if also speculative.[2] It is "very doubtful", according to Macdonell and Keith,[3] whether the *Ṛgveda* recognizes the truth of the moon shining by the borrowed light of the sun. But in the passages that may be construed to signify such awareness,[4] there is no trace of the Aśvins or Sūryā. Where the Aśvins are called the "husbands" (*patī*),[5] and Sūryā their "wife" (*patnī*),[6] there seems no room for doubt or disagreement. Abstruse explanations apart, the evidence is quite straight and clear. Had polyandry been anathema to the ordinary Āryan, his poets and priests would have refrained from perpetrating this allegorical sacrilege in poetry. The practice was known and not yet viewed with disapprobation; hence the gods, too, could be innocently described as polyandrous. The poet could certainly not invent a non-existent equation to drive home even a mythological or symbolic proposition.[7]

1 *RV.*, X.85.40, *somaḥ prathamo vivide gandharvo vivida uttaraḥ / tṛtīyo agniṣṭe patisturīyaste manuṣyajāḥ /.* Cf. also verse 41.

2 Cf. Upadhyaya, *op. cit.*, pp. 120, 121. We must remember that sunset plays but little part in Vedic worship.

3 *Vedic Index*, II, pp. 467, 468.

4 Cf. *RV.*, IX.71.9, *ukṣeva yūthā pariyannarāvī dadhi tviṣīradhita sūryasya / divyaḥ suparṇo'va cakṣata kṣāṁ somaḥ pari kratunā paśyate jāḥ /.* Also *ibid.*, IX.76.4; 86.32; I.190.3. Cf. Hillebrandt, *Vedische Mythologie*, 3, pp. 467, 468.

5 *RV.*, I. 119.5, etc.

6 *Ibid.*, X.39.11. *yamaśvinā suhavā rudravartanī purorathaṁ kṛṇuthaḥ patnyā saha.*

7 Cf. H. D. Griswold, *The Religion of the Ṛgveda*, London, 1923, pp. 259-260.

The Aśvins' chariot has three seats,[1] and is said to have three supports fixed in it to lay hold of,[2] certainly to secure the riders' balance when the vehicle is in rapid motion. It is quite appositely made for three, the twin Aśvins and their consort Sūryā, a happy union perhaps symbolically signified by the three wheels of their chariot.[3] Some scholars believe that the Aśvins are not merely mythical, but hark back to a tribe of horsemen who were known for their swift movements as well as proficiency in the arts of healing and curative magic. These people later became synonymous with their dual kings of great celebrity, who were translated into "deities of the dawn and destroyers of darkness and disease".[4] Przyluski suggested that names like Satvant, Sātvata and Nāsatya have a non-Āryan radical *sata* which appears in the modern Muṇḍa languages in the form of *sadam*, meaning "horse."[5] Of the two radicals meaning "horse", *sat* is non-Āryan, *aśva* is Āryan. Some breed of the horse or pony (*sāda* as in Sanskrit *sādin*=rider) must have been known to the Austric speaking pre-Āryan peoples of India.[6] The Aśvins are also often known and addressed as Nāsatyā in the *Ṛgveda* and even outside India, as in the famous Hatti-Mitanni and Mitanni-Hatti treaties.[7] Their name Nāsatya may thus connect the Aśvins

[1] Cf. *RV.*, I.34.9; I.47.2; I.118.1; I.157.3; VII.71.4, etc.

[2] *Ibid.*, I.34.2, *trayaḥ skambhāsaḥ skabhitāsa ārabhe.*

[3] See f.n. 2 on p. 44.

[4] Walker, Benjamin, *Hindu World*, vol. I, p. 93.

[5] Przyluski, "Hippokoura et Satakarni", *JRAS*, 1929, p. 273 ff.; "Satvant, Sātvata and Nāsatya", *IHQ*, IX, 1933, pp. 88-91.

[6] Chatterji, S. K., in *The Vedic Age*, p. 150; also, "Polyglottism in Indo-Aryan", *Seventh Oriental Conference*, pp. 183-185; "Non-Aryan Elements in Indo-Aryan", *Journal of the Greater India Society*, Calcutta, vol. III, p. 42. Also see Przyluski, "Asses, Horses and Gandharvas", *Indian Culture*, vol. III, 1936-37, p. 617; Singh, S. D., *op. cit.*

[7] Cf. Konow, Sten, "The Aryan gods of the Mitanni People", *Kristiania Etnografiske Museums Skrifter* Bind 3 Hefte I, 1921, p. 38; Thieme, Paul, "The Aryan gods of the Mitanni Treaties", *JAOS*, vol. 80, 1960, p. 306.

also with some of these pre-Āryan peoples, and lend greater substance to their somewhat nebulous physical forms. There is no doubt that there was an early fusion of races as of languages,[1] and also of social usages,[2] of which polyandry was one. The Āryans and the Asuras had also commingled quite early in their history; many brāhmaṇas had come from the Asura stock;[3] many Vedic gods were called Asuras. Many scholars derive the Vedic *asura* from *assur*,[4] which is not improbable, and may point to the reminiscences of contacts outside India. We know that Assyria was a Mitanni dependency for a period during the second millennium B.C.[5] And Przyluski and others see in the Sumerian speech of Chaldea a language allied to primitive Austric.[6] Be that as it may, what interests us in the present context and makes all this linguistic evidence relevant is the

[1] Cf. *The Vedic Age*, pp. 151, 152, 155, 228; also Hall, *Bronze Age Greece*, p. 288.

[2] Cf. Chatterji in *The Vedic Age*, p. 167: "Many of our social institutions and conventions (e.g., certain usages regarding prohibited degress in marriage, and customs like a wife being on familiar terms with her husband's younger brother...) and a good many of our wedding and other customs... are of non-Aryan origin." Also see Chattopadhyay, K. P., *Ancient Indian Culture Contacts and Migrations*, Calcutta, 1970.

[3] *Ibid.*

[4] Cf. *JRAS*, 1916, pp. 363-364; Bhandarkar's *Aśoka*, Third edn., pp. 194, 195, 196 ff.; *JDL*, XI, 1924, pp. 178-179; *ABROI*, vol. 31, p 41. There are many other indications of contact. The word *lú šušanu*, signifying a horse-trainer in the Assyrian records, has been traced to an Indo-European etymology. Cf. Ebeling, E., *Bruchstücke einer mittelassyrischen Vorschriftensammlung für die Akklimatisierung und Trainierung von Wagenpferden*, Berlin, 1951, p. 11. For Indian horse-terms in the Akkadian text of the Nuzi documents, see Soden, W. von, and Kronasser, H., in *Wiener Zeitschrift für die Kunde des Morgenlandes*, vol. LIII, 1957, p. 181ff. Also see *The Vedic Age*, p. 216.

[5] Cf. *Encyclopaedia Britannica*, Micropaedia, vol. I, 1974, *s.v.* Assyria.

[6] *The Vedic Age*, p. 155. For Austric influence on Iranian see Przyluski, J., "Emprunts anaryens en Indo-aryes", *Le Monde Oriental*, vol. 28, 1934, pp. 140 ff.

fact that the earliest known proof of polyandry comes from Sumer. There "relics of polyandry are apparent until the time of Uru-Kaggina (c. 2900 B.C.). The women of that period were owned by two men."[1] We may also here recall the Harappan civilization's links with ancient Sumer, which must indeed have resulted in a measure of social and cultural interaction.

If, then, the Nāsatyas or Aśvins practise polyandry without compunction, we need neither be shocked nor surprised. They are indeed likened to bulls,[2] who rush to the aid of eunuchs' wives.[3] There are repeated references to their positive response to the call of Puraṁdhi Vadhrimatī, whom they bless with a son.[4] Celestial healers, they help alike with love, potion and benediction.

What the Aśvins do is by no means unexampled or solitary. The *Ṛgveda* refers in vivifying verses to the *sādhāraṇī* wife of the Maruts, Rodasī, who with her hair dishevelled and mind fixed on her lords, woos them to unite with her, like Sūryā mounting the chariot of the twin Aśvins.[5] And the bright Maruts cling

[1] Meissner, Bruno, *Babylonien und Assyrien*, I, 401, Vorderasiatische Bibliothek, tom. 1.

[2] *RV.*, X.39.9, *vṛṣaṇā*.

[3] *Ibid.*, VI.62.7, *vi jayuṣā rathyā yātamadriṁ śrutaṁ havaṁ vṛṣaṇā vadhrimatyāḥ*...

[4] *Ibid.*, 1.116.13, *ajohavīnnāsatyā karā vāṁ mahe yāman purubhujā puraṁdhiḥ | śrutaṁ tacchāsuriva vadhrimatyā hiraṇyahastamaśvināvadattaṁ*; cf. 1.117.24, *hiraṇyahastamaśvinā rarāṇā putraṁ narā vadhrimatyā adattaṁ*. Cf. also 1.117.19; X.39.7; 65.12. *Vadhrimatī* means the wife of an impotent man. Macdonell and Keith go beyond the warrant of the Ṛgvedic text when they suggest that the Aśvins gave her a son by restoring her husband's virility. Cf. *Vedic Index*, *s.v.*, *vadhrimatī*. In the *Mahābhārata*, for example, they sire the princes Nakula and Sahadeva on Mādrī through *niyoga*, and not by restoring the sexual efficacy of her husband Pāṇḍu. Cf. also Zimmer, *Altindisches Leben*, p. 398.

[5] *RV.*, 1.167.5, *joṣad yadīmasuryā sacadhyai viṣitastukā rodasī nṛmaṇāḥ | ā sūryeva vidhato rathaṁ gāt tveṣapratīkā nabhaso netyā*.

to their young wife, who belongs to them all.[1] "Upon their chariot the youths have set the maiden wedded to glory."[2]

Another Ṛgvedic verse thus addresses the Maruts: "Go ye heroes, far away, ye bridegrooms with a lovely spouse."[3] Rodasī is called their common wife more than once,[4] "ihre gemeinsame Frau", as Geldner[5] describes her. She is their beloved,[6] their young and radiant wife.[7]

The Maruts are in fact the most numerous among the gods,[8] and are apparently thought of on the analogy of commoners on the earthly plane. And if they are described as having a common wife, the analogy points back to the common people.[9] The explanation that the Maruts are the storm-gods or clouds, and that Rodasī is the lightning associated with them,[10] fails to satisfy the question why she is called their common beloved and wife. The association could indeed have been brought out in other inoffensive similes that would not lend themselves to blasphemous or immoral interpretations. The thought of blasphemy or immorality in such a description does not in fact even occur to the poets in question. The erotic predilections

[1] *Ibid.*, 1.167.4, *parā śubhrā ayāso yavyā sādhāraṇyeva maruto mimikṣuḥ | na rodasī apa nudanta ghorā juṣanta vṛdhaṁ sakhyāya devāḥ.*

[2] *Ibid.*, 1, 167.6, *āsthāpayanta yuvatiṁ yuvānaḥ śubhe nimiślāṁ vidatheṣu pajrāma.*

[3] *Ibid.*, V.61.4, *parā vīrāsa etana maryāso bhadrajānayaḥ.*

[4] Cf. *Ibid.*, VI.50.5.

[5] *Der Rig-Veda, HOS*, vol. 36, Vierter Teil, p. 96.

[6] *RV.*, 1.64.9.

[7] *Ibid.*, 1.101.7; V.61.4

[8] Cf. *Ibid.*, VIII.96.8; *SV.*, II.IX.3.3.2; *AV.*, IV.27.7; TS., V.4.7, designates the Maruts as "the people". Cf. *ŚB.*, II. 5.1.13; IX.3.1.25.

[9] The Maruts are repeatedly identified with the people; cf. *TS.*, V. 4.7.7; *ŚB.*, II. 5.2.27, 34, 36; IV.3.3.6.

[10] Cf. Upadhyaya, *op. cit.*, pp. 121-22.

of the Maruts are on the other hand frankly emphasized in the Ṛgvedic verses.[1]

Polyandry in the divine sphere does not end with the Maruts and Rodasī. The Viśvedevas, too, follow suit. "Two with one dame ride on with winged steeds and journey forth like travellers on their way."[2] Mythological features such as these[3] mirror the persistence of the polyandric tradition in the early Āryan society. And it is to that society that we now turn to find proof of the practice of polyandry among men.

RV., VII.33 refers to the celebrated sage Vasiṣṭha as the son of Mitra and Varuṇa from the nymph Urvaśī. To quote from Geldner's translation :

> Und du Vasiṣṭha, bist der Sohn
> Von Mitra und Varuṇa, von

[1] *RV.*, V.52.3, 6.

[2] *Ibid.*, VIII.29.4, *vibhirdvā carata ekayā saha pra pravāseva vasataḥ.*

[3] Pṛthivī is, for example, the wife of Dyaus in the dual compound *dyāvā-pṛthivī*. Cf. *RV.*, I.159.2; VII.53.2; X.65.8. But she is also sometimes called the wife of Parjanya, the rain-giving cloud, elsewhere (*RV.*, VII.102.1) called the son of Dyaus. And in the *Vaitāna Sūtra*, XV.3, Pṛthivī is referred to as the wife of Agni. Of husbands she indeed has more than one. Uṣā also has many lovers. She is the wife of the Sun, *sūryasya yoṣā* in *RV.*, VII.75.5, and *patnīḥ sūro* in *ibid.*, VI.5.13. But she is also the beloved or *priyā* of Dyaus in *ibid.*, I.46.1; and of Agni in *ibid.*, I.69.1; VII.10.1; cf. X.3.3. She is often associated with the twin Aśvins, as in *ibid.*, I.44.2; 183.2; III.58.1; IV.52.2,3; VIII.9.17; X.39.12. And she is also once connected with the moon in *ibid.*, X.85.19. Sūryā was wooed by Soma, and chosen by the Aśvins, whom she herself chose (*vṛṇīta*), and whose chariot she then mounted. Cf. *ibid.*, X.85.9; IV.43.6; I.119.5; VII.69.4; V.73.5; VIII.8.10; I.34.5; 116.17; 118.5; VI. 35.5; I.117.13; IV.43.2. Though the Aśvins are her "husbands" (*patī*), the gods elsewhere give her to Pūṣan. Cf. *ibid.*, VI.58.4, *pūṣā subandhurdiva ā pṛthivyā iḷaspatirmaghavā dasmavarcāḥ. yaṁ devāso adaduḥ sūryāyai kāmena kṛtaṁ tavasaṁ svañcaṁ.*

der Urvaśī aus dem (blossen)
Gedanken geboren, O Hoherpriester.[1]

The legend clearly suggests that prominent *ṛṣi* families saw nothing improper or unseemly in the idea of two persons sharing a wife, and in tracing their ancestry to such a union. Indeed, the *Ṛgveda* repeatedly refers to the plurality of husbands in relation to a single wife.[2] Reluctant to accept the existence of polyandry, Macdonell and Keith admit that "it is difficult to be certain of the correct explanation of each separate instance of this mode of expression".[3] Is the plural here a so called plural of majesty ?[4] They doubt it themselves, but tell us that the mythological explanation proposed by Delbrück[5] is "probably right".[6] The plural "husbands" actually occur at a number of places in the *Vedas* and the *Sūtras*; and the assertion that the expression is "simply generic" does not carry conviction. *RV.*, X.85.37 is quite explicit when it says :

Send, O Pūṣan, her, most propitious, in whom men scatter
seed; who, eager, shall part her thighs for us;
in whom, we, eager, may insert the member.[7]

The bride is candidly described as "desirous of", or "loving

[1] *RV.*, VII.33.11, *utāsi maitrāvaruṇo vasiṣṭhorvaśyā brahman manaso'dhijātaḥ.* Cf. Geldner, *Der Rig-Veda*, Zweiter Teil, *HOS*, vol. 34, p. 213. Also VII.33.10, *vidyuto jyotiḥ pari saṁjihānaṁ mitrāvaruṇā yadapaśyatāṁ tvā / tat te janmotaikaṁ vasiṣṭha' gastyo yat tvā viśa ājabhāra //* See Geldner, *loc. cit.*, pp. 210-213.

[2] *RV.*, X.85.37, *tāṁ pūṣañchivatamāmerayasva yasyāṁ bījaṁ manuṣyā vapanti / yā na ūrū uśatī viśrayāte yasyāmuśantaḥ praharāma śepaṁ //* and verse 38, ...*punaḥ patibhyo jāyām dā agne prajayā saha.*

[3] *Vedic Index*, I, p. 479.

[4] Weber, *Indische Studien*, 5, 191; cf. Zimmer, *AL*, p. 326.

[5] Delbrück, *Die indogermanischen Verwandtschaftsnamen*, p. 543.

[6] *Vedic Index*, I, p. 479.

[7] See n. 2 above.

her brothers-in-law" in some verses,[1] which seem to hint at their status as her secondary husbands. The very word for brother-in-law, *devṛ=devara,* is derived from the Sanskrit root *div,* meaning "to play", emphasizing the free and flippant familiarity of the *devṛ* with his sister-in-law.[2] The reference to "fathers-in-law"[3] elsewhere points to the polyandry of the groom's parents, thus indicating the time-honoured, hereditary character of the custom.[4]

We do not know if the three previous divine husbands of the maiden, Soma, Gandharva and Agni, may "be best understood as a relic of a gradually disused custom of polyandry, which was transformed into an allegory, most probably representing the life stages of a maiden till marriage".[5] Says the *Ṛgveda* :

> Soma obtained her first of all; next the Gandharva was her lord. Agni was thy third husband. Now one born of woman is thy fourth.[6]

[1] Cf. *RV.*, X.85.44, *devakāmā*. The *AV.* mss. are divided between *devakāmā* and *devṛkāmā* in XIV.2.17 and 18. See Whitney's translation, II, pp. 756, 757. According to Sarkar, *Some Aspects of the Earliest Social History of India*, p. 80, the variant reading *devakāmā* "shows an attempt at conscious emendation". But *deva,* too, means "husband's brother"; see Monier Williams' Skt.-English Dictionary, *s. v.*

[2] For the etymology of *devṛ* and *devara* see Yāska, *Nirukta*, III.15.

[3] Cf. *RV.*, X.95.12, *śvaśureṣu.*

[4] In present-day joint Hindu households in the Indian countryside, women may refer to their father-in-law and uncle-in-law generally as *vaśura* or Hindi *sasura,* though there is no polyandry in their families. But more often than not, they would refer to them as *sasura* for father-in-law, and *caciyā or taiyā-sasura* for the uncle-in-law. In the Vedic context, however, the mention of "fathers-in-law" in contradistinction to "father-in-law" would seem to suggest the practice of polyandry, particularly in relation to their relevant occurrence.

[5] Sarkar, *op. cit.*, p. 80.

[6] *RV.*, X.85.40, *somaḥ prathamo vivide gandharvo vivida uttaraḥ | tṛtīyo agniṣṭe patisturīyaste manuṣyajāḥ.*

> Soma gave thee to the Gandharva, the Gandharva gave thee to Agni, and Agni has given thee to me for wealth and sons.[1]

The commentator Sāyaṇa explains:

> While yet the desire for sexual intercourse has not arisen, Soma enjoys a girl; when it has just begun, the Gandharva takes her, and at marriage transfers her to Agni, from whom man obtains her for producing wealth and sons.[2]

These gods are, then, the mythical husbands or guardians of the girl before her marriage to a man. They betoken the Āryan belief that a girl is always married to the gods before she is to man; and also the principal roles visualized for her, of wifedom and maternity. The sexual imagery employed in conjuring up these successive "matrimonial" relationships in the *Ṛgveda* and later literature, making man the fourth husband of the girl, finds nothing repugnant or reprehensible in the thought of many husbands in theory, if not in practice.

Ṛgveda, X.109 refers to the wife of a brāhmaṇa taken to a kṣatriya's home, and later returned. Its expanded version found in the *Atharva Veda*, to be discussed a little later, attests the existence of polyandrous practices.

While some scholars tell us that *niyoga* or levirate has nothing to do with polyandry,[3] others are equally insistent that it typifies an attenuated relic of polyandry.[4] The appointed kinsman

[1] *Ibid.*, X.85.41, *somo dadadgandharvāya gandharvo dadadagnaye / rayiṁ ca putrāṁś-cādādagnirmahyamatho imām.*

[2] Sāyaṇa on the above verses.

[3] Cf. *Vedic Index*, s. v.

[4] Cf. McLennan, *Primitive Marriage*, Chicago, 1970, pp. xxv, 81-82, 90, 97; Briffault, *The Mothers*, I, 681-682.

performs *niyoga* for the restricted purpose of begetting a son; but the Vedic *devṛ*–marriage knows no such limits. When a man's funeral rites are performed, the *didhiṣu* (wooer) brother-in-law claims the widow as full wife for love, property and progeny. Thus the priest addresses her:

> Rise, come unto the world of life, O woman,
> come, he is lifeless by whose side you lie.
> Wifehood with this your husband was your
> portion, who took your hand and wooed you
> as a lover.[1]

The brother of the deceased also takes from the latter's lifeless hand the bow it carried, so that "it may be our power and might and glory. There are you, there: and here with noble heroes may we overcome all hosts that fight against us."[2] The alarums and excursions of inevitable warfare dictate the need for able-bodied men and brave sons to fight shoulder to shoulder against their ubiquitous foes; and widows of child-bearing age are incompatible with the whole pattern of early Āryan existence. The widow therefore grasps the hand of her brother-in-law and becomes his wife even before the obsequies end; there is no formal ceremony of marriage, for none is required. Their relationship is taken for granted; and the ease of transition prompts the presumption that the brother-in-law had been a secondary husband of the woman even during his departed brother's lifetime. The funeral notwithstanding, the poet declares: "We have come forth for dancing and for laughter."[3] They take death in their stride, for life must go on. As their warriors fall, many more are born to take their places. They defeat the

[1] *RV.*, X.18.8, *udīrṣva nāryabhi jīvalokaṁ gatāsumetamupa śeṣa ehi / hastagrābhasya didhiṣostavedaṁ patyurjanitvamapi saṁ babhūtha.*

[2] *Ibid.*, 9, *dhanurhastādādadāno mṛtasyā'sme kṣatrāya varcase balāya / atraiva tvamiha vayaṁ suvīrā viśvāḥ spṛdho abhimātīrjayema.*

[3] *Ibid.*, X.18.3,.. *prāñco agāma nṛtaye hasāya..*

designs of death by their virility and irrepressible will to live. And as we know from later examples down to the present day, polyandry prospers among people whose men are preoccupied with war, leaving the care of their women to those males who are obliged to stay behind. The early Āryan scene doubtless illustrates a classic combination of circumstances conducive to the practice of polyandry in some sections of a migratory society.

Another verse, addressed to the Aśvins, thus interrogates them:

> Where were you at night, where during the day?
> O Aśvins, where do you do the necessary things,
> Where do you dwell? Who takes you to bed
> in a dwelling place, as a widow bedward
> draws her husband's brother, as the
> wife attracts the husband.[1]

It clearly shows that the Aśvins are polyandrous and share a common bed with a common partner. The homely simile of the widow drawing her husband's brother to bed reminds us of the bride desirous of mating with her brothers-in-law (*devṛkāmā*, *devakāmā*), and of the *didhiṣu* character of the *devara*. Yāska comes to our aid in understanding the true purport of this allusion, and tells us that the *devara* or husband's brother is called the second husband of a woman, as his designation itself suggests one who indulges in amorous frolics with her.[2] Our thoughts

[1] *Ibid.*, X.40.2, *kuha svid doṣā kuha vastoraśvinā kuhābhipitvaṁ karataḥ kuhoṣatuḥ | ko vāṁ śayutrā vidhaveva devaraṁ maryaṁ na yoṣā kṛṇute sadhastha ā.*

[2] Yāska, *Nirukta*, 3.15, *kva svit rātrau bhavathaḥ|kva divā | kva abhiprāptiṁ kuruthaḥ| kva vasathaḥ | ko vāṁ śayane vidhaveva devaraṁ (devaraḥ kasmāt? dvitīyo vara ucyate) | vidhavā vidhātṛkā bhavati | vidhavanād vā vidhāvanād vā iti carmaśirāḥ| api vā, 'dhavaḥ' iti manuṣyanāma | tadviyogāt vidhavā | devaro dīvyatikarmā | maryo manuṣyaḥ mara-*

quite naturally go back to the common Indo-European custom of *niyoga* or levirate,[1] which was also practised by the Hebrews,[2] and is still practised by others.[3]

Thus the *Ṛgveda* reveals the Āryans as a free and easy, fun-loving people, fully conversant with the uses of marriage, which they sanctify with due ritual and ceremony. We find evidence of great variety of conjugal relationships including monogamy,[4] polygyny[5] as well as polyandry. And if monogamy is approved in a few passages,[6] polyandry is alike acceptable and present

---

ṇadharmā | yoṣā yauteḥ | ākurute sahasthāne ||

Cf. Bakshi, M. J. (ed.), *The Nirukta of Yāska Muni,* I edn., Nirnayasagar Press, Bombay, 1930; Sarup L.,(ed.) *The Nighaṇṭu and the Nirukta,* Delhi, 1967. According to Sarup, p. 48 of his translation, the passage "he is so called because he is the second husband" is an interpolation. We cannot, however, be certain. The etymology of *devara* given by Yāska quite agrees with the meaning of this passage.

1 Cf. Xenophon, *Rep. lac.,* 1.9; Plutarch, *Lives,* pt. I, ch. iii, sec. 3 and sec. 5; Caesar, *Commentaries,* bk. IV, ch. XIV; *Deut.,* XXV.5; *St. Matthew,* XXII,24; *Manu,* IX.57-68; *Gautama,* XVIII. 4.5; *Baudhāyana,* II. IV. 9-10, etc.

2 Cf. Loth, David, *The Erotic in Literature,* London, 1961, pp. 47, 48.

3 Cf. Chie Nakane, "A Plural Society in Sikkim: A study of the Interrelations of Lepchas, Bhotias and Nepalis", in Fürer-Haimendorf (ed.), *Caste and Kin in Nepal, India and Ceylon,* Bombay, 1966, pp. 243-245. She comes to the conclusion that "the widespread levirate ideology among both Lepchas and Bhotias paves the way for polyandrous marriage". See p. 244. Cf. also Fürer-Haimendorf, *The Sherpas of Nepal,* London, 1964, for a description of polyandry among them.

4 Cf. *RV.,* I. 124. 7; IV. 3.2; X. 71.4, etc.

5 *Ibid.,* I. 62.11; 71.1; 104.3; 105. 8; 112.19; 186.7; VI.53.4; VII. 18.2; 26.3; X.43.1; 101.11. Cf. Muir, *Sanskrit Texts,* 5, 455 *et seq.;* Schrader, *Prehistoric Antiquities,* p. 387. Jolly, *Recht und Sitte,* p. 64; von Schroeder, *Indiens Literatur und Cultur,* pp. 430, 431; Delbrück, *Die indogermanischen Verwandtschaftsnamen,* pp. 539, 540; Hopkins, *JAOS,* Vol. 13, p. 353; Bloomfield, *Zeitschrift der Deutschen Morgenländischen Gesellschaft,* vol. 48, p. 561.

6 See f.n. 4 above.

in circles both human and divine. The reference to the well-known sage Dīrghatamas[1] by his metronymic, Māmateya,[2] alone, in many passages of the *Ṛgveda* strongly suggests the use of metronymics particularly in relation to the offspring of polyandrous households. He is also called Aucathya or "son of Ucatha".[3] The *Bṛhaddevatā*[4] tells us his interesting story woven out of fragments of *RV.*, I. 140–164, attributed to him:

> There were (once) two seer's sons, Ucathya and Bṛhaspati. Now Ucathya's wife was Mamatā by name, of the race of Bhṛgu.[5]
>
> Bṛhaspati, the younger (of the two), approached her for sexual intercourse. Now at the time of impregnation the embryo addressed him:[6]
>
> "Here am I previously engendered; you must not cause a commingling of seed." Bṛhaspati, however, could not brook this remonstrance about the seed.[7]
>
> (So) he addressed the embryo: "Long darkness shall be your lot." And (hence) the seer, Ucathya's son, was born with the name Dīrghatamas (Long Darkness).[8]

1 *RV.*, I. 158.1,6; cf. *Śāṅkhāyana Āraṇyaka*, 14; *AB*. VIII. 23.

2 *RV.*, I. 147. 3; 152.6; 158.6; IV.4.13.

3 *Ibid.*, I. 158.1.

4 *Bṛhaddevatā*, IV. 11-15; 21-25.

5 *Ibid.*, IV.11, *dvāvucathyabṛhaspatī ṛṣiputrau babhūvatuḥ/āsīducathyabhāryā tu mamatā nāma bhārgavī //*

6 *Ibid.*, IV.12, *tāṁ kanīyānbṛhaspatir maithunāyopacakrame / śukrasyotsargakāle tu garbhastaṁ pratyabhāṣata //*

7 *Ibid.*, IV.13, *ihāsmi pūrvasaṁbhūto na kāryaḥ śukrasaṁkaraḥ/ tacchukrapratiṣedhaṁ tu na mamarṣa bṛhaspatiḥ //*

8 *Ibid.*, IV.14, *sa vyājahāra taṁ garbhaṁ tamaste dīrghamastviti/sa ca dīrghatamā nāma babhūvarṣirucathyajaḥ //*

> He when born distressed the gods, having become suddenly blind. The gods, however, gave him (the use of) his eyes (*tannetre*); so he was cured of his blindness.[1]

The story is retold in the *Mahābhārata*, which we propose to discuss later. The present account is quite categorical, in as much as it establishes that though Mamatā was known as the wife of Ucathya, his younger brother Bṛhaspati had free and rightful access to her. The latter could indeed force himself upon her despite her physical condition or remonstrance. This is a clear case of fraternal polyandry, in which the legitimacy of the progeny is properly assured by Mamatā's it nuptial knot with the elder brother. What is significant is that the text finds no fault with the conduct of Bṛhaspati. There is not a word of expostulation or condemnation, for his kind of behaviour is expected and accepted in his society.

The Ṛgvedic evidence also shows that a wife desirous of a son in her husband's absence,[2] or despite his impotence,[3] can have one, if necessary, even through agencies other than the *devṛ* or the husband's brother.

The *Atharva Veda* contains some unmistakable references to

[1] *Ibid.*, IV. 15, *sa jāto'bhyatapaddevān akasmādandhatāṁ gataḥ / dadurdevāstu tannetre tato' nandho babhūva saḥ //* Cf. Macdonell, A. A. (ed. and tr.), *The Bṛhad-devatā attributed to Śaunaka, A Summary of the Deities and Myths of the Rig-Veda*, Parts I and II, *HOS*, vols. 5 and 6, Second Issue, Delhi, 1965. The text and translation are taken from this work.

[2] *RV.*, IV.42.8, *asmākamatra pitarasta āsan tṣapta ṛṣayo daurgahe badhyamāne / ta āyajanta trasadasyumasyā indraṁ na vṛtraturamardhadevaṁ.*
9, *purukutsānī hi vāmadāśaddhavyebhir indrāvaruṇā namobhiḥ / athā rājānaṁ trasadasyumasyā vṛtrahaṇaṁ dadathurardhadevaṁ.* If we identify the Ṛgvedic Purukutsa with his namesake of the Purāṇic list, then the son of Purukutsānī was obtained through her *devara*.

[3] *RV.*, I. 116. 13; 117. 24; VI. 62. 7; X. 39. 7; of. X. 65.12.

polyandry, which go far to corroborate the conclusions drawn from the Ṛgvedic material. It is fully conscious of the significance of marriage and family in contemporary society; and it is in the marriage hymns themselves that we find some telling allusions to polyandry. Let us allow the text to speak for itself:

> Be thou supreme among fathers-in-law, supreme also among brothers-in-law; be thou supreme over sister-in-law, supreme also over mother-in-law.[1]
>
> ..What is lovely (*vāma*) for the fathers who came together here; joy to the husbands for embracing the wife.[2]
>
> The well-flowered (*sukiṁśuka*) all-formed bridal-car (*vahatu*), golden-coloured, well-rolling, well-wheeled, do thou mount O Sūryā, to the world of the immortal; make thou a bridal car pleasant to husbands.[3]
>
> For thee in the beginning they carried about Sūryā, together with the bridal car; mayest thou, O Agni, give to us husbands the wife, together with progeny.[4]
>
> Be thou pleasant to fathers-in-law....[5]

The verses are indeed quite revealing. The pointed reference to "fathers-in-law" in contradistinction to "mother-in-law" shows that the groom's parents are polyandrous. And where the

[1] *AV.*, XIV.1.44, *samrājñedhi śvaśureṣu samrājñuta devṛṣu,* etc. The translations of the *AV.*, are taken from Whitney, who tries to be as literal as possible.

[2] *Ibid.*, XIV.1.46, . . *vāmaṁ pitṛbhyo ya idaṁ samīrire mayaḥ patibhyo janaye pariṣvaje.*

[3] *Ibid.*, XIV.1.61, *sukiṁśukaṁ vahatuṁ viśvarūpaṁ hiraṇyavarṇaṁ suvṛtaṁ sucakraṁ| ā roha sūrye amṛtasya lokaṁ syonaṁ patibhyo vahatuṁ kṛṇu tvaṁ.*

[4] *Ibid.*, XIV.2.1 . . *sa naḥ patibhyo jāyāṁ dā agne prajayā saha.*

[5] *Ibid.*, XIV.2.27, *syonā bhava śvaśurebhyaḥ* . .

poet talks of the joy of the "husbands" in embracing the wife, the implication is obvious. The bridal chariot carries the bride together with her "husbands", who doubtless enjoy themselves. The prayer to Agni for a wife for "husbands" for the sake of progeny clearly suggests fraternal polyandry, in which it is not necessary for all the brothers to go through the ritual of marriage together with their elder brother. *Patibhyo* in *AV.*, XIV.1.61, instead of *patye* in *RV.*, X.85.20, of which it is a variant, makes the former a deliberate and meaningful emendation. To go back to the *Atharva Veda*:

> Her not brother-slaying, O Varuṇa; not cattle-slaying, O Bṛhaspati; not husband-slaying, possessing sons, O Indra—bring (her) for us, O Savitar.[1]

> (As) a soulful cultivated field hath this woman come; in her here, O men, scatter ye seed; she shall give birth to progeny for you from her belly, bearing the exuded sperm of the male.[2]

> With an eye not terrible, not husband-slaying, pleasant, helpful, very propitious, of easy control for the houses, hero-bearing, loving brothers-in-law, with favouring mind—may we thrive together with thee.[3]

[1] *Ibid.*, XIV.1.62, *abhrātṛghnīṁ varuṇāpaśughnīṁ bṛhaspate / indrāpatighnīṁ putriṇīmāsmabhyaṁ savitarvaha.*

[2] *Ibid.*, XIV.2.14, *ātmanvatyurvarā nārīyamāgan tasyāṁ naro vapata bījamasyāṁ/ sā vaḥ prajāṁ janayad vakṣaṇābhyo bibhratī dugdhamṛṣabhasya retaḥ.*
Women are often likened to a field, cf. *Manu*, IX.33 ff.; Aeschylus, *Septem*, 753; Sophocles. *Ant.*, 569; *Eurip. phoen.* 18, etc. Cf. also *Koran*, II.22: "Your women are your plough-land".

[3] *AV.*, XIV.2.17, *aghoracakṣurapatighnī syonā śagmā suśevā suyamā gṛhebhyaḥ/ vīrasūr-devṛkāmā saṁ tvayaidhiṣīmahi sumanasyamānā.* Cf. *RV.*, X. 85.44.

> Not brother-in-law slaying, not husband-slaying be thou here, propitious to the cattle, of easy control, very splendid, having progeny, hero-bearing, loving brothers-in-law, pleasant, do thou worship this household's fire.[1]

> Send, O Pūṣan, her, most propitious, in whom men scatter seed, who, eager, shall part our thighs; in whom we, eager, may insert the member.[2]

Language, of course, could not be more explicit. There is no doubt that all the brothers of the bride-groom have fully approved and desired access to the bride. She comes to them as a field, in which they may scatter their seed for the sake of progeny. The simile could not be more apt or appropriate; a field engages many hands for tilling, sowing and reaping, just as the bride engages not only the groom, but also his brothers in love-play for the solidarity and prosperity alike of the family. She should be auspicious to her husband and to his brothers, and should give birth to noble sons. She should indeed be desirous of mating with her husband's brothers, as the word *devṛkāmā* shows. We have here a picture of sibling solidarity promoted by polyandry in a joint family, the household fire of which is tended and worshipped by their common spouse.

Another Atharvavedic passage talks of a maiden "given to husbands" to enable her to find one according to her wish.[3] The oft-repeated reference to "husbands" of a girl raises no eyebrows, because it is commonplace; because it does not offend against the norms of the Āryan society. The present passage

[1] *AV.*, XIV. 2.18, *adevṛghnyapatighnīhaidhi śivā paśubhyaḥ suyamā suvarcāḥ| prajāvatī vīrasūrdevṛkāmā syonemamagnim gārhapatyam saparya.*

[2] *Ibid.*, XIV. 2.38, *tām pūṣam chivatamāmerayasva yasyām bījam manuṣyā vapanti | yā na ūrū uśatī viśrayāti yasyāmuśantaḥ praharema śepaḥ.* Cf. *RV.*, X.85.37.

[3] *AV.*, II.36.7, *..ete patibhyastvāmaduḥ pratikāmāya vettave.*

seems to indicate that the girl will find a man after her heart among her husbands, presumably brothers.

The *Atharva Veda* repeats the Ṛgvedic belief that every girl is always married; that Soma is her first husband; Gandharva the second and Agni the third; and that the fourth husband is of human birth.[1] Soma passes her on to Gandharva, who gives her to Agni; and Agni gives her to man.[2] This mystical allegory is clearly pregnant with the traces of polyandry, and certainly not innocent of it. Later explanatory texts do not describe the three gods as mere guardians; but as enjoying the girls in a most mundane and matter-of-fact manner.[3] That divinity does not taint, must indeed be a comforting thought for the human husband. And if polyandry is permissible without fuss in the divine sphere, is it an ideal of yore, from which men are departing with the passage of time?

There are some truly baffling verses in the *Ṛgveda*[4] and the *Atharva Veda*[5] expressive of the notion that every virgin contains a demon who leaves her with the nuptial blood, causing some risk to her husband. And they have been interpreted to mean that a proxy for the husband took the risk and then disappeared.[6] There are verses,[7] however, that hint at the defloration of the bride by the husband himself and no other person. Be that as

[1] *Ibid.*, XIV.2.3.

[2] *Ibid.*, XIV.2.4 Cf. *RV.*, X.85.40, 41.

[3] *Romakāle tu saṁprāpte somo bhuṅktetha kanyakāṁ / rajo dṛṣṭvā tu gandharvāḥ kucau dṛṣṭvā tu pāvakaḥ. Saṁvarta* verse 64, quoted by *Sm. C.*, I, p. 79 and *Gr. R.*, p. 46. Cf. Kane, *History of Dharmaśāstra*, Vol. II. Part I, Second edn., 1974, p. 443.

[4] Cf. *RV.*, X.85.28, 29, 34, 35, etc.

[5] *AV.*, XIV.1.9, 25, 26, 28, 29, 30; XIV.2.66, 67.

[6] Cf. Sumner, *Folkways*, p. 353; Zimmer, *Altindisches Leben*, pp. 313-314.

[7] *AV.*, XIV.1.27.

it may, the use or otherwise of a proxy has nothing to do with polyandry.[1]

Patent proof of polyandry is provided by other passages in the *Atharva Veda*. *AV*., V. 17 takes up the theme of a brāhmaṇa's wife, who was returned to her husband by King Soma after a while.[2] The eighth verse of this hymn makes a preposterous claim for the brāhmaṇa:

> And if there are ten former husbands of a woman, not brāhmaṇas, provided a brāhmaṇa has seized her hand, he is alone her husband.[3]

And the ninth repeats it to leave no room for doubt:

> A brāhmaṇa is indeed her husband, not a noble (rājanya), not a vaiśya; this the sun goes proclaiming to the five races of men.[4]

This extravagant claim is characteristic of the ravenous brahmanical rapacity that comes quite unabashedly to the fore in the *Atharva Veda*. The brāhmaṇa goes out of his way to lay

[1] See *Introduction*, above, for such practices elsewhere, and for the exercise of the right of the lord to the bride of one of his subjects in the form of *jus primae noctis* in medieval Europe. For a review of such practices in Babylonia, Cyprus, Lydia, Anatolia, Armenia, Egypt and parts of Europe, see Briffault, *The Mothers*, III, pp. 218 ff.

[2] *AV.*, V.17.2; cf. *MS.*, III.7.3.

[3] *AV.*, V.17.8, *uta yat patayo daśa striyāḥ pūrve abrāhmaṇāḥ | brahmā ceddhastama grahīt sa eva patirekadhā.*

[4] *Ibid.*, V.17.9, *brāhmaṇa eva patirna rājanyo na vaiśyaḥ | tat sūryaḥ prabruvanneti pañcabhyo mānavebhyaḥ.* I. B. Horner, *Women under Primitive Buddhism*, makes a mistake when she refers her readers to *RV.*, X.109. 89. *RV.*, X. 109 has only seven verses. She probably meant *AV.*, V. 17.8 and 9, cited here.

a claim to the wives of others, when he cannot even defend his own. For, the return of the brāhmaṇa's wife is the central theme of the hymn. What, however, these verses clearly show is that a woman may have as many as ten husbands at a time. They must be contemporaries, so that it becomes essential for the brāhmaṇa to stress his supersessive primacy. That polyandry was well-known and being practised in the age of the *Atharva Veda*, cannot be doubted.

Two more verses elsewhere in the *Atharva Veda* deserve notice:

> Whoever (fem.) having gained a former husband, then gains another later on, if they shall give a goat with five rice dishes, they shall not be separated.[1]

> Her later husband comes to have the same world with his remarried spouse who (masc.) gives a goat with five rice dishes, with the light of sacrificial gifts.[2]

These verses have been taken as proof of widow remarriage;[3] but the original talks only of a twice married woman, not of a widow. The arrival of the second husband does not necessarily mean the death or departure of the first. According to Keith,[4] the spell secures that a woman married twice may be united in the next world with her second husband, not the first. There is nothing in the original, though, to preclude the presence of the

[1] *AV.*, IX.5.27, *yā pūrvaṁ patiṁ vitva' thānyaṁ vindate' paraṁ / pañcaudanaṁ ca tāvajaṁ dadāto na vi yoṣataḥ.*

[2] *Ibid.*, IX.5.28, *samānaloko bhavati punarbhuvā' paraḥ patiḥ / yo' jaṁ pañcaudanaṁ dakṣiṇājyotiṣaṁ dadāti.* Delbrück, *Die indogermanischen Verwandtschaftsnamen*, pp. 553-555, realizes that the first husband is still alive, and surmises that he is probably impotent or *patita*, fallen from his caste. There is no basis for such an assumption. Also see *Vedic Index*. I, p. 477.

[3] Cf. *The Vedic Age*. p. 457.

[4] Keith, in Hastings (ed.) *Encyclopaedia of Religion and Ethics*, vol. 8, p. 452.

former husband in the life beyond. We must indeed be looking at a potentially polyandrous situation in paradise !!

The funeral verses in the *Atharva Veda*, like those of the *Ṛgveda* discussed earlier,[1] give us a vivid glimpse of the act a widow puts on by lying beside her dead husband, only to get up soon enough to grasp the outstretched hand of her husband's brother:

> This woman, choosing her husband's world,
> lies down (*ni-pad*) by thee that art departed,
> O mortal, continuing to keep (her) ancient duty;
> to her assign thou here progeny and property.[2]
>
> Go up, O woman, to the world of the living;
> thou liest by this one who is deceased; come!
> to him who grasps thy hand, thy spouse
> (*didhiṣu*), thou hast now entered into the
> relation of wife to husband.[3]

The *didhiṣu* brother-in-law's immediate and acknowledged claim on his brother's widow is a significant pointer to the probability that he was a secondary husband even before her widowhood. The husband's brother is always to be loved and desired, as we have already seen. Whitney's translation of the second verse here (*AV.*, XVIII. 3.2) renders *didhiṣostavedaṁ* as "thy second spouse",[4] even though there is no word signifying "second" in this passage. We find reference to this custom

[1] See above, p. 54.

[2] *AV.*, XVIII.3.1, *iyaṁ nārī patilokaṁ vṛṇānā ni padyata upa tvā martya pretaṁ / dharmaṁ purāṇamanupālayantī tasyai prajāṁ draviṇaṁ ceha dhehi.*

[3] *Ibid.*, XVIII.3.2, *udīrṣva nāryabhi jīvalokaṁ gatāsūmetamupa śeṣa ehi / hastagrābhasya didhiṣostavedaṁ patyurjanitvamabhi saṁ babhūtha.*

[4] Whitney's translation, vol. II, p. 848.

in many other texts of the later Vedic period.[1]

It looks as though polyandry was common among the non-Āryans, specially the Austrics;[2] and was also found among the Āryans, the brāhmaṇas and the *ṛṣis* in particular.[3] The *Atharva Veda* is perhaps the most important testament of the Āryan-unārya fusion, and records many traditions and practices that go back to earlier antiquity. And the picture that emerges from the examination of many passages in the foregoing discussion proves the presence of polyandry beyond the shadow of any doubt. And we need not be taken aback. Polyandry was a widespread practice among the Indo-European peoples. Of that, however, a little later.

The *Taittirīya Saṁhitā* speaks of a woman being given to the Gandharvas. She also goes to the gods, as they sing. "So if there is in a family one person who knows thus (i.e., sings), men give their daughters in wedlock to that family, even if there be other (wooers) in plenty."[4] Keith's opinion that "there is no real suggestion of polyandry",[5] cannot be accepted, when we view the present passage side by side with later ones which expressly tell us that a girl is given to a famliy;[6] and some of which call it reprehensible.[7]

[1] *TA.*, VI.1.3. The text reads *abhi sambabhūva,* which the commentator explains by *ābhimukhyena samyak prāpnuhi.* Cf. *Kauśika Sūtra,* 80.45; *Āśvalayana GS.*, IV.2.18.

[2] Cf. Meyer, *SLAI,* vol. 1, pp. 115-116; Jolly, *Recht und Sitte,* p. 48.

[3] This point will be elaborated later, though some of the foregoing evidence already establishes it.

[4] *TS.*,VI.1.6. Cf. Keith, *The Veda of the Black Yajus School,* Part II, *HOS,* vol. 19, p. 493.

[5] *Ibid.,* f.n. 6.

[6] Cf. *Āp. Dh. S.,* II.10.27. 2-4...."A bride is given to a family (of brothers and not to one alone)." Cf. Kane, *loc. cit.,* vol. II, Pt. I, p. 555.

[7] Bṛhaspati quoted in *Smṛticandrikā,* I. 10.

Elsewhere,[1] too, the *Taittirīya Saṁhitā* refers, as do the other *saṁhitās*, to "noble husbands" and "fair offspring" in relation to a single wife, whatever we may take that to mean.

The Vedic texts often speak of the sale of a daughter,[2] which must be viewed and understood in the context of the Vedic injunction that the younger brothers and sisters should not marry before their elders do so.[3] If the current practices in polyandrous societies including those descended from the ancient Āryans[4] serve as any guide, the younger brothers contribute to the amount of bride-price paid to the girl's father, and enjoy socially sanctioned access to the common wife as her co-husbands. The eldest brother is almost invariably the first to marry; and not all the younger brothers care to contract individual marriages.

[1] *TS.*, III.5.6.

[2] *MS.*, I.10.11; *TS.*, II.3.4.1; *Taitt. B.*, I.1.2.4; *Kāṭhaka Saṁhitā*, XX.VI.5. Cf. *Manu*, III.53; VIII. 204; IX.98; Megasthenes in McCrindle's translation, p. 70; Weber, *Indische Studien*, 5, p. 407; Hopkins, *JAOS*, 13, pp. 345 ff.; Schrader, *Prehistoric Antiquities*, p. 381; Pischel, *Vedische Studien*, 2, pp. 78 ff.; Hillebrandt, *Vedische Mythologie*, 3, p. 86, n.; Jolly, *Recht und Sitte*, p. 52; *Vedic Index*, I, p. 482. Cf. also *RV.*, 1.109.2.

[3] Cf. Delbrück, *Die indogermanischen Verwandtschaftsnamen*, pp. 578 ff. Those who break the common rule of conduct are censured as sinful and given derogatory epithets, such as *pari-vividāna* or *agre-dadhus*, meaning the man who, though a younger brother, marries before his elder brother; the latter is then called *parivitta*. *Agre-didhiṣu* is the man who weds a younger daughter, while her elder sister is yet unmarried. All these epithets have a connotation of disapproval. Cf. *MS.*, VI.1.9; *VS.*, XXX. 9;*Āp. Dh. S.*, II. 5. 12, 22; *Vedic Index*, I, p. 476.

[4] Cf. Majumdar, D. N., *Races and Cultures of India*, pp. 167, 172, 192 ff.;"Some Aspects of the Cultural Life of the Khasas of the cis-Himalayan Region", *Journal and Proceedings of the Royal Asiatic Society of Bengal*, Third Series, vol. 6, 1940, pp.1 ff.; Parmar, Y. S., *Polyandry in the Himalayas*, Delhi, 1975, pp. 20-24 54 ff. Majumdar makes an interesting observation in the article referred to above. Polyandry, according to him, enabled the Khasas to retain their racial purity.

Among the Khasas mentioned earlier, polyandry, monogamy as well as group marriage are in simultaneous evidence.[1]

Marriages by capture are also known to the *Vedas*, including the *Ṛgveda* itself,[2] thus anticipating the *rākṣasa* mode of marriage mentioned in the later *dharmaśāstra* texts.[3] This is doubtless another form of marriage associated with polyandry in early antiquity. The references in the Vedic literature, though, do not specify whether some of these marriages were polyandrous in character.

Macdonell and Keith believe that metronymics denote sons of maidens (*kumārī-putra*), such as Satyakāma Jābāla in the *Chāndogya Upaniṣad*[4], and the teachers (?) of the lists (*vaṁśas*) given in the *Bṛhadāraṇyaka Upaniṣad*.[5] But if the Ṛgvedic example of Māmateya is any indication, metronymics may point as much to polyandry as to polygyny or promiscuity. Their suggestion would make most of these ancient teachers sons of maidens, which is on the face of it an absurd proposition.

Twice or thrice in the later Vedic literature, we come across opposition to the practice of polyandry, which only serves to

[1] See above, p. 35.

[2] Cf. *RV.*, I. 112.19; 116.1; 117.20; X.39.7; 65.12. Also see the chapter on the ethics of war in my *Ancient Indian Warfare*.

[3] Cf. Hopkins, *JAOS*, 13, pp. 361-362; Jolly, *Recht und Sitte*, pp. 50 ff.; Pischel, *Vedische Studien*, I, p. 29; Schrader, *Prehistoric Antiquities*, p. 383.

[4] Cf. *Vedic Index*, I, p. 481. *Ch. U.*, IV.4.1,2,4.

[5] *Vedic Index*. In f.n. 70, on p. 481, they say, "the custom may be due simply to polygamy", and refer to Keith, *Aitareya Āraṇyaka*, p. 244, n.2. Had they meant both polyandry and polygyny by polygamy, we would have been in total agreement. But they use the term "polygamy" for polygyny. We also find the use of metronymics in some early Indian epigraphs, at Pabhosa, Bharhut, etc.

illustrate the incipient morality of a succeeding epoch. Says the *Taittirīya Saṁhitā* :

> On one sacrificial post he passes round two girdles, so one man secures two wives; that he does not pass one girdle round two posts, so one wife does not obtain two husbands.[1]

The *Aitareya Brāhmaṇa* once asserts that a man has several wives, "but one wife has not many husbands at the same time".[2] And that ends the registration of protest.

Why did Brahmanism seek to oppose something that was non-existent? Critical opposition is directed only against an obtaining practice that might become obnoxious or repugnant to certain sections of a given society. When male jealousy asserts itself alongside increasing male dominance, this is the kind of protest males would mouth. These rare voices of opposition indeed presuppose the presence of polyandry.

Polyandry, thus, is neither un-Vedic nor merely un-Āryan. It is true that both before and after their arrival in India, the Āryans were "in the closest possible contact with populations among whom polyandry was an established social usage".[3] But to nail polyandry down to the names of the non-Āryan, Tibetan or Dravidian tribes or castes to the exclusion of the Āryans would amount to a falsification of history. They were also likewise polyandrous. This is not to say that they did not know monogamy or polygyny. The trend was undeniably in the

[1] *TS.*, VI.6.4.3, *yannaikāṁ raśanāṁ dvayoryūpayoḥ parivyayati tasmannaikā dvau patī vindate.* Cf. also *TS.*, VI.5.1.4; Kane, *History of Dharmaśāstra*, vol. II, Part I, pp. 550-551.

[2] *AB.*, XII.11, *tasmādekasya bahvyo jāyā bhavanti naikasyai bahavaḥ sahapatayaḥ.*

[3] Briffault, *The Mothers*, vol. I, p. 688.

direction of monogamy, as many passages testify;[1] and the *Atharva Veda* even compares a pair of human spouses to the inseparable *cakravākas*, the proverbial poetic pair of loving birds :

> Here, O Indra, do thou push together these two spouses like two *cakravākas*; let them, with [their] progeny, well-homed, live out all their life-time.[2]

The marriage hymns of the *Vedas* consist of *mantras* of different origins, truly reflecting the variety of the usages of marriage in the Āryan society. Not in India alone, polyandry was practised among other members of the Indo-European group as well. It was a well established form of marriage among the Medes of the upland country,[3] as it was common also among the Get-ti of Bactria and Sogdiana, and among the tribes of the Hindu-Kush.[4] The kings of the Medes, according to Strabo,[5] were polygynous; but the masses were polyandrous; and the women reckoned it an honour to have many husbands. Indeed, to have less than five was accounted a misfortune.[6]

Speaking of the Tapyri or the present-day Mazanderan, Strabo again refers to the polyandry of the Medes. In the country extending along the southern shores of the Caspian, together with the adjacent province of Azerbaijan, the Holy Land of the *Avesta* and of the Medic religion, it was customary

[1] Cf. *RV.*, I. 124.7; IV.3.2; X.71.4.

[2] *AV.*, XIV.2.64, *ihemāvindra saṁ nuda cakravākeva dampatī / prajayainau svastakau viśvamāyurvyaśnutāṁ //*

[3] The Aryan was the ruling race there. Cf. Sykes, Sir P., *A History of Persia*, vol. 1, p. 95.

[4] Briffault, *loc. cit.* I, pp. 671, 691-692.

[5] Strabo. XI.13.11.

[6] *Ibid.*

to exchange wives between friends.[1] Exchange of wives is not polyandry; but we learn from later sources that, right down to Islamic times, the women of Azerbaijan "were esteemed in proportion to the number of their husbands."[2]

Fraternal polyandry was a legally recognized institution in Greece.[3] "In Sparta", we are told, "several brothers had often one wife between them, and the children were brought up in common."[4] Wives were also lent as tokens of friendship, or in order to get vigorous offspring.[5] The Spartan women, too, enjoyed the recognized right to take "secondary husbands" in the absence of their own husbands.[6]

Theopompos informs us that wives were held in common among the Etruscans in accordance with their legal institutions.[7]

Plutarch refers to the polyandrous practices of the Romans, and tells us that the second Cato lent his wife to Quintus Hortensius, and took her back after the death of the latter.[8] Strabo speaks of the same in a more revealing vein:

> In our own day Cato lent his wife to Hortensius, upon

[1] *Ibid.*, XI.9.

[2] Balfour, E., *The Cyclopaedia of India and of Eastern and Southern Asia*, vol. III, p. 244; Briffault, *loc. cit.*, p. 692.

[3] *Ibid.*

[4] Polybius, XII.6; cf. Plutarch, *Vit. Lycurgus*, 15; Xenophon, *R. Lacedemoniae*, 1.7,8,9.

[5] *Ibid.*; cf. Sumner, *Folkways*, p. 351. Wives were often offered to strangers, cf. Nicholas Damascenus, in *Fragmenta Historicorum Graecorum* vol. III, p. 458.

[6] Briffault, *loc. cit.*, p. 693.

[7] Athenaeus, XII.14.

[8] Plutarch, *Cato Secundus*, XXV.

> the latter's request, followng in this an ancient custom of the Romans.[1]

It was quite customary among the barbarians of northern Europe to exchange wives.[2] It was a socially approved and legal practice in Germany until quite late in the Middle Ages to introduce a relative or friend to one's own wife to try to have a baby, if the marriage otherwise proved infructuous.[3] The usage lingered right down to modern times among the peasants of the remoter districts of Germany.[4]

The goddess Frigga in Nordic and Teutonic mythology cohabits with the brothers of her husband Odin, when he goes out on a journey.[5]

Caesar informs us that the ancient Britons had their wives in common, brothers sharing wives among themselves.[6] In the epitome of Xiphilinus, Dio Cassius makes queen Boadicea cry, exhorting her soldiers:

> It is our Britons that I rule,....men who have all things in common, who have even their wives and their children in common.[7]

[1] Strabo, XI.9.In *Stichus*, a comedy by Plautus, two slaves are said to have one wife. Roman epithets reveal two men jointly celebrating a common wife. Cf. Pellison,M., *Roman Life in Plinys' Time*, (trans.), Meadville, Pennsylvania, 1897, p. 100.

[2] Gjerset, K., *History of the Norwegian People*, vol. I, p. 92.

[3] Grimm, I., *Deutsche Rechtsalterthümer*, pp. 443 *et. seq*. Cf. Gierke, O. von, *Der Humor in deutschen Recht*, p. 56.

[4] Maurer, G. L. von, *Geschichte der Dorfverfassung in Deutschland*, vol. I, pp. 338 ff.

[5] Weinhold, K., *Altnordisches Leben*, p. 249.

[6] Caesar, *De bello Gallico*, V. 14.

[7] Xiphilinus, epitome of Dio Cassius, *Hist. Rom.*, lxii, 6; cf. Bardesanes, in Eusebius, *Praeparatio evangelica*, VI.10.

Bardesanes also tells us the same thing: "In Britain several men have one wife between them."[1] And of the Caledonians and the other tribes of the border we are told:

> They live in tents, naked and bare-footed, having wives in common, and rearing the whole progeny.[2]

St. Jerome thus describes the Britons of the north before the introduction of Christianity :

> The nation of the Scots have no individual wives; and, as if they had been reading Plato's 'Republic', or wished to imitate the example of Cato, a man, amongst them, has no wife of his own, but each one indulges his lasciviousness according to his pleasure, after the manner of beasts.[3]

As late as Chaucer's day, the Wife of Bath tells her tale of five husbands, and seems to be looking for the sixth. We are not sure if they are all dead or alive, despite the description in the past tense;[4] and even if they were dead and gone, she is an unrepentant practitioner of what may be described as staggered or sequential polyandry. God created the organs of generation. To use them for their intended purpose is to fulfil God's intention:

> Tell me also, to what conclusion
> Were membres maad of generacion...
> Glose whoso wole...
> I sey this, that they maked ben for bothe

[1] *Ibid.*
[2] Xiphilinus, epitome of Dio Cassius, *Hist. Rom.*, lxxvi, 12.
[3] Jerome, *Adversus Jovinianum*, VII, in Migne, *Patrologiae Cursus Completus*, vol. XXIII, col. 296.
[4] Cf. Huppé, Bernard F., *A Reading of Canterbury Tales*, New York, 1964, pp. 109-110.

This is to sey, for office, and for ese
Of engendrure, ther we nat God displese.[1]

Strabo refers to the report that the old Irish had free access to one another's wives, and even did not bar incestuous relations.[2] The *Ulster Saga* tells us that the princess Clothru married three brothers; and her son, Lugaid Riab n-Derg, who became supreme king of Ireland, had thus three fathers.[3] Mythological texts also refer to multiple fatherhood.[4] In the Celtic family on the mundane plane, property was indivisible, and brothers lived together forming one common household. "The name and symbol of that fraternal household was not the house, but significantly enough the bed; the Celtic family was called 'com lebaid', 'the common bed' in Irish, 'gwely', 'the bed' in British."[5]

All this evidence clearly establishes the presence of polyandry or practices closely akin to it among different peoples of the Indo-European family. Coming back to Asia, polyandrous institutions were once common in the Hindu-Kush and Chitral regions,[6] and extended as far west as the western shores of the Caspian. In Turkestan, according to Ma-twan-lin, polyandrous marriage was obligatory.[7] It was a species of fraternal polyandry, in which brothers shared a wife, and in their absence cousins or clan brothers did so.

1 *Canterbury Tales, The Wife of Bath's Prologue*, 115-128. Cf. also Loth, David, *The Erotic in Literature*, p. 61.
2 Strabo, IV.5.4
3 Windisch, W. O. E., *Irische Texte*, vol. III, pp. 332, 415; Thurneysen, R., *Die irischen Helden-und Königsage*, p. 584; Stokes, Whitley, "On the death of some Irish Heroes", *Revue Celtique*, XXIII, p. 333.
4 McCulloch, J. A., *The Religion of the Ancient Celts*, p. 224.
5 Briffault, *loc. cit.*, p. 697.
6 Called Panchir by Alberūnī, to be discussed later.
7 Briffault, *loc. cit.*, p. 671.

The references to polyandry in the early Indian Āryan texts are therefore as natural as they are expected. We know that polyandry was by no means unknown or uncommon around the shores of the Caspian, whence according to the latest authorities the Āryans came to India. Mayrhofer[1] believes that Central Asia was their original home; and Diakonov[2] agrees. The Soviet archaeologists connect them with the Andronovo culture of Kazakhistan and Southern Siberia.[3]

[1] Cf. Mayrhofer, M. *Die Indo-Arier im alten Vorderasien*, Wiesbaden, 1966.
[2] Diakonov, I. M., *Istoriya Midii*, Moscow, 1956, pp. 124-125.
[3] Burrow, T., "The Proto-Indo-Aryans", *JRAS*, 1973, no. 2, pp. 123-140.

CHAPTER THREE

Polyandry: c. 600 B.C.–400 A.D.

The limitless variety of human relationships figures alike in texts, Brahmanical, Buddhist and Jaina; but is nowhere better illustrated than in the *Mahābhārata* and the *Rāmāyaṇa*. Traditions as colourful as they are vivid, mirror the myriad patterns of social evolution in a sphere of action larger than that of mere mundane existence. It would be stressing the obvious, but nevertheless worthwhile to say that the Indian society would remain a riddle to an observer ignorant of the Epics and their enduring hold on the Indian modes of life and thought. We often discover in them whatever, indeed, we may be looking for; we have 'proofs' of promiscuity and unregulation; of polyandry and polygyny; of group-marriage and monogamy; of celibacy and license; and of *niyoga* at times almost indistinguishable from polyandry or cicisbeism. The evidence of the Vedas is corroborated and elaborated in more ways than one; and our conclusions in the preceding chapter receive a remarkable reinforcement from the interminable string of stories woven into the scheme of epic narration.

Āpastamba[1] and Baudhāyana[2] make a veiled allusion to a period when little or no value was placed on the conjugal faith of a woman.[3] And the *Mahābhārata*, as we have seen before,[4] clearly visualizes

1 Āpastamba, II. 13.7.
2 Baudhāyana, II. 3.34.
3 Jolly, J., *Hindu Law and Custom*, Calcutta, 1928, p. 105.
4 See above, p. 7, n. 2.

an age of unrestricted sexual expression, innocent of the later taboos of incest and avoidance. Pāṇḍu tells his wife Kuntī of a time when women were free to cohabit with anybody they chose without a trace of sin. They went uncloistered, and were their own mistresses, taking their pleasure where it pleased them.[1] This, Pāṇḍu says, was the ancient Law *(dharma)* witnessed by the "great-spirited, law-minded seers".[2] He goes on:

> From their childhood onwards they were unfaithful to their husbands, but not lawless, for such was the Law in days gone by.[3] Even today, the animals follow this ancient Law, without any passion or hatred. This Law, witnessed of old, was honoured by the great seers.[4] O (Kuntī) of the softly tapering thighs, it still prevails amongst the northern Kurus; this is the eternal Law favouring women.[5]

Pāṇḍu explains how and by whom the present rule was laid down.[6] There was once a great seer named Uddālaka, who had a hermit son called Śvetaketu. It was this Śvetaketu, who laid down the new Law for women in a fit of rage. It so transpired that a brāhmaṇa took Śvetaketu's mother by the hand in full view of the father and son, and said, "Let us go".[7] The sight of his mother being

[1] *Mbh.* I. 113. 4, *anāvṛtāḥ kila purā striya āsanvarānane| kāmacāravihāriṇyaḥ svatantrāścārulocane ||*

[2] *Ibid.*, I. 113. 3,. . . .*purāṇamṛṣibhirdṛṣṭaṁ dharmavidbhirmahātmabhiḥ.*

[3] *Ibid.*, verse 5, *tāsāṁ vyuccaramāṇānāṁ kaumārātsubhage patīn | nādharmo' bhūdvarārohe sa hi dharmaḥ purābhavat ||*

[4] *Ibid.*, verse 6,. . . .*purāṇadṛṣṭo dharmo'yaṁ pūjyate ca maharṣibhiḥ.*

[5] *Ibid.*, verse 7, *uttareṣu ca rambhoru kuruṣvadyāpi vartate | strīṇāmanugrahakaraḥ sa hi dharmaḥ sanātanaḥ ||*

[6] *Ibid.*, verse 8 ff.

[7] *Ibid.*, verse 11, *śvetaketo kila purā samakṣaṁ mātaraṁ pituḥ | jagrāha brāhmaṇaḥ pāṇau gacchāva iti cābravīt ||*

led away, as if by force, infuriated Śvetaketu[1], but his father counselled: "Do not get angry, son. This is the eternal Law. The women of all classes are uncloistered on earth. Just as the cows do, so do the other creatures in their respective classes."[2]

Śvetaketu refused to condone or acquiesce in the prevailing practice, and laid down the present *maryādā* or restrictive rule for men and women.[3] "From today onwards", he legislated, "a woman's infidelity to her husband shall be a sin tantamount to aborticide, an evil that will engender misery. Seduction of a chaste and constant wife avowed to her husband shall also be a sin on earth. And a wife, who is enjoined by her husband to conceive a child, and refuses, shall incur the same sin."[4]

This legend would lead one to believe that promiscuity prevailed in particular among the *ṛṣis* and brāhmaṇas, and that, in their sequestered settlements, their women were held in common. However, there are repeated references to sexual unregulation among all classes of men, in which even the gods participate. When, for example, the maiden Kuntī invokes the sun-god (Sūrya) in her sprightly curiosity, the latter, delighted, proposes coitus, from which she vainly seeks to shy away. Sūrya tells her that there would be nothing wrong in their act of love; and of a maiden's right to cohabit with a person of her choice. It is none of her parents' or elders' business to stop her.[5] An unmarried girl is called *kanyā*, for she is one to be liked and desired (from the root *kan*); and she

[1] *Ibid.*, I. 113. 12, *ṛṣiputrastataḥ kopaṁ cakārāmarṣitastadā| mātaraṁ tāṁ yathā dṛṣṭvā nīyamānāṁ balādiva ||*

[2] *Ibid.*, I. 113. 13-14. . . . *yathā gāvaḥ sthitāstāta sve sve varṇe tathā prajāḥ.*

[3] *Ibid.*, verse 15, *ṛṣiputro'tha taṁ dharmaṁ śvetaketurna cakṣame | cakāra caiva maryādāmimāṁ strīpuṁsayorbhuvi ||*

[4] *Ibid.*, I. 113. 17-19.

[5] *Ibid.*, III. 291, 12, 14.

can choose her love-mate without let or hindrance.[1] Sūrya refers to the natural freedom of men and women in matters of sex, and to the artificiality of later restrictions.[2] He even tells Kuntī that she would regain her maidenhood after coition and consequent childbirth.[3]

Karṇa calls Śalya, the ruler of the Madras, a *pāpadeśaja*[4], i.e., a person born in a country of sin, and in an outburst of remarkable candour, so describes the people thereof :

> Fathers, mothers, sons, mothers-in-law, fathers-in-law, maternal uncles, sons-in-law, daughters, brothers, grandsons and other relations, friends of the same age, guests, male and female slaves, mix freely and without constraint; and the women, according to their will, enjoy the company of men known and unknown[5] .... They drink spirituous liquor, eat beef, dance and giggle; and indulge in acts of sex without any inhibition whatsoever[6] ....

And again :

> Inebriated with spirits, the women fling their clothes away and dance, and engage in unrestricted sexual intercourse with

[1] *Ibid.*, III. 291. 13.

[2] *Ibid.*, verse 15, *anāvṛtāḥ striyaḥ sarvā narāśca varavarṇini / svabhāva eṣaṃ lokānāṁ vikāro' nya iti smṛtaḥ //*

[3] *Ibid.*, verse 16 ... *punaḥ kanyā bhaviṣyasi.*

[4] *Ibid.*, VIII. 27. 68.

[5] *Ibid.*, VIII. 27. 75-76:

pitā mātā ca putraśca śvaśrūśvaśuramātulāḥ /
jāmātā duhitā bhrātā naptā te te ca bāndhavāḥ // 75
vayasyābhyāgatāścānye dāsīdāsaṁ ca saṁgataṁ /
puṁbhirvimiśrā nāryaśca jñātājñātāḥ svayecchayā // 76

[6] *Ibid.*, verses 77-78.

yāni caivāpyabaddhāni pravartante ca kāmataḥ /
kāmapralāpino' nyonyaṁ teṣu dharmaḥ kathaṁ bhavet // 78

whomsoever they will. How can their son, a Madraka, dare talk of *dharma* ?[1]

Madra, Sindhu-Sauvīra, Gāndhāra and the Bāhlika region are alike 'notorious' for the laxity of their sexual codes.[2] We find a measure of confusion between the Bāhlikas and the Vāhīkas in the different recensions of the *Mahābhārata*. Karṇa actually tells us that the region between the Indus and the five rivers is beyond the bounds of *dharma*.[3] The Vāhīkas enjoy copulation in the open, and joyously follow the dictates of their free will.[4] Despite fulminations of so-called righteous wrath[5], people of the north and north-west include both brāhmaṇas and kṣatriyas; and two Kaurava queens hail from Madra and Gāndhāra.

The land of Uttara-Kuru is far-famed as a region of heavenly felicity in food and freedom, where Indra "rains wishes; where women make love as they choose; where jealousy is unknown amongst men and women."[6] The Rāmāyaṇa,[7] too, refers to

[1] *Ibid.*, VIII. 27.85:

vāsānsyutsṛjya nṛtyanti striyo yā madyamohitāḥ |
mithune' saṁyatāścāpi yathākāmacarāśca tāḥ |
tāsāṁ putraḥ kathaṁ dharmaṁ madrako vaktumarhati ||

Karṇa refers to the shamelessness of the Madra women, who urinate standing, like she-camels and asses. Cf. VIII. 27.86.

[2] *Ibid.*, VIII. 27. 80, 91; VIII. 30.68. Cf. also the Gita Press Ed., VIII. 44 and VIII. 45.

[3] *Ibid.*, VIII. 44.7, 31, 32, 47; 45. 6, 7, 8, 29, Gita Press Edn.

[4] *Ibid.*, VIII. 44. 13, ... *anāvṛtā maithune tāḥ kāmacārāśca sarvaśaḥ.* Gita Press Edn.

[5] Cf. *Ibid.*, VIII. 45.23, ... *malaṁ pṛthivyāṁ vāhīkāḥ strīṇāṁ madrastriyo malaṁ.* Gita Press Edn. VIII. 30.68 of Critical Edn. has *malaṁ pṛthivyā bāhlīkāḥ...*

[6] *Ibid.*, XIII. 102. 26, *yatra śakro varṣati sarvakāmān yatra striyaḥ kāmacārā bhavanti | yatra ceṛṣyā nāsti nārīnarāṇāṁ* ... Gita Press Edn.

Cf. also I. 113.7, Critical Edn.; Hopkins, *Epic Mythology*, p. 186, where he describes the Uttara-Kurus as a class of northern saints and seers.

[7] *Rāmāyaṇa*, *Ayodhyā*, 91. 19.

Uttara-Kuru as a land of lovely women, who still practise promiscuity with impunity.[1] Even the Buddhist literature speaks of this land as a place where women are nobody's chattel, and where there is no private property.[2] The references to this millennium of sensual bliss, peace and plenty, indicate envy, but no condemnation.

Sahadeva sees similar freedom being enjoyed by the women of Māhiṣmatī, who go about making love with any person of their choice without incurring any blot or blemish, owing to a boon granted by the fire-god Agni.[3] A land of fire-worshippers, presumably of the Āryan stock, poised on the border between the north and south, Māhiṣmatī is located in the heart of India; and whatever happens there is characteristic of contemporary brahmanical India. Westermarck's easy observation that such stories in the *Mahābhārata* "may allude to the laxity of morals among the non-Āryan people of India and the Himālayas",[4] is as unfounded as it is unjust.

Social restraints are relaxed and inhibitions are shed in the infectious gaiety of occasional revelries. Such an occasion is the Yādava festival on the Mount Raivataka, from where Arjuna elopes with Subhadrā;[5] or a pleasure excursion organized by Kṛṣṇa and Arjuna on the bank of the Yamunā, where women with big swaying hips and heavy breasts enliven the scene with their beautiful eyes and tipsy gait, enjoying themselves as they please.[6]

[1] *Mbh.*, I. 113. 7; cf. note 5 on p. 77.

[2] *Dīgha Nikāya*, Rhys Davids' Translation, pt. III, p. 192.

[3] *Mbh.*, II. 28. 24, *evamagnirvaraṁ prādātstrīṇāmaprativāraṇe / svairiṇyastatra nāryo hi yatheṣṭam pracarantyuta //*

[4] Westermarck, *History of Human Marriage*, I, p. 106.

[5] Cf. *Mbh.*, I. 211; 212.

[6] *Ibid.*, I. 214. 21, f.n. 20, 2101 (Critical Edn.); I. 221. 21 (Gita Press Edn.):
striyaśca vipulaśroṇyaścārupīnapayodharāḥ /
madaskhalitagāminyaścikrīḍurvāmalocanāḥ //

The authors of the Epic do not gloss over these cultural traits because of their importance even during the period when the *Mahābhārata* undergoes various revisions. A proof of this is furnished by the later commentator Nīlakaṇṭha describing the *gaṇa* of Utsavasaṁketa[1] as a republic of seven promiscuous tribes with no fixed laws of marriage.

Most of the usages found in the Epics are also reflected in the *dharmaśāstra* literature. Thus, though Āpastamba upholds the ideal of monogamy, he is quite familiar with polyandry despite his disapproval thereof :

> One shall not make over (his wife) to strangers, but only to one who is a *sagotra;* for they declare that a wife is given to the family (of brothers and not to one brother alone); that is forbidden on account of the weakness of men's senses.[2]

That polyandry, like levirate, did not disappear from the land, is proved alike by the Epics and Bṛhaspati, a *dharmaśāstra* author assigned to c. 200-400 A. D.[3] For he tells us that group-marriage (*kule kanyāpradānaṁ*) is still prevalent "in other regions", taken by

[1] *Mbh.*, II. 24. 15. Arjuna conquered the hilly regions, including the *gaṇa* of Utsavasaṁketa.

[2] *Āpastamba Dh. S.*, II. 10.27. 2-4,... *kulāya hi strī pradīyata ityupadiśanti* ... Cf. Jolly, *Hindu Law and Custom*, p. 102; Hopkins, *JAOS*, XIII, p. 355; Keith *Encyclopaedia of Religion and Ethics*, vol. VIII, p. 453. Kane, *History of Dharmaśāstra*, vol. II, Pt. I, p. 555, grudgingly concedes that "in the Dharmaśāstra works there are traces of the knowledge of the practice of polyandry." Jolly, *loc. cit.*, is quite right in pointing out that though the commentary on Āpastamba connects the whole passage with *niyoga*, "the wording goes against such an interpretation." Cf. p. 102, n. 3. Cf. also *Pāraskara Gṛhya Sūtra*, I. 7. 3: "Mayst thou give back, Agni, to the husbands the wife together with offspring." *SBE*, vol. XXIX, p. 283.

[3] Kane, *loc. cit.*, vol. I, pp. 210-211; vol. II, Part I, p. 555.

Jolly[1] and Keith[2] to mean the south, but understood by Kane as signifying "other countries (but not Aryan India)".[3] Kane argues that Bṛhaspati first refers to "the practice of marrying a maternal uncle's daughter as prevalent amongst the southerners (dākṣiṇātyas) in his day and then adds that a practice of giving a girl to the family is in vogue in other countries".[4] A careful examination of the passage reveals that Bṛhaspati is illustrating the contrary practices of the south to back up his advice that a king should not interfere with popular usages despite their impropriety. He speaks of the reprehensible practice of marrying a maternal uncle's daughter; of the "exceedingly odious" custom of a brother taking (as wife) the widow of his deceased brother; of a girl being given to a family seen in other regions; and of the Pārasīkas (Persians) marrying their mothers.[5] *Deśeṣvanyeṣu* may here refer to "other regions" of the south as well as the north not excluding "Aryan India" and lands beyond India. We know that both polyandry and levirate have been in evidence in the south since time immemorial; and it would be wishfully unrealistic to assume Bṛhaspati's ignorance thereof.

The law-givers portray society as they would like it to be. Their class interests, dreams and ideals are woven into patterns of dharmik formulation; but the Epics, despite a deal of didactic moralising, editorial deletions and additions, still present a picture of society in many ways as it was, and as it continues to be. Protes-

1 Jolly, *Hindu Law and Custom*, p. 102.
2 Keith, in *ERE*, vol. VIII, p. 453.
3 Kane, *op. cit.*, vol. II, Pt. I, p. 555.
4 *Ibid.*
5 *viruddhāḥ pratidṛśyante dākṣiṇātyeṣu saṁprati |
svamātulasutodvāho mātṛbandhutvadūṣitaḥ ||
abhartṛkabhrātṛbhāryāgrahaṇaṁ cātidūṣitaṁ |
kule kanyāpradānaṁ ca deśeṣvanyeṣu dṛśyate |
tathā mātṛvivāhopi pārasīkeṣu dṛśyate |*
Bṛhaspati quoted in the *Smṛticandrikā*, 1.10.

tations of disapproval notwithstanding, polyandry is a fact of life in the period of the *Mahābhārata.* That both brāhmaṇas and kṣatriyas practise it, remains incontrovertible. That the temper of later morality increasingly opposes it, is also patently visible. That the otherwise dictatorial and cantankerous priesthood approves of Draupadī's polyandry, though some frustrated kṣatriyas question it, is equally clearly significant.

Long-tressed, deep-bosomed and slender-waisted, lovely and delicate, with eyes like lotus petals, the flawless Draupadī[1] is the central heroine of the great Epic, and the most celebrated practitioner of polyandry. She is the daughter of King Drupada of Pāñcāla; and the *Mahābhārata* gives a graphic description of her marriage with the five Pāṇḍavas. It is a case of classical polyandry,

[1] Cf. *Mbh.*, I. 175. 5 ff. IV. 8. 10-13, contain an exhaustive description of Draupadī's charms:

gūḍhagulphā saṁhatorustrigaṁbhīrā ṣaḍunnatā /
raktā pañcasu rakteṣu haṁsagadgadabhāṣiṇī // 10
sukeśī sustanī śyāmā pīnaśroṇipayodharā /
tena tenaiva saṁpannā kāśmīrīva turaṅgamā // 11
svarālapakṣmanayanā bimboṣṭhī tanumadhyamā /
kambugrīvā gūḍhasirā pūrṇacandranibhānanā // 12
Kā tvaṁ brūhi yathā bhadre nāsi dāsī kathañcana /
yakṣī vā yadi vā devī gandharvī yadi vāpsarāḥ // 13

Queen Sudeṣṇā tells Draupadī that her ankles are not prominent; her thighs are close-set and well developed; her navel is deep, and her nose, ears, eyes, breasts, nails, etc., are all well-formed. Her soles, palms, corners of eyes, lips, tongue and nails are healthily ruddy; and her voice is happy like that of swans. Her hair is beautiful; her breasts are lovely; her complexion is dark; both her breasts and buttocks are delightfully heavy. She has every auspicious mark like a mare from Kāśmīra. Her eye-lashes are dark and winsomely arched; her lips are red like the ripe *bimba* fruit. Her waist is slender, and her neck wrests the beauty of the śaṅkha. Her veins are deep and scarcely visible; and her face puts to shame the beauty of the full moon. That is why Sudeṣṇā asks her whether she is a yakṣī, or a goddess, or a gandharvī or an apsarā ?

and the details of the proceedings are as revealing as they are important for a proper appraisal of our subject.

King Drupada organizes a *svayaṁvara* for the marriage of his matchless daughter, and has an extremely hard bow made, almost impossible to bend. He has a device built in the sky, and to that device he gets a target fixed. "The man who can string this bow and, when he has strung it, can shoot arrows through this device into the target, will have my daughter," declares Drupada.[1] The Pāṇḍavas proceed to the *svayaṁvara* disguised as brāhmaṇas, in the company of other wandering brāhmaṇas.[2] Drupada's challenge, proclaimed far and near, attracts kings, princes, seers and brāhmaṇas; and prospective suitors and spectators add to the throng of people in his capital.

An arena built on an even and consecrated piece of land north-east of the city is surrounded by stands on all sides. Around it also runs a wall and a moat; and it is adorned with grand gateways. Entirely shaded by colourful awning, the whole arena echoes with the music of myriad instruments, and wafts the fragrance of sandal water and decorative flowers to a fair distance. Well-enclosed, high-rising pavilions scratch the sky like the peaks of Kailāsa, embellished with mosaics of precious stones and gently rising flights of steps; with fine canopied seats and lovely carpets. A hundred wide doors provide access to these magnificent many-storeyed pavilions furnished with superb seats brought to life by the brave kings who sit there, outdoing one another with the adornment of their persons. Townsmen and country-folk converge on the arena to enjoy the great spectacle of Kṛṣṇā (Draupadī), and sit all about on their own rich platforms, staring at the might and

[1] *Mbh.* I. 175. 9 ff.
[2] *Ibid.*, I. 175.20.

majesty of proud kings, defenders of their realms loved and applauded for their hallowed good deeds.[1]

The Pāṇḍavas take their seats with the brāhmaṇas and marvel at the matchless wealth of the king of Pāñcāla. The audience grows for many days, heaped with royal largesses and entertained by actors and dancers. Finally on the sixteenth day, watched by an eager crowd, Draupadī appears, bathed and bedecked with new clothes. As she carries the golden goblet of the champion into the arena[2], the priest of the Pāñcālas, proficient in the spells, strews sacred grass around and makes an apposite oblation of butter in the fire. After propitiating the fire and the brāhmaṇas, and blessing the day, he stops the music. As the audience waits in hushed silence, Draupadī's brother Dhṛṣṭadyumna strides to the centre of the ring and speaks in a voice as loud as thunder:

Hear ye all kings who are gathered here
Mark bow and target, and mark these arrows.
You must hit the mark with these five arrows
By shooting through this hole in the wheel.
Whoever of lineage, beauty, and might
Accomplished this most difficult feat,
To him shall go my sister Kṛṣṇā
To be his wife, and I say sooth.
When Drupada's son had spoken to them,
He thereafter spoke to Draupadī,
And heralded the assembled princes
By name and lineage and by their feats.[3]

The irresistible Draupadī steals the hearts of the assembled

[1] *Ibid.*, I. 176. 12-25.
[2] *Ibid.*, I. 176. 26-30.
[3] *Ibid.*, I. 176. 31-36. Buitenen's translation.

kings who, with "their limbs besieged by the arrows of love", proceed to the pit for her sake. Rivalry turns friends into foes,[1] while the gods and other divine beings watch the proceedings from the sky.[2]

> The many sons and grandsons of kings,
> Their eyes, mind and mettle to Kṛṣṇā gone,
> Stared as she walked, flexing their muscles,
> Biting their lips, with copper-red faces.[3]
> The wide-armed sons of Pāṇḍu by Pṛthā
> And the two heroic and powerful twins,
> They all kept looking at Draupadī,
> They were all struck by the arrows of love.[4]

Despite their strength and exertions, the princes fail to bend and cord the tough bow, which recoils and flings them into the dust.

> The hardwood bow cried out in pain
> And shattered and ground their bracelets and earrings.
> Their feelings of love for Kṛṣṇā departed,
> The circle of kings was woe-begone.[5]

When Karṇa sees all the kings laid in the dust by the unbendable bow, he goes forward, swiftly snatches it up from the ground, raises it and strings it, and sets the arrows on it. The sons of Pāṇḍu deem

[1] *Ibid.*, I. 178. 5.

[2] *Ibid.*, I. 178. 6-7.

[3] *Ibid.*, I. 178. 11. Buitenen's translation.

[4] *Ibid.*, I. 178. 12. Buitenen's translation.

tathaiva pārthāḥ pṛthubāhavaste
vīrau yamau caiva mahānubhāvau /
tāṁ draupadīṁ prekṣya tadā sma sarve
kandarpabāṇābhihitā babhūvuḥ //

[5] *Ibid.*, I. 178. 17. Buitenen's translation.

the splendid mark to be already shot through and down to the ground. But when Draupadī sees him, her voice rings out loud and clear: "I will choose no sūta." Looking up towards the sun with an angry laugh, the redoubtable Karṇa lets drop the springing bow.[1]

Arjuna then arises in the midst of the brāhmaṇas, some of whom cheer him, while the others derisively question his temerity. Some of them wonder, and feel that his failure would make them a laughing stock of the people around.[2]

Arjuna takes his stand beside the bow, walks around it in a solemn circumambulation, and bows his head to it. Resolute and confident, he takes it in his hand,[3] and :

> In a twinkling of the eye he strung the bow
> And took the arrows that counted five.
> He pierced the target and brought it down,
> Hit through the hole, and it fell with a might.[4]

There is applause, both human and divine; flowers rain on the head of the victor; and there is music, as the bards lift their voices

[1] *Ibid.*, I. 186. 21-23, Gita Press Edn.
sarvān nṛpānstān prasamīkṣya karṇo dhanurdharāṇāṁ pravaro jagāma |
uddhṛtya tūrṇaṁ dhanurudyataṁ tat sajyaṁ cakārāśuyuyoja bāṇān || 21
dṛṣṭvā tu taṁ draupadī vākyamuccairjagāda nāhaṁ varayāmi sūtaṁ |
sāmarṣahāsaṁ prasamīkṣya sūryaṁ tatyāja karṇaḥ sphuritaṁ dhanustat || 23

[2] *Ibid.*, I. 179. 1 ff., Critical Edn.

[3] *Ibid.*, I. 179. 15.

[4] *Ibid.*, I. 179. 16. Buitenen's translation.
sajyaṁ ca cakre nimiṣāntareṇa
śarānśca jagrāha daśārdhasaṁkhyān |
vivyādha lakṣyaṁ nipapāta tacca
chidreṇa bhūmau sahasātividdhaṁ ||

in praise.[1] Kṛṣṇā (Draupadī) beholds the target hit, and, with a festoon of white flowers, goes smilingly up to the Indra-like Arjuna.[2]

Having won in the lists, he took the woman,
Whilst the twice-born brahmins paid him homage.
And the miracle-monger strode from the pit,
And after him followed she, his wife.[3]

Angered by the king's readiness to give the maiden to the triumphant brāhmaṇa, the kṣatriyas are loud and bitter in their protest. They cannot stand the sight of the king passing them by as though they were straw, and giving his daughter Draupadī, the finest of women, to a brāhmaṇa.[4] Brāhmaṇas, indeed, have no title to the choosing; the bridegroom choice is for the kṣatriyas alone. The scriptures are categorically clear on the point. Hostilities commence as the assembled princes advance on Drupada with upraised weapons.[5] Arjuna and Bhīma, however, rush to their host's rescue, and the attackers are all beaten off.[6]

As Bhīma and Arjuna arrive with Draupadī at the place where they have been staying, they find their mother Kuntī at home, and speak to her of their prize. "Look what we found", they tell her; but she is inside the house, and without seeing them, simply

[1] *Ibid.*, I. 179. 17-20.
[2] *Ibid.*, I. 179. 22.
[3] *Ibid.*, I. 179. 23:

sa tāmupādāya vijitya raṅge
dvijātibhistairabhipūjyamānaḥ |
raṅgānnirakrāmadacintyakarmā
patnyā tayā cāpyanugamyamānaḥ ||

[4] *Ibid.*, I. 180. 1 ff.
[5] *Ibid.*, I. 180. 5 ff.
[6] *Ibid.*, I. 180. 15 ff.; 181. 1-35.

says: "Now you share that together." But a little later, Kuntī sees the girl and cries out, "Woe. O what have I said!"[1] Afraid of *adharma*, and ashamed, she leads the exceedingly trustful Draupadī to Yudhiṣṭhira, and thus addresses him:[2] "This daughter of king Drupada was presented to me by your younger brothers, and I carelessly told them, as I am used to do, 'now you share that together.' Now tell me, ... how this word of mine may not become a lie; and how the daughter of the Pāñcāla ruler may not incur an *adharma*, such as never has been!"[3]

The short-lived horror of Kuntī seems to be an editorial afterthought, in view of the fact that her husband advocated sex relations outside the bounds of marriage, and made her beget three

[1] *Ibid.*, I. 182. 1-2:

gatvā tu tāṁ bhārgavakarmaśālāṁ
pārthau pṛthāṁ prāpya mahānubhāvau |
tāṁ yājñasenīṁ paramapratītau
bhikṣyetyathāvedayatāṁ narāgryau || 1
kuṭīgatā sā tvanavekṣya putrā-
nuvāca bhuṅkteti sametya sarve |
paścāttu kuntī prasamīkṣya kanyāṁ
kaṣṭaṁ mayā bhāṣitamityuvāca || 2

[2] *Ibid.*, I. 182. 3:

sā dharmabhītā hi vilajjamānā
tāṁ yājñasenīṁ paramapratītāṁ |
pāṇau gṛhītvopajagāma kuntī
yudhiṣṭhiraṁ vākyamuvāca cedaṁ ||

[3] *Ibid.*, I. 182. 4-5:

iyaṁ hi kanyā drupadasya rājña-
stavānujābhyāṁ mayi sannisṛṣṭā |
yathocitaṁ putra mayāpi coktaṁ
sametya bhuṅkteti nṛpa pramādāt || 4
kathaṁ mayā nānṛtamuktamadya
bhavetkurūṇāmṛṣabha bravīhi |
pāñcālarājasya sutāmadharmo
na copavarteta nabhūtapūrvaḥ || 5

sons from Dharma, Vāyu and Indra.[1] He wanted her to have more, but Kuntī, tired, said 'no'.[2] Pāṇḍu actually told her that a wife had to be faithful to her husband during her *ṛtu* only; and that at all other times she was free to exercise her own choice.[3] Kuntī had a son even before her marriage; and her first lover Sūrya had told her that unregulation was more natural than artificial constraints on sexual fulfilment.[4]

Yudhiṣṭhira considers the question, comforts Kuntī and addresses Arjuna: "By you was Draupadī won, O Pāṇḍava; and by you she will be satisfied. Let a fire be lit and an offering made. Take her hand with a proper rite."[5]

Arjuna's reply is most significant : "O King, do not make me share in *adharma* or lawlessness. This is not the *dharma* or Law accepted by others. You should yourself be the first to marry, and then the strong-armed Bhīma of wondrous deeds.[6] I come next, with Nakula after me, and Sahadeva the last of us all. Vṛkodara (Bhīma), I and the twins, O King, all hold that the girl should go

[1] Cf. *Ibid.*, I. 114.

[2] *Ibid.*, I. 114 64-65. Kuntī protests:

nātaścaturthaṁ prasav:māpatsvapi vadantyuta |
ataḥ paraṁ cāriṇī syāt pañcame bandhakī bhavet || 65

"They do not speak of a fourth son even in times of distress. After three she is loose; after four she is a harlot." But Pāṇḍu manages to have five sons in all by sending his second wife Mādrī to the twin Aśvins. Cf. I. 115. 15 ff.

[3] *Ibid.*, I. 113. 25-26. The Gita Press Edition omits these verses, though the Critical Edition retains them.

[4] See above, pp. 78-79.

[5] *Mbh.*, I. 182. 7.

[6] *Ibid.*, I. 182. 8,

mā māṁ narendra tvamadharmabhājaṁ
kṛthā na dharmo hyayamīpsito' nyaiḥ |
bhavānniveśyaḥ prathamaṁ tato' yaṁ
bhīmomahābāhuracintyakarmā ||

to you![1] What ought now to be done at this juncture? Think and do whatever brings *dharma* and honour, and pleases the prince of Pāñcāla. Tell us, for we are all under your authority!"[2]

They all stare at the curvacious Draupadī, who captivates their hearts with her peerless beauty. They look at one another, as Yudhiṣṭhira rightly reads their manifest feelings.[3] Lest a breach should occur among them, he declares without a ruffle: The lovely Draupadī shall be the wife of us all!"[4]

The decision is delivered by the eldest brother; and the sons of Pāṇḍu placidly ponder the meaning thereof.[5] Kuntī apparently happily accepts the proposition of Yudhiṣṭhira, even though he does not yet make any reference to the sanctity and sanction of past tradition in this regard. Nor does any of the Pāṇḍavas raise the faintest murmur of expostulation. What is perhaps most important, and what almost all the scholars discussing this marriage fail to mention, is the significant but eloquent silence of Draupadī. She is neither appalled nor outraged by the prospect of Pāṇḍava polyandry. She could be, when occasion demanded, signally bold and

[1] *Ibid.*, I. 182. 9,
ahaṁ tato nakulo' nantaraṁ me
mādrīsutaḥ sahadevo jaghanyaḥ /
vṛkodaro' haṁ ca yamau ca rāja-
nniyaṁ ca kanyā bhavataḥ sma sarve //

[2] *Ibid.*, I. 182. 10,
evaṁgate yatkaraṇīyamatra
dharmyaṁ yaśasyaṁ kuru tatpracintya /
pāñcālarājasya ca yatpriyaṁ syā
ttadbrūhi sarve sma vaśe sthitāste //

[3] *Ibid.*, I. 182. 11-14.

[4] *Ibid.*, I. 182. 15:
abravītsa hi tānbhrātṛnmithobhedabhayānnṛpaḥ /
sarveṣāṁ draupadī bhāryā bhaviṣyati hi naḥ śubhā //

[5] *Ibid.*, I. 183. 1.

outspoken, as we know from her immediate and forthright rejection of Karṇa earlier.[1] She is quite calm, cool and happy. The idea of five husbands does not seem to suggest any moral atrocity. It does not appear to be a custom unknown or unpalatable to her. She is "exceedingly trustful" and as willing as a woman could be, if her deportment serves as any guide. Kuntī's initial sense of horror is put into her mouth by the later narrators of the great Epic, who could not otherwise gloss over her insistence that whatever she said must yet be accomplished. The ready decision of Yudhiṣṭhira is enough to please her and win her willing acceptance. The ripples of doubt and questioning are caused by later moralists in the otherwise quiet pool of Pāṇḍava polyandry.

When Kuntī leaves it to Yudhiṣṭhira to find a solution to the problem posed by her, he asks Arjuna to marry Draupadī, as the latter had won her in the competitive contest. But Arjuna would have none of it. He points out that Yudhiṣṭhira being the eldest should be the first to wed, and only then might Bhīma and the others also do so, in order of seniority. He therefore asks Yudhiṣṭhira himself to marry Draupadī. This suggestion clearly shows that it was possible for the winner of the girl to marry her to any or all of his brothers. It would not be unreasonable to assume that Arjuna, the best archer of them all, actually took part in the competition to win the girl for himself as also for his brothers, who were all equally desirous of her. That is why, the others did not even try.

Society looked upon the marriage of a younger brother before that of his elder with distinct disapproval not unmixed with resentment. For such an offence the didactic portions of the Epic prescribe proper penitence, and call upon the *parivettā* (the younger brother marrying before the elder) and the *parivitti* (the unmarried elder brother), together with the former's wife, to redeem themselves

[1] See above. p. 88.

with the *kṛcchra* or *cāndrāyaṇa* penance.[1] The Rāmāyaṇa classes the *parivettā* with "the murderer of king or brāhmaṇa, the cow-slayer, the thief, he who rejoices in destroying living creatures, and the atheist", who all "go to hell."[2] Baudhāyana[3], Manu[4], and Parāśara[5] likewise tell us that the unmarried elder brother, the married younger brother and his wife, the girl's guardian and the sacrificial priest who officiated at the ceremony, all alike go to hell.

The didactic portions of the *Mahābhārata* are supposed to be later in point of time, but even therein we find the wife of the younger brother being offered to the unmarried elder brother as a *snuṣā* or daughter-in-law, or a woman unenjoyed (*abhuktā*) according to the commentator; and then with his permission, the younger brother weds her again.[6] *Snuṣām* in this verse seems to be a later garbling

[1] Cf. *Mbh.*, XII. 165. 68-69, Gita Press Edn.:
parivittiḥ parivettā yā caiva parividyate |
pāṇigrahāstvadharmeṇa sarve te patitāḥ smṛtāḥ || 68
careyuḥ sarva evaite vīrahā yad vrataṁ caret |
cāndrāyaṇaṁ carenmāsaṁ kṛcchraṁ vā pāpaśuddhaye || 69
Cf. also *ibid.*, XII. 35. 27 and 28, Gita Press Edn.; XII. 35. 4-5, Critical Edn.

[2] *Rāmāyaṇa, Kiṣkindhā*, 17. 36:
rājahā brahmahā goghnaścoraḥ prāṇivadhe rataḥ |
nāstikaḥ parivettā ca sarve nirayagāminaḥ ||

[3] *Baudhāyana*, II. 1. 1. 39. According to II. 1. 1. 40, the two brothers, the priest at the wedding, and the bestower of the bride, must cleanse themselves by a twelve days' *kṛcchra* penance. The wife should observe a fast for three days.

[4] *Manu*, III. 172.

[5] *Parāśara*, IV. 23-24. Cp. *Viṣṇu*, XXXII. 13 ff.; LIV. 16; *Yājñavalkya*, III. 234 ff.

[6] *Mbh.*, XII. 165. 70, Gita Press Edn.:
parivettā prayaccheta tāṁ snuṣāṁ parivittaye |

for an earlier *jāyāṁ*, as Vasiṣṭha[1] tells us that the two brothers must undergo the prescribed penances called *kṛcchra* and *atikṛcchra;* the younger brother must hand over his wife to the elder, and the latter take her as his own wife, and then give her back to the former, who must get married to her again. Even if this offer became symbolic with time, it certainly appears to hark back to a period when the brothers shared their wives in common; when the eldest brother was usually the first to marry, and his younger brothers were also deemed his wife's husbands or secondary husbands.[2]

The *Mahābhārata* also speaks derogatively of the younger sister who marries before the elder (*agredidhiṣu*), and the husband of the elder sister who marries after the younger sister (*didhiṣūpati*). Vasiṣṭha ordains that the man who marries a younger sister before the elder, must observe twelve days' *kṛcchra* penance, and then marry the elder one as well. The husband of an elder sister married after the younger one must make atonement with *kṛcchra* and *atikṛcchra*, and hand over his wife to the husband of the younger one.[3] This is a somewhat baffling suggestion. The girls to be thus offered to each other's husbands may indicate a relic or remnant of group marriage, or the right of brothers-in-law to one another's wives, or of the sisters to one another's husbands, approximating to group marriage inclusive of the inevitable polyandrous principle.

---

jyeṣṭhena tvabhyanujñāto yavīyānapyanantaraṁ |
evaṁ ca mokṣamāpnoti tau ca sā caiva dharmataḥ ||

Cf. also Meyer, *Sexual Life in Ancient India*, vol. I., p. 105.

1 *Vasiṣṭha*, XX. 7-10. Cf. also Meyer, *loc. cit.*, pp. 106-107, n. 1.

2 Cf. the Vedic evidence in the preceding chapter, and Yāska, *Nirukta*, III. 15.

3 *Vasiṣṭha*, XX. 7-10. Cf. Bühler, *SBE*, XIV, p. 103; Meyer, *loc. cit.*; *Viṣṇu*, XXXVII, 15-17; LIV, 16; *Baudhāyana*, IV. 6. 7, 6; *Āpastamba*, II. 5. 12. 22-23; *Gautama*, XV. 16 ; *Yājñavalkya Smṛti*, I. 223.

It is thus quite easy to understand, in the light of these dharmik formulations, why Arjuna refuses to marry Draupadī before Yudhiṣṭhira and Bhīma. Even before the prescribed ceremonies take place, Kuntī accepts Kṛṣṇā as her daughter-in-law, and entrusts her with the household chores.[1] And that daughter of a king quite cheerfully does as she is told, and distributes the food around, giving the great glutton Bhīma the lion's share.[2] She certainly acts as a delighted daughter-in-law, nothing daunted by the prospect of five husbands. They all lie down together on a kuśa grass bed on the ground; Kuntī, the mother, sleeps by the side of the heads of the Pāṇḍava heroes, while Kṛṣṇā lies athwart their feet:[3]

> So she lay on the floor with the sons of Pāṇḍu,
> As though rendered a foot pillow on the grass :
> And no grievance arose in her for that.
> Nor did she despise the bulls of the Kurus.[4]

After finding out where his daughter is staying with her winners, King Drupada sends his family priest to them.[5] The latter praises the Pāṇḍavas and entreats them to disclose their identity, and to marry Kṛṣṇā according to Law.[6] Yudhiṣṭhira orders water and guest-gift to be offered to the priest, and tells him that King Drupada set a test for winning his daughter, who was duly won by

[1] *Mbh.,* I. 184. 4-6.
[2] *Ibid.,* I. 184. 6-7.
[3] *Ibid.,* I. 184. 8-9.
[4] *Ibid.,* I. 184. 10, Buitenen's translation.
aśeta bhūmau saha pāṇḍuputraiḥ
pādopadhāneva kṛtā kuśeṣu /
na tatra duḥkhaṁ ca babhūva tasyā
na cāvamene kurupuṅgavānstān //
[5] *Ibid.,* I. 185. 14.
[6] *Ibid.,* I. 185. 15-19.

Arjuna. Questions of class, living, lineage or family of the victor are therefore alike irrelevant and irksome:[1]

> She has been bestowed by the fact of the bow
> Being corded, the fact of the mark being hit.
> And thus the great-spirited man has won
> This Kṛṣṇā amidst the hosts of the kings.[2]

A second messenger arrives from the Pāñcāla court to announce that a feast has been prepared for the bridegroom's party, and to ask the Pāṇḍavas to proceed together with Kṛṣṇā to Drupada's palace.[3] The Pāṇḍavas send the priest back ahead of themselves; and follow with Kuntī and Kṛṣṇā on chariots provided for their ride.[4] King Drupada extends warm-hearted hospitality, and the finest food is served around in dishes and bowls of silver and gold. Kuntī goes with Draupadī into the king's female apartments, where she receives the homage of the inmates.[5] The king and his son, and their councillors, pay court to the Pāṇḍavas;[6] and then Drupada requests Yudhiṣṭhira to reveal whether they are brāhmaṇas or kṣatriyas. When the latter tells him that they are kṣatriyas, he is exceedingly happy, and the Pāṇḍavas are invited into the palace.[7]

The King and his sons later ask for Arjuna to take the hand of Draupadī in ritual fashion,[8] whereupon Yudhiṣṭhira, "the son of

[1] *Ibid.,* I, 185. 23.
[2] *Ibid.,* I. 185. 24. Buitenen's translation.
[3] *Ibid.,* I. 185. 28; 186. 1.
[4] *Ibid.,* I. 186. 2-3.
[5] *Ibid.,* I. 186. 4-13.
[6] *Ibid.,* I. 186. 15.
[7] *Ibid.,* I. 187. 1 ff.
[8] *Ibid.,* I. 187. 19:

gṛhṇātu vidhivatpāṇimadyaiva kurunandanaḥ /
puṇye'hani mahābāhurarjunḥa kurutāṁ kṣaṇaṁ /

Law" (*Dharmaputra*) tells Drupada, "Then I must also take my wife, O lord of the people."[1] Drupada then requests Yudhiṣṭhira to take Kṛṣṇā's hand by the ritual, or assign her to whomsoever he wishes.[2] But Yudhiṣṭhira says:

> Draupadī shall be the common queen of us all....for this is what my mother said....I am yet unmarried, and so is Bhīmasena Pāṇḍava. Your daughter was won by Pārtha, and she is a treasure. We have a covenant that we share together every treasure, O King, and we do not want to break our covenant now. According to Law, Kṛṣṇā will be the common queen of us all. She will take the hand of each of us, one after the other, before the fire.[3]

Drupada opposes the proposition, and thus addresses Yudhiṣṭhira :

> It is laid down that a man may have many queens, but never that a woman may have many men (husbands), O scion of Kuru ! You should not commit such a breach of *dharma*,

[1] *Ibid.*, I. 187. 20:
tatastamabravīdrājā dharmaputro yudhiṣṭhiraḥ |
mamāpi dārasaṁbandhaḥ kāryastāvadviśāṁ pate ||

[2] *Ibid.*, I. 187. 21:
bhavānvā vidhivatpāṇiṁ gṛhṇātu duhiturmama |
yasya vā manyase vīra tasya kṛṣṇāmupādiśa ||

[3] *Ibid.*, I. 187. 22-25:
sarveṣāṁ draupadī rājanmahiṣī no bhaviṣyati |
evaṁ hi vyāhṛtaṁ pūrvaṁ mama mātrā viśāṁ pate || 22
ahaṁ cāpyaniviṣṭo vai bhīmasenaśca pāṇḍavaḥ |
pārthena vijitā caiṣā ratnabhūtā ca te sutā || 23
eṣa naḥ samayo rājanratnasya sahabhojanaṁ |
na ca taṁ hātumicchāmaḥ samayaṁ rājasattama || 24
sarveṣāṁ dharmataḥ kṛṣṇā mahiṣī no bhaviṣyati |
ānupūrvyeṇa sarveṣāṁ gṛhṇātu jvalane karaṁ || 25

> contrary to *Veda* and the world, Law-minded and pure as you are, O Kaunteya! Whence this sort of scheme in your mind?[1]

These frequent appeals to the *Vedas* by the later apologists are often as funny as they are irrelevant and inaccurate. Resolute and not to be dissuaded, Yudhiṣṭhira is quite categorical:

> The Law (*dharma*) is subtle, O mahārāja; we do not know its course. One after the other, we follow the path that was trodden by the ancients. My voice tells no lies; my mind does not hold *adharma*. Thus has my mother spoken; and such is also my desire. This is the lasting Law (*dharmo dhruvo*), O King, obey it without vacillation. You should have no doubts about it, whatsoever, my prince![2]

Drupada requests Yudhiṣṭhira, Kuntī and Dhṛṣṭadyumna to deliberate on what is to be done. Just then, the great sage Dvaipāyana Vyāsa arrives there, and after the formalities of welcome, Drupada asks him the great question of the moment: How can a woman be the wife of many men without breaking the Law?[3] Vyāsa wants to hear the arguments for and against the proposal, and Drupada says it would result in a breach of the Law; it would

1 *Ibid.*, I. 187. 26-27:
ekasya bahvyo vihitā mahiṣyaḥ kurunandana |
naikasyā bahavaḥ puṁso vidhīyante kadācana || 26
lokavedaviruddhaṁ tvaṁ nādharmaṁ dhārmikaḥ śuciḥ |
kartumarhasi kaunteya kasmātte buddhirīdṛśī || 27

2 *Ibid.*, I. 187. 28-30:
sūkṣmo dharmo mahārāja nāsya vidmo vayaṁ gatiṁ |
pūrveṣāmānupūrvyeṇa yātaṁ vartmānuyāmahe || 28
na me vāganṛtaṁ prāha nādharme dhīyate matiḥ |
evaṁ caiva vadatyambā mama caiva manogataṁ || 29
eṣa dharmo dhruvo rājanścarainamavicārayan |
mā ca te'tra viśaṅkā bhūtkathaṁcidapi pārthiva || 30

3 *Ibid.*, I. 188. 5.

be contrary to the *Veda* and the world; for one wife of many men is not found.[1] He does not regard polyandry as an "eternal Law", and cannot decide to put it into practice in a mental state of moral misgiving.

Dhṛṣṭadyumna, however, gives the lie to his father's alleged ignorance of polyandry or of its practice in the past, when he says: "But how can an elder brother have congress with his younger brother's wife, O brāhmaṇa, best of the twice-born, and yet be steadfast in his virtue, O ascetic?[2] *Dharma* is too subtle for us to know its course in full. People like us cannot decide whether it is *dharma* or a breach thereof (*adharma*), O brāhmaṇa! I, therefore, come to no decision, whatever, on whether Kṛṣṇā should be the queen of the five."[3]

Dhṛṣṭadyumna, thus, offers no objection to polyandry as such; he remained silent even before the arrival of Vyāsa, when his father alone sought to protest. What he finds hard to condone is that the elder brother would have access to the wife of the younger brother. The younger brother, then, could have access to the elder's wife without violating Dhṛṣṭadyumna's code of ethics. Draupadī's brother is apparently familiar with that type of polyandry, in which a woman married to the eldest brother serves as the common wife of the younger brothers as well. Therefore, the eldest brother is the first to marry; and his younger brothers follow him. It may not even be necessary for the younger brothers to go through the ritual of marriage to be deemed the co-husbands of

[1] *Ibid.*, I. 188. 7, ... *na hyekā vidyate patnī bahūnāṁ dvijasattama.*

[2] *Ibid.*, I. 188. 10:

yavīyasaḥ kathaṁ bhāryāṁ jyeṣṭho bhrātā dvijarṣabha |
brahman samabhivarteta sadvṛttaḥ saṁstapodhana ||

Dvijarṣabha, literally "bull of the twice-born", is better translated as "the best of the twice-born".

[3] *Ibid.*, I. 188. 11-12.

their eldest brother's wife. Dhṛṣṭadyumna seems to be aware of this restricted species of polyandry, in which the elder brother would not go to the wife of a younger brother, i.e., a woman married only to a younger brother. The line of his argument clearly shows that he is not so sure of his father's objections, or of the Law in the matter.

Yudhiṣṭhira speaks again:

> My voice tells no lies ; my mind does not hold *adharma*. As my thoughts favour it, it cannot in any way be a breach of *dharma*. We hear in the ancient lore (*purāṇa*) that a girl of the Gautama gotra named Jaṭilā, eminent amongst the upholders of *dharma*, lay with the seven seers.[1] So also did Vārkṣī, the daughter of Muni (Kaṇḍu), marry the ten Pracetasa brothers of one name, of souls purified by their penance.[2] O most Law-wise sage, the word of a *guru* is said to be *dharma*, and of all the *gurus* the mother is the greatest. And she has spoken the words, "Share as you share the alms." Therefore, I take it to be *dharma*, O most excellent of the twice-born ![3]

[1] *Ibid.*, I. 188. 13-14:

na me vāganṛtaṁ prāha nādharme dhīyate matiḥ |
vartate hi mano me'tra naiṣo'dharmaḥ kathaṁcana || 13
śrūyate hi purāṇe'pi jaṭilā nāma gautamī |
ṛṣīnadhyāsitavatī sapta dharmabhṛtāṁ varā || 14

I don't agree with the reading *vara* at the end of this verse, given in the *Critical Edition*, and have, therefore, adopted *varā* of the other editions because of its obviously greater relevance in the present context.

[2] *Ibid.*, I. 195. 15, Gita Press Edn.:

tathaiva munijā vārkṣī tapobhirbhāvitātmanaḥ |
saṁgatābhūd daśa bhrātṛnekanāmnaḥ pracetasaḥ ||

This śloka is, questionably, relegated to the footnotes in the *Critical Edition*; Cf. f.n. 14: 1910 on p. 756 of the *Ādiparva*.

[3] *Ibid.*, I. 188. 15-16, Critical Edn.:

guruśca vacanaṁ prāhurdharmaṁ dharmajñasattama |
gurūṇāṁ caiva sarveṣāṁ janitrī paramo guruḥ || 15

Kuntī reaffirms her wish in no uncertain terms : "It is just as the dharma-abiding Yudhiṣṭhira says. My fear of lying is indeed excessive; how can I escape (the sin of) lying?"[1] This fear of lying is a clever expression of the inner wish, now out in the open, that Draupadī should marry the five Pāṇḍavas.

The great Vyāsa gives his verdict in favour of the proposal, and assures Kuntī that she would escape the sin of lying. He agrees that whatever Yudhiṣṭhira said was in perfect harmony with *dharma* without a shadow of doubt. "This is the eternal Law", he declares, and takes the king inside a royal chamber to confide to him alone, how the Law came to be ordained.[2]

While the Pāṇḍavas, Kuntī and Dhṛṣṭadyumna await their return, Vyāsa tells the king how the Law came to be that many men would have one wife (*bahūnāmekapatnitā*).[3] He recounts the story of five Indras incarcerated in a cave by the great God for their insolence, and then sent down to the earth to be reborn.[4] Begotten by Dharma, Vāyu, Indra and the Aśvins in accordance with their wish, the five Indras are born as the five Pāṇḍavas. As Draupadī is Lakṣmī, they are destined for each other. Vyāsa conjures up a vision of the former celestial bodies of the Pāṇḍavas, and also of Śrī who is now Draupadī, for the king to see. Drupada is pleased and surprised.[5]

---

sā cāpyuktavatī vācaṁ bhaiṣavadbhujyatāmiti |
tasmādetadahaṁ manye dharmaṁ dvijavarottama || 16

1 *Ibid.*, I. 188. 17..... *anṛtānme bhayaṁ tīvraṁ*
mucyeyamanṛtāt kathaṁ || 17

2 *Ibid.*, I. 188. 18-19 : .... *yathā ca prāha kaunteyastathā*
dharmo na saṁśayḥ || 19. Also 20.

3 *Ibid.*, I. 188. 22, ... *ācakhyau tadyathā dharmo*
bahūnāmekapatnitā.

4 *Ibid.*, I. 189.

5 *Ibid.*, I. 189. 30-45.

Draupadī is thus an incarnation of Śrī, who is even otherwise polyandrous, as we shall see later. The role of Draupadī, therefore, could not be more apposite or appropriate !

The story of the Indras was indeed invented as a sop to later morality. But the Indras were still five in number, not one, and in their present incarnations begotten by different deities. The explanation only pushes polyandry into the precincts of the gods.

As if one explanation is not enough, Vyāsa furnishes another, which can be equally easily laughed out of court. He now tells the story of the daughter of a "great-spirited" sage. Despite her beauty, she failed to find a suitable husband. Determined, however, to achieve her objective, she satisfied Śaṁkara with severe austerities; and the Lord asked her to "choose a boon". The girl said, "I want to have a husband who has all the virtues", and repeated it again and again. The benevolent Lord of the gods gave her the desired boon : "You shall have five excellent husbands."[1] Five times she had asked him for a husband, and so it would be in a following incarnation.[2]

The god Śaṁkara himself sees nothing wrong or reprehensible in conferring on a maiden the bliss of five husbands. Polyandry is clearly blessed by divinity, deriving its sanction directly from Śiva. If a girl asks for a husband five times, the benign god in his irrepressible generosity gives her five, blameless in the form of divine benediction. This, too, clearly shows that polyandry was not so long ago a practice of common occurrence.

Finally, says Vyāsa:

> The effulgent goddess sought by the gods,
> Sole wife to the five by the acts she performed,

[1] *Ibid.*, I. 189. 41-44.
[2] *Ibid.*, I. 189. 45 ff.

The Creator created as wife to the gods,
And hearing this, Drupada, act as you wish.[1]

The Creator, the gods and the goddess are all alike parties to the polyandrous marriage of Draupadī. It is only man conditioned by the growth of later morality, who wavers and vacillates. We are looking at a period of social and moral transition, when polyandry is going out of fashion in the Middle Country (*madhyadeśa*). What was once commonplace, called for laboured justification in the later editions of the great Epic; and we shall not be wrong in assuming that, in its original form, the story of Draupadī's marriage must have been a straightforward account, with no trace of ethical opprobrium clouding the practice of polyandry.

Drupada acquiesces in the polyandrous proposition. What can puny man do against the divine ?[2]

Since Kṛṣṇā had said in the days of yore
"May the blessed Lord give me many a husband",
He pronounced his boon in the way she asked.
The God surely knows the best of it.[3]

The father understands that his daughter had herself asked for "many a husband", and the Lord obliged. Whether it is *dharma* or *adharma*, he would bear no guilt whatsoever. He asks them to take her hand in the ritual way, "for to them is Kṛṣṇā ordained."[4]

[1] *Ibid.*, I. 189. 49. Buitenen's translation.
[2] *Ibid.*, I. 190. 1-2.
[3] *Ibid.*, I. 190. 3, Buitenen's translation.
yathaiva kṛṣṇoktavatī purastā
nnaikānpatīnme bhagavān dadātu /
sa cāpyevaṁ varamityabravīttāṁ
devo hi veda paramaṁ yadatra //
[4] *Ibid.*, I. 190. 4.

This is later morality squirming still in the mouth of Drupada. It may indeed be that polyandry was not universally practised among all Āryan tribes; that some upheld it, while others derided or detested it. God, however, certainly sanctioned it. It is not necessary to suppose with Hopkins that the Pāṇḍavas were "an unknown folk", who "attacked the stronghold of Brahmanism in the holy land about the present Delhi", simply because they were polyandrous.[1] We have already seen that polyandry was definitely known to the Āryans and practised by them even before the bands of Indo-European tribes descended on India. Hence, we do not have to speculate with Altekar either, that the Pāṇḍavas derived their polyandry from the peoples of Tibet and Kashmir, because "they belonged to a stock of Āryans different from that of the Kauravas," who "entered India via the Gilgit pass in Kashmir and through Nepal."[2] Times without number, the *Mahābhārata* refers to the Pāṇḍavas as Kauravas; Pāṇḍu is patently called "*kurukulodvahaḥ*";[3] and so is Yudhiṣṭhira elsewhere.[4] Patañjali[5] knows Bhīma, Nakula and Sahadeva as Kurus; the *Dasa-Brāhmaṇa Jātaka*[6] calls a scion of Yudhiṭṭhila a Koravya; and the *Kurudhamma Jātaka*[7] refers to Dhanañjaya as a Kuru king. We must also bear in mind the permissive land of the Uttara-kurus; and the matrimonial bonds of the Kauravas with the Madras and the Gāndhāras, whose lives are free from the sanctimonious sex

[1] Hopkins, *The Religions of India*, pp. 466-67; *CHI*, vol. I, p. 230.

[2] Altekar, *The Position of Women in Hindu Civilization*, IInd edn,. Delhi, 1973, p. 114.

[3] *Mbh.*, I. 117.31.

[4] *Ibid.*, II. 46. 5, Gita Press Edn.; III. 18. 9, Critical Edn. Cf. I. 187. 19 and 26, Critical Edn., where King Drupada of Pāñcāla addresses Arjuna and Yudhiṣṭhira as *Kurunandana*.

[5] Patañjali, IV. 1. 4 ; cf. *Ind. Ant.*, I, p. 350.

[6] Cowell's *Jātaka*, vol. IV, p. 227.

[7] *Ibid.*, vol. II, p. 251.

restrictions of other climes. The *Śatapatha Brāhmaṇa*[1] in fact refers to a Kauravya king (*kauravyo rājā*) called Bahlika Prātipīya; and the great Epic leaves us in no doubt about the free life of the Bāhlikas.[2] There is no valid reason to support the supposition that the Pāṇḍavas were neither Kauravas nor Āryas. 'Pious' preconceptions alone lead to such a suggestion, the absence of proof notwithstanding.

The Epic gives us a detailed description of the ceremonies that follow. Drupada asks Yudhiṣṭhira to "take Kṛṣṇā's hand first of all", as the day is one of good augury, when the moon is conjoined with Puṣya.[3] The king gives a great deal of wealth to the bridegroom's party. The blushing bride appears, bathed and bedecked with sparkling jewels;[4] the friends, relatives, ministers and councillors of the king, the brāhmaṇas and the notables of the town, are all there to watch the wedding; and crowds of beggars complete the picture of the local populace.[5] The young sons of the king of the Kauravas,[6] elegantly robed, ornamented and scented, perform the prescribed hallowing rites, and enter the assembly hall with Dhaumya, their family priest, in proper pomp one after the other, in order of seniority.[7] The Veda-wise Dhaumya then lights a fire, makes offerings with proper hymns, and joins Yudhiṣṭhira with Kṛṣṇā with *mantras* prescribed for the purpose. He makes them both walk, hands joined, the deasil around the fire to complete the rite of marriage.[8]

1 *Śatapatha Brāhmaṇa,* XII. 9. 3. 3,....
bahlikaḥ prātipīyaḥ...kauravyo rājā.

2 Discussed earlier.

3 *Mbh.,* I. 190. 5.

4 *Ibid.,* I. 190. 6

5 *Ibid.,* I. 190. 7-8.

6 *Ibid.,* I. 190. 9. Here, too, Pāṇḍu is called *kauravarāja.*

7 *Ibid.,* I. 190. 10. Even today, the wedding parties carry their own priests.

8 *Ibid.,* I. 190. 11-12.

It is indeed a classical instance of polyandry, with the eldest brother the first to marry, still practised in the Himālayas and elsewhere with local variations.

> One after the other, a day apart,
> The warrior sons of the king of men,
> The beautiful scions of Kuru's line,
> Took each the hand of the choicest of brides.[1]
> And this great wonder the seer declared.
> A wonder surpassing the power of man.
> That the beautiful wife of majestic might
> Each day became a virgin again.[2]

This preoccupation with virginity may be a later superimposition on a polyandrous union, where the husbands, of necessity, have to take turns. Or else, the priest of the Pāṇḍavas performed their nuptial rites according to a form which supposedly enabled the bride to regain her virginity after each individual marriage and its consummation. The sage Dhaumya was fully familiar with polyandry and the rituals that accompanied it. His role and Vyāsa's support alike indicate unambiguous brahmanical acceptance of polyandry. Sarkar[3] makes the interesting point that "the Gautama (Āṅgirasa), Vāsiṣṭha and Kāśyapa brāhmaṇs were all familiar with polyandric marriages, as much as the princes and people of Indraprastha, Matsya and Pāñcāla." That polyandry was more common among

1 *Ibid.*, I. 190. 13, Buitenen's translation.
krameṇa cānena narādhipātmajā
varastriyāste jagṛhustadā karaṁ |
ahanyahanyuttamarūpadhāriṇo
mahārathāḥ kauravavaṁśavardhanāḥ ||
Here, again, the Pāṇḍavas are clearly called Kauravas.

2 *Ibid.*, I. 190. 14, Buitenen's translation.

3 Cf. Sarkar. *Some Aspects of the Earliest Social History of India*, p. 152, n. 4.

brāhmaṇas, is revealed by Draupadī's regret elsewhere that she and her husbands were not born as brāhmaṇas, for amongst the kṣatriyas she was derisively called a "cow" by Duryodhana.[1] The polyandrous marriage of the brāhmaṇa lady Jaṭilā Gautamī was well and widely known; for when the victorious Pāṇḍavas later entered the city of Hastināpura together with Draupadī, they were admired by the populace, and the women exclaimed:

> Hail, Pāñcālī, you serve these five good men, like Gautamī serving her ṛṣi husbands.[2]

We do not hear even the faintest whisper of disapproval from the ranks of the Pāñcāla people who witness the marriage of Draupadī. So, too, later, she conceals her identity in the country of the Matsyas by professing to be the common wife of five gandharvas. Queen Sudeṣṇā is neither surprised nor shocked by the statement of the *sairaṁdhrī* (maid-servant).[3] The people of Matsya doubtless know polyandry and practise it. Their queen Sudeṣṇā knows it from the country of Kaikeyas adjacent to the Punjab hills, whence she herself hails, and where polyandry is still practised. The intermingling of races and settlement of some Āryans in the sub-Himalayan regions are facts beyond doubt or dispute.

To come back to the marriage of Draupadī, it is both celebrated and consummated by the five husbands in the home of the bride herself. Her father gives the Pāṇḍavas costly gifts, including chariots, horses, elephants, a hundred handmaids in beautiful

1 *Mbh*, III. 37. 25-27, Gita Press Edn.; III. 38. 21, Critical Edn.

2 *Ibid.*, XII. 38.5, Gita Press Edn.; XII. 39. 5, Critical Edn.
dhanyā tvamasi pāñcāli yā tvaṁ puruṣasattamān /
upatiṣṭhasi kalyāṇi maharṣīniva gautamī //

3 *Ibid.*, IV. 8. 27-33, Critical Edn. Draupadī served this queen in the disguise of a maid-servant.

youth, robes and ornaments.[1] They bask like the equals of Indra in the sunshine of Pāñcāla hospitality.[2]

Drupada's ladies come to Kuntī, mention their names and touch her feet with their heads. Kṛṣṇā, too, dressed in a linen raiment, with the marriage thread duly tied, pays homage to her mother-in-law and, hands folded, stands bowed before her. Lovingly, Kuntī blesses her; and the benediction would bear quotation:

> ....Bear live children, bear man-children, and be, my dear, joined with much happiness, favoured with love, and gifted with joy. Be thou the Wife at their sacrifices, strict in thy vows, and, may the years for ever go by thee in the solemn homage of guests that come, of holy men, of children, of the old, and of your elders. Be thou anointed queen.... What precious treasures the earth may hold, O treasure of virtue, obtain them in happiness for a hundred autumns. As I bless thee now, bride, in thy linen raiment, so shall I bless thee again when thou hast virtuously borne a son.[3]

When the Kauravas view with misgiving the prosperity of the Pāṇḍavas, Karṇa tells Dhṛtarāṣṭra and Duryodhana that the five brothers cannot be alienated from one another: "Men in love with one and the same wife are not split".[4] Nor could anyone alienate Kṛṣṇā from them; for she chose them even when they were indigent, let alone their present prosperity. "Women

[1] *Ibid.*, I. 190. 15-17.

[2] *Ibid.*, I. 190. 18.

[3] *Ibid.*, I. 191. 2 ff. Buitenen's translation. The formal relations between the ladies of the two households (the bride's and the bridegroom's) are still much the same as they were in the days of the Epic. Kuntī's blessing voices the wish of every modern Indian mother-in-law for grandsons.

[4] *Ibid.*, I. 194. 6,...*ekasyāṁ ye ratāḥ patnyāṁ na bhidyante parasparaṁ.*

deem it a desirable attribute to have more than one husband. Kṛṣṇā (Draupadī) having managed to secure them, would not be alienated so easily !"[1]

This is a most significant utterance, in as much as it shows Karṇa's full familiarity with the practice of polyandry. He knows all its attributes. It fosters family or sibling solidarity and discourages division. Men in love with a common wife do not split. She keeps their property and goods together. Karṇa also knows that a woman likes to have several husbands. He uses the term *bahubhartṛtā* to denote polyandry; while elsewhere[2] it is described as *bahūnāmekapatnitā*.

Droṇa advises the Kauravas to send a soft-spoken man to Drupada's court with rich presents for the Pāṇḍavas. He should speak of the great growth of fortune arising out of this alliance; he should state that Dhṛtarāṣṭra and Duryodhana are immensely pleased; he should present to Draupadī jewelry of sparkling gold and propose the Pāṇḍavas' return to Hastināpura.[3]

Not a word is uttered by any of the Kauravas or brāhmaṇas against Draupadī's polyandrous marriage. They are neither disgusted nor even surprised. There is no aversion to a polyandrous alliance as such, hailed by the brāhmaṇa Droṇa as most felicitous. The grounds of opposition to the Pāṇḍavas lie elsewhere, in family dissension and the question of succession to the kingdom. It is only later that the discomfited contenders for her hand in her *svayaṁvara*, Karṇa and Duryodhana deprecate

[1] *Ibid.*, I. 194. 6-8 :
īpsitaśca guṇaḥ strīṇāmekasyā bahubhartṛtā |
taṁ ca prāptavatī kṛṣṇā na sā bhedayituṁ sukhaṁ|| 8

[2] *Ibid.*, I. 188. 22.

[3] *Ibid.*, I. 196. 1-10.

Draupadī's polyandrous union with the Pāṇḍavas. The importance of all this evidence has not been realized before.

Dhṛtarāṣṭra dispatches Vidura with lavish presents to bring the Pāṇḍavas and their wife home.[1] Vidura tells King Drupada that "all the first ladies of the Kurus, and the city, and the country, are waiting to see Kṛṣṇā Pāñcālī..."[2] There is no poohpooing of polyandry here, but only full acceptance and eagerness to meet the new bride.

The Pāṇḍavas return to a joyous welcome, and are given the Khāṇḍava tract, half of the kingdom, in a settlement of their claims.[3] They are later visited by the famous seer Nārada, who advises them: "O Pāṇḍavas, the renowned Pāñcālī is the one lawful wife (*dharmapatnī*) of you all. You should therefore devise (proper) policy, so that there may not be any dissension here."[4] He tells them of Sunda and Upasunda, two Asura brothers of times past, who always lived together, and could not be killed by anyone else except themselves, owing to a boon they received from Brahmā. They had one kingdom and one home. They slept in one bed, sat on one seat, and ate together. But despite deep love mutually reciprocated, they killed each other for the sake of possessing the *apsarā* Tilottamā.[5]

Brahmanical practice and acceptance of polyandry is again evidenced in Nārada's reference to Draupadī as a *dharmapatnī*. He praises her, but cautions the Pāṇḍavas against jealous dissension.

1 *Ibid.*, I. 198. 1-5.
2 *Ibid.*, I. 198. 15 ff.
3 *Ibid.*, I. 199.
4 *Ibid.*, I. 200. 17 :
pāñcālī bhavatāmekā dharmapatnī yaśasvinī /
yathā vo nātra bhedaḥ syāt tathā nītirvidhīyatām //
5 *Ibid.*, I. 200. 18-19.

The story of Sunda and Upasunda shows that the two asura brothers shared everything in life including their bed and their women. Since they committed great atrocities, Brahmā at the instance of afflicted seers decided to destroy them. At his command, Viśvakarmā created a divine woman of unexcelled beauty by gathering everything lovely from the three worlds and investing her body with the lustre of numerous gems. She was asked by Brahmā to go to Sunda and Upasunda and act so as to raise a quarrel between the two brothers over her and her perfect body.[1]

She was made to be irresistible.[2] The two asuras,[3] given to pleasure with women presumably shared, one day went to enjoy themselves on a Vindhyan rock plateau, amid śāla trees with flowering crowns. Their women went with them and waited on them with music and dance. It was there that Tilottamā appeared, plucking flowers in the woods in a provocative garb of one red piece of cloth.[4] The two brothers were smitten as soon as they saw her full swaying hips and fine buttocks; they leapt from their seats and rushed towards her. Crazed by love, Sunda took her by the right hand, and Upasunda by the left. They then began shouting to each other: "She is my wife and your *guru*", said Sunda; "she is mine and your sister-in-law", said the other.[5] "She is not yours, she is mine", they shouted at each other; "me first, me first", they cried, as blinded by their rage and love for her they fought and slew each other.[6]

"Me first, me first", shout the two, as they die. It is precedence that matters more than sharing, which would have

1 *Ibid.*, I. 203. 10-19.
2 *Ibid.*, I. 203. 20 ff.
3 We have talked of asura polyandry before.
4 *Ibid.*, I. 204. 6-9.
5 *Ibid.*, I. 204. 16,...*mamabhāryā tava gururiti*...
6 *Ibid.*, I. 204. 10 ff.; verse 18, *ahaṁ pūrvamahaṁ pūrvamityanyonyaṁ nijaghnatuḥ*.

been amicably arranged,[1] but for the fact that Tilottamā had been expressly created to kindle instant irrepressible lust calculated to destroy the two asuras. The context of the story also shows that Nārada sees nothing wrong or remiss in brothers sharing a wife. The only moral he seeks to convey is that there should be no misunderstanding between the brothers. They should so order their relations with their common wife, that they all enjoy her without detriment to one another.[2]

The Pāṇḍavas make a covenant with one another then and there: "If one of us sees the other while he is sitting with Draupadī, he must live in the forest as a hermit for twelve years."[3]

1 Cf. *Ibid.*, I. 204. 25, *evaṁ tau sahitau bhūtvā sarvārtheṣvekaniścayau*...Cf. Sarkar, *op. cit.*, p. 150, n. 2, where he examines the allusions to Sunda and Upasunda in the *Rāmāyaṇa* and the *Purāṇas*. Cf. also *Brahmāṇḍa*, III. 5. 34 ff.; *Vāyu*, 67. 72-3.

2 *Mbh.*, I. 204. 26,...*yathā vo nātra bhedaḥ syāt sarveṣāṁ draupadīkṛte*...

3 *Ibid.*, I. 204. 28, *draupadyā naḥ sahāsīnamanyonyaṁ yo'bhidarśayet | sa no dvādaśavarṣāṇi brahmacārī vane vaset ||* There are various ways of arranging access to the common wife in polyandrous societies. Either each sharer in the marriage takes his turn on his fixed days, or a sign at the woman's door warns the others. Such a *cave canem* at the entrance to the common love-paradise differed from place to place. Among the Massagetae it was the quiver of the man with her at the moment hanging to the wife's waggon; among the Nasamones in Libya the man left his staff at the door; and so also among the Arabians and Sabaeans. The staff, arrow or shoe kept the others away among the old Arabs. Cf. Meyer, *op. cit.*, p. 112, n.1. Strabo, XVI. 4, 25, says of pre-Islamic Arabia : "...A daughter of a certain king who had fifteen brothers all much in love with her tried to keep her room to herself by getting sticks like her husbands' to put at the door. One of the brothers found the stick at the door when he knew that the whole family were in the market-place, and suspecting the presence of an adulterer, he runs to the father, who comes up, and it is found that the man has falsely accused his sister." The reference to "sister" here is "habitually explained by saying that as the eldest brother-husband was often called 'father', the common wife was looked upon as his daughter, and hence a 'sister' of her other husbands." Prince Peter, *op. cit.*, p. 60. The Tiyan in Malabar places a knife in the door-frame as a warning sign; and the Izhuva or Tandan in south Malabar puts a vessel with water before the entrance. Cf. Hartland, *Primitive Paternity*, II, pp. 165 ff.

The covenant is faithfully kept, and the Pāṇḍavas live happily together for a long time. Their wife fulfils all their wishes, and is as pleased with them as they are with her.[1] But one day, while Yudhiṣṭhira is with his wife Draupadī, Arjuna is asked for immediate help by a brāhmaṇa, whose cows have been stolen.[2] Arjuna tells him to have no fear; but his weapons are in the room occupied by the king and Kṛṣṇā. He recognizes the urgent priority of protection sought by the brāhmaṇa, enters the room, takes his bow with the king's permission, goes out and scatters the robbers.[3] The brāhmaṇa's property is recovered; but Yudhiṣṭhira's privacy with Kṛṣṇā is transgressed. So, on his return, Arjuna says to his brother: "...I have violated the covenant by seeing you (together). I shall go and live in the forest, for that was the agreement we made."[4]

Yudhiṣṭhira, however, calls him blameless, and tells him that he forgave him and bore him no grudge, whatever. "It is not an offence if a younger brother enters at his elder's; it is violative of the law (*vidhilopakaḥ*), if the eldest enters at his younger brother's."[5] Yudhiṣṭhira asks him to desist from his design, since no offence was taken where none was meant; but Arjuna is adamant and goes into banishment.[6]

During the course of his self-imposed exile, Arjuna marries Ulūpī[7] and Citrāṅgadā[8]; and both these marriages remain matrilocal. Vora's statement that the Pāṇḍavas show traces of

[1] *Mbh.*, I. 205. 1-4.
[2] *Ibid.*, I. 205. 5-9.
[3] *Ibid.*, I. 205. 10-22.
[4] *Ibid.*, I. 205. 24.
[5] *Ibid.*, I. 205. 27.
[6] *Ibid.*, I. 205. 25-30.
[7] *Ibid.*, I. 206.
[8] *Ibid.*, I. 207.

matriliny, is open to grave doubt, if not altogether wrong.[1] The influence of Kuntī or of her relative Kṛṣṇa is not enough to substantiate the supposition. This type of maternal influence is an inseparable part of the Indian patrilineal set-up even today, as it was yesterday.

Arjuna later elopes with Subhadrā, and comes back with her to Khāṇḍavaprastha. He goes to Draupadī, who, torn by jealousy, thus addresses him: "Why have you come here, O son of Kuntī? Go where the daughter of the Sātvata is; for however tightly you may tie a load, the first knot becomes loose when you tie it again."[2] Arjuna consoles her and repeatedly apologizes;[3] Draupadī is yet supreme. Subhadrā, too, pays her homage and meekly tells Draupadī, "I am your slave."[4]

Thus, some of the Pāṇḍavas individually acquire more wives. Yudhiṣṭhira, though, has only one wife, Draupadī, common to them all. We have to reckon with a situation where polyandry and polygyny coexist in close proximity.

Though he had earlier shown great understanding of the motivating factors behind polyandry,[5] Karṇa insults Draupadī and calls her a courtesan (*bandhakī*) because she is "under many",[6]

[1] Cf. Vora, *Evolution of Morals in the Epics*, p. 9.

[2] *Mbh.*, I. 213. 15:

tatraiva gaccha kaunteya yatra sā sātvatātmajā |
subaddhasyāpi bhārasya pūrvabandhaḥ ślathāyate ||

[3] *Ibid.*, I. 213. 16.

[4] *Ibid.*, I. 213. 19, *vavande draupadīṁ bhadrā preṣyāhamiti cābravīt.*

[5] *Ibid.*, I. 194. 6-8.

[6] *Ibid.*, II. 61. 35 :

eko bhartā striyā devairvihitaḥ kurunandana |
iyaṁ tvanekavaśagā bandhakīti viniścitā ||

when Yudhiṣṭhira loses her to Duryodhana with everything else in a gambling game. But the fact that she is asked to choose a new husband in the Kaurava court, clearly shows that polyandry has by no means besmirched her.[1] Elsewhere, Jayadratha importunes her to leave her five husbands and become his queen.[2] Kīcaka, too, madly wants her.[3] Thus, previous polyandrous connections do not at all impede later marriage or marriages with others in the social climate of the *Mahābhārata.*

That Karṇa's abusive outburst against Draupadī is expressive of personal pique rather than current social attitudes, becomes quite clear from the statement of Dhṛtarāṣṭra in that very court: "You are the best of all my daughters-in-law, O Draupadī, devoted to *dharma* and a *satī.*"[4] Yudhiṣṭhira pays a glowing tribute to his wife before he bets and loses her. Beautiful beyond words, she is the model of a woman whom every man would like to love and own. She is modest, serviceable and diligent, so much so that she goes to bed even after the shepherds and cowherds, and knows all about the work done or yet to be done.[5] Despite her peerless charm and extraordinary qualities, though, she is bet

---

This is doubtless later morality in the mouth of the same man who, almost in the same breath, asks Draupadī to choose anyone of the Kauravas as her husband, thereby implying that she is quite unsoiled and acceptable.

1 *Ibid.*, II. 63. 3, *anyaṁ vṛṇīṣva patimāśu bhāmini...*

2 *Ibid.*, III. 251. 18, *bhāryā me bhava suśroṇi tyajainān sukhamāpnuhi...*

3 *Ibid.*, IV. 13. 6-12:

tyajāmai dārānmama ye purātanā
bhavntu dāsyastava cāruhāsini /
ahaṁ ca te sundari dāsavat sthitaḥ
sadā bhaviṣye vaśago varānane // 12

4 *Ibid.*, II. 63. 27, *vadhūnāṁ hi viśiṣṭā me tvaṁ dharma-paramā satī.* Cf. also verse 33, *tvaṁ hi sarvasnuṣāṇāṁ me śreyasī dharmacāriṇī.*

5 *Ibid.*, II. 58. 32-37. It is a remarkably candid description of his wife's faultless beauty and other qualities of head and heart.

and lost by a doting husband who is also a compulsive gambler. And that indicates the total mastery of a husband over his wife.[1] This incident in particular demonstrates the supreme authority of the seniormost husband in a polyandrous union.

Draupadī gives birth to five sons sired by her five husbands: Prativindhya by Yudhiṣṭhira; Sutasoma by Bhīmasena; Śrutakarman by Arjuna; Śatānīka by Nakula; and Śrutasena by Sahadeva.[2] They are all born a year apart one after the other, and are devoted to one another's well-being.

It is worthy of notice that two of Draupadī's husbands, Nakula and Sahadeva, have no blood relationship with the other brothers. And on the eve of the *Mahābhārata* war, Kṛṣṇa has a secret conference with Karṇa, in which he tries to win him over to the Pāṇḍava side.[3] Kṛṣṇa tells the first son of Kuntī that he is a *kānīna* son of Pāṇḍu in consonance with *dharma*;[4] and also that he would become king as the eldest brother if he espoused the Pāṇḍava cause. He finally attempts to lure Karṇa with the promise that the beautiful Draupadī would approach him, too, as a wife, when the sixth turn came.[5] Needless to stress, Kṛṣṇa has the prior consent of Draupadī to enlarge the scope of her polyandry, so as to include Karṇa in its fold.

[1] It is noteworthy that Yudhiṣṭhira thus loses her, without any protest from Arjuna who had won her. Yudhiṣṭhira also gambles himself and his brothers away into slavery, together with his wife. The loss of a wife in a betting game is also described in an English novel, *The Mayor of Casterbridge*, by Thomas Hardy.

[2] *Mbh.*, I. 213. 71-78.

[3] *Ibid.*, V. 138. 6 ff.

[4] *Ibid.*, V. 138. 9, *pāṇḍoḥ putro'si dharmataḥ*.

[5] *Ibid.*, V. 138. 15, *ṣaṣṭhe ca tvāṁ tathā kāle draupadyupagamiṣyati*. This shows that her five husbands took their turns according to an understanding between them.

A conversation between Satyabhāmā and Draupadī reveals how the latter manages to please all her five husbands, so that they are always under her control and never angry with her.[1] Draupadī says she eschews false pride, desire and anger in order to serve the Pāṇḍavas and even their other women.[2] She wins the hearts of her husbands only with the wish to serve, and allows no quarter to self-conceit or vanity.[3] She is careful in speech and cultured in her movements. She does not sit or stand at undesirable places; she does not shamelessly fling her glances around. She refrains from evil action, and is ever on her guard against indiscretion of any kind.[4] She does not feel any attraction towards other men or even the gods, and bestows all her love on her husbands.[5] She does not eat without first feeding them and even their attendants. She bathes after she has bathed them, and sleeps only when they are asleep.[6] Whenever her husbands come from outside, she gets up to greet them, and offers them seats and water.[7] She keeps her kitchen clean, prepares wholesome meals and feeds them at proper hours. She keeps her discipline and her promises.[8] She refrains from insulting anyone; and keeps aloof from the company of evil women. She is never lazy, and ever pleasant to her husbands.[9] She laughs only when they joke, and keeps away from dirty or lonely places. She does not stand at the door to stare at others; she does not talk to men of questionable character. She does not allow discontent a lodgement in her heart; she is never too talkative

[1] *Ibid.*, III. 222. 5 ff.
[2] *Ibid.*, III. 222. 18 ff.
[3] *Ibid.*, verse 19.
[4] *Ibid.*, verses 20-21.
[5] *Ibid.*, verse 22.
[6] *Ibid.*, verse 23.
[7] *Ibid.*, verse 24.
[8] *Ibid.*, verse 25.
[9] *Ibid.*, verse 26.

or too angry. In fact, she does not allow opportunities for anger to arise; always speaks the truth and serves her husbands; and does not desire to live anywhere without them.[1] She desists from adornment and performs *vrata* or penance in the absence of her husbands.[2] If her husbands do not eat or drink, she too gives up.[3] She adorns her person only to please them.[4] She maintains the traditions and rites of the family, as instructed by her mother-in-law.[5] She is always afraid of her husbands, while serving them;[6] for the husband is the refuge of the wife and her destiny. No woman would like to do a thing disliked by her husband.[7]

She keeps herself in proper check, and never speaks ill of her mother-in-law.[8] She personally helps Kuntī with her bath, clothes and food.[9] She gives her the same type of clothes and ornaments as she would herself like to wear, and always praises her.[10] It is indeed a very happy relationship.

Draupadī organizes the munificence of Pāṇḍava hospitality, and knows all the servants by their faces and names. She also knows what they do from day to day, and what remains yet to be done. She knows even the shepherds and cowherds in royal service, and keeps count of the horses and elephants in the royal stables. The first to rise, the last to retire, she maintains accounts of income and expenditure, and serves her lords without caring for

1 *Ibid.*, verses 27-28.
2 *Ibid.*, verse 29.
3 *Ibid.*, verse 30.
4 *Ibid.*, verse 31.
5 *Ibid.*, verse 32.
6 *Ibid.*, verse 34.
7 *Ibid.*, verse 35.
8 *Ibid.*, verse 36, *nāpi parivade śvaśrūṁ...*
9 *Ibid.*, verse 38.
10 *Ibid.*, verse 39.

her own comforts. Devotion and service are the twin talismans of her hold over her husbands.[1]

Doubtless, Draupadī's is a great and majestic presence. Her beauty is as compelling as her demeanour; her charm is as eloquent as her virtue. She is vigilant, hospitable, hardworking and intelligent, devoted to her husbands and their prosperity. She is a woman of grit and determination, with a sharp and incisive mind, intent on dominating when she can; and outspoken if the occasion so demands. She may be initially jealous of a co-wife; but is then perfectly equable and dignified, gentle and obliging, as her senior. She personally serves and supervises the comforts of her mother-in-law, and is the paragon of a polyandrous wife, who radiates the glory of her limitless charm around, and wins hearts by her unfailing warmth and lavish hospitality. She is the Indian deity of beatific polyandry.

It is indeed remarkable that the Epic in its present form "moulded under direct sacerdotal influence" did not suppress the story of Pāṇḍava polyandry. "Those ballads which described too plainly the independence of the military caste, and their successful opposition to the sacerdotal, were modified, obscured by allegory, or rendered improbable by monstrous mythological embellishments. Any circumstance which appeared to militate against the Brahmanical system was speciously explained away, glossed over, or mystified."[2] It would therefore be wholly wrong to suppose that the Pāṇḍavas portrayed as the models of piety could adopt from conquered races "a practice to which even a shadow of moral reprobation was attached in ancient Aryan thought."[3] Later moralists, however, offered ingenious explana-

[1] *Ibid.*, III. 222. 40 ff.

[2] Monier-Williams, M., *Indian Epic Poetry*, pp. 10 sq.

[3] Briffault, *The Mothers*, vol. I., p. 684. n.

tory excuses. Thus Kumārilabhaṭṭa asserted that there were really five Draupadīs, very much alike, married separately to the five Pāṇḍavas; and that the Epic only figuratively spoke of one alone.[1] Such a statement is merely symptomatic of a change in outlook with the passage of time, even though the Indian society has always known polyandry in certain sections of her vast and variegated fold. Nīlakaṇṭha, for instance, in his comment on *Ādi.* 104. 35 (Bombay Edn.) refers to the practice of one woman having two or three husbands among the low castes of his day.

The *Mahābhārata* contains clear evidence of the incidence of polyandry among the brāhmaṇas, as among the kṣatriyas. Though it is undeniable that polyandry is a recessive social phenomenon running into increasing opposition from the protagonists and practitioners of the evolving Āryan ideal, it is equally true that old practices die hard, and continue to linger here and there, leaving their echoes in corners far and wide. We have already noted the polyandrous marriages of Vārkṣī and Jaṭilā Gautamī. The *Ādi Parva*[2] also speaks of the seer Utathya, who had a wife named Mamatā, held in great esteem by her husband. Utathya had a younger brother called Bṛhaspati, who was the priest of the gods, and who, possessed of great virility, lusted after Mamatā.[3] Once, however, approached by her brother-in-law who was a great arguer, Mamatā remonstrated: "Stop ! I am with child by your elder brother. This child of Utathya's in my womb has learned the *Veda* and its six branches... You would spill your seed in vain. And since

[1] *Tantravārtika*, p. 209, *athavā bahvya eva tāḥ sadṛśarūpā draupadya ekatvenopacaritā iti vyavahārārthāpattyā gamyate.* Cf. Kane, *op. cit.*, vol. II, Part I, p. 555.

[2] *Mbh.*, I. 98. 6.

[3] *Ibid.*, I. 98. 7.

utathasya yavīyāṁstu purodhāstridivaukasām |
bṛhaspatirbṛhattejā mamatāṁ so'nvapadyata ||

this is the case, you must stop today."[1] Despite her protest, Bṛhaspati was unable to check himself, and lay with his sister-in-law. But as he ejaculated his seed, the child in the womb spoke: "O little uncle, there is no room here for two ! You have wasted your seed, and I was here first !"[2]

Livid with rage, the blessed seer Bṛhaspati cursed the son of Utathya in the womb : "Since you spoke as you did at a moment cherished by all creatures, you shall enter a long darkness." Mamatā gave birth to a son who was congenitally blind owing to his uncle's curse, and hence became famous as Dīrghatamas, his uncle's peer in might.[3]

The story harks back to the *Ṛgveda*. and is told in the *Bṛhaddevatā*.[4] It is not a 'fantastic fabrication' except perhaps in details seeking to explain the etymology of Dīrghatamas. What is strikingly noteworthy is the fact that Mamatā sees nothing new or unknown in the conduct of Bṛhaspati. This is by no means *adharma*; and she seems quite used to such a relationship. The ground of her present objection is her physical condition, and not any moral aversion. The right of the younger brother to have sexual relations with the wife of his elder brother is fairly clearly recognized. To quote Meyer:[5]

[1] *Ibid.*, I. 98. 8-10.
[2] *Ibid.*, I. 98. 11-13.
[3] *Ibid.*, I. 98. 14 ff.
[4] See above, pp. 57-58.
[5] Meyer, *Sexual Life in Ancient India*, vol. I, pp. 114-115. In the *Daśakumāracarita*, p. 209 of Meyer's translation, cited in n.1, p. 115 of his *SLAI*, the "devilish wiles" of the gods and holy men are illustrated, among other things, by the visits of Bṛhaspati to the wife of Utathi. Cf. *Samayamātṛkā*, IV. 20-35. Bṛhaspati's own wife Tārā was abducted by the god Soma, and was later restored to her husband only through Brahmā's intervention. She gave birth to a son called Budha, who was claimed by both Bṛhaspati and Soma as theirs. Tārā settled the dispute by declaring that Soma, not Bṛhaspati, was the father of

It is, indeed, a strange thing to find a usage, which aroused the moral feelings of the Indian, unhesitatingly ascribed to this priest of the gods, Brihaspati, and to his brother, as also to other Rishis and holy men; and one feels tempted to look on such things as echoes from a time when, among even the Aryans also, group-marriage may have been a recognized institution. But such a conclusion would seem to be at least a highly uncertain one; for what stories are not told among the different peoples of gods and holy men! The Indian has often declared, in the Epic, too, that such divine figures as these are not tied down to the laws of earth, that mankind indeed must follow a loftier ethic than they. True enlightened views such as these belong to a later time, of noble spiritual and emotional culture, and can hardly be assumed in the age when such myths were being shaped, or in the days before it.

He cannot make up his mind !

Mamatā seems to have been the wife of both Utathya and Bṛhaspati, for the latter also got a son, Bharadvāja, through her. This Bharadvāja was so called because he was "born of two fathers", who both entrusted Mamatā with his maintenance.[1] He was also known as *dvyāmuṣyāyaṇa*, generally explained as referring to his adoption by Bharata, so that he was the son of a priest by birth, and of a king by adoption.[2] The details of his tradition,[3]

Budha. Cf. Walker, B., *Hindu World,* vol. I, p. 177. This clearly shows that both Bṛhaspati and Soma had access to Tārā at the time of her conception. Cf. *Varāha Purāṇa,* XXXII. She was also desired by Dharma, a brother of Bṛhaspati, who was, however, obstructed by her paramour Soma.

1 Sarkar, *op. cit.,* p.147.

2 *Ibid*

3 Cf. *Brahma,* XIII. 58-60; *Matsya,* 49. 11-34; *Viṣṇu,* IV. 19. 4-8; *Vāyu,* 99.

however, reveal that it was not Bharadvāja, but his son or descendant Vitatha or Vidathin, who was adopted. And this Vitatha was in all probability a *kṣetraja* son of Bharata through Sunandā, so that his was not really a case of adoption at all. The *Mahābhārata* tells us that Bharata got a son called Bhumanyu through the good offices of Bharadvāja, and that the line continued through Bhumanyu's progeny.[1] Bharadvāja was, therefore, a *dvyāmuṣyāyaṇa* because he was himself a son of two fathers, Utathya and Bṛhaspati, borne by their common wife Mamatā, just as Dakṣa was the son of ten fathers. The *Śrautasūtras,* too, mention the *dvyāmuṣyāyaṇa* or the *dvipitṛ*;[2] and we find, besides the descendants of Bharadvāja, "three other Āṅgirasa and eight (or twelve) Kāśypa families designated 'dvāmuṣyāyaṇas'; all of their forefathers cannot have been similarly adopted by childless kings, and they have no evident connexions with any dynasty; but these brāhmaṇ clans may well have had some sort of a biandric custom originally."[3]

Dīrghatamas, probably predisposed this way in his mother Mamatā's womb by his uncle's unrestrained lust, later learnṣ from Saurabheya the "custom of the cattle", and then practises it with great yearning and without fear. This "custom of the cattle" may connote "public copulation" as understood by Nīlakaṇṭha. But there is nothing in particular to be learnt about public indulgence; and promiscuity rather than "public copulation" seems to be intended. Meyer is "inclined to think of the joyous heat, painted by Boccaccio, of the stallions and mares on the Thessalian

[1] *Mbh.,* I. 94. 22, Gita Press Edn.,...*lebhe putraṁ bharadvājād bhumanyuṁ nāma bhārata.* Cf. Critical Edn., I. 90. 34.

[2] Jolly, *Hindu Law and Custom,* p. 156, Cf. Caland, *Altind. Ahnencult,* p. 197.

[3] Sarkar, *op. cit.,* p. 148. In note 1 on p. 150, Sarkar suggests that brāhmaṇa *gotra* names such as Āṅgirasa or Kāśyapa "may be Sanskritized forms of Dravidian clan names(meaning 'magician' and 'mat-seated father', respectively)."

plains,"[1] because enjoyment of the sex act like animals also seems to be implied. The other seers, however, charge Dīrghatamas with a breach of morality, and "mistakenly" consider him unfit to live in the hermitage. When his wife, together with her sons, refuses to keep him, Dīrghatamas declares: "From this day on the course of the Law in the world is laid down by me. One husband is for the woman the first thing and the last so long as she lives. Whether he be dead or alive, she shall have no other man. But if a wife goes to another man, then, without fail, she sinks out of her caste."[2]

This is indeed important, in as much as the passage evinces the birth of a new brand of morality in the restrictions imposed upon women and the prejudice against widow-remarriage. Clearly, till then, women had relations with more men than one, especially in the family or clan of Dīrghatamas, and practised polyandry of a kind. The constraint put upon his wife by Dīrghatamas connotes that she, too, was polyandrous like her mother-in-law Mamatā before her.

The *Mahābhārata* tells us the story of princess Mādhavī, charmingly illustrative of the polyandrous practices of that epoch. A pious disciple of the sage Viśvāmitra, named Gālava, completes his studies and then insists on paying his teacher's fee. Incensed, the teacher demands as his fee 800 noble, moon-white steeds, each with one black ear.[3] Gālava vainly seeks the rare horses around the world, and then, in despair, goes to the king Yayāti. The king does not have the horses, but dreads the consequence of disappointing a holy suppliant. He, therefore, gives Gālava his daughter Mādhavī of peerless beauty, and tells him that the rulers of the world would

[1] Cf. Meyer, *SLAI*, vol. I, p. 124, n. 1.

[2] *Mbh.*, I. 104. 22 ff., Bombay Edn. The Critical Edn., I. 98, drops this part of the story.

[3] *Ibid.*, V. 104. 26, Critical Edn.

give up their kingdoms to have her, let alone the 800 horses demanded by Viśvāmitra. The king would, however, like to have her sons perform the ancestral sacrifice for him. Gālava takes the girl in the springtide of her youth to King Haryaśva, who becomes love-sick at her first sight. He, though, has only 200 such horses to offer,[1] for which he is allowed to beget but one son with her. Mādhavī herself tells Gālava: "I was granted a boon by a man versed in the *Veda:* 'after each birth you will become a maid again." Give me to the king, so soon as you have received 200 peerless steeds. By means of four kings you will thus get full 800 horses, and I shall get four sons."[2] She lives with Haryaśva until she bears him a son for one fourth of the price, and then by the power of her wish becomes a maid again to go with Gālava to King Divodāsa, who rejoices greatly at her arrival. But he, too, can give only 200 such horses, and is therefore allowed to beget but one son with her.[3] Gālava and the girl, a maid again, then proceed to the court of King Uśīnara, who readily gives 200 horses and enjoys himself with her, till after a son's birth, she is demanded back.[4] The mythical bird Garuḍa now tells Gālava that there are no more than these 600 horses on earth, and the latter therefore offers Mādhavī to his *guru* to make up for the unavailability of 200 more such horses yet required.[5] A discerning judge of feminine charms, Viśvāmitra is quite satisfied, and says: "O, why did you not give her to me here immediately at the beginning ? Then I should have got four sons from her to carry on the line."[6] She bears him a son, and Viśvāmitra withdraws into the forest, giving her up to Gālava, who takes her back to her father. Yayāti, her father,

[1] *Ibid.*, V. 114. 8-9.
[2] *Ibid.*, V. 114. 10-12.
[3] *Ibid.*, V. 115.
[4] *Ibid.*, V. 116.
[5] *Ibid.*, V. 117.
[6] *Ibid.*, V. 117. 15.

holds a *svayaṁvara* for her; but she takes to the life of a penitent in the forest.

This is a rather revealing account of things. When Yayāti gave his daughter to Gālava, he knew what she was in for. When Gālava took her to Haryaśva, she showed that she was willing and even eager to marry that king, though she knew full well that she would have to marry other kings, too, to secure more horses for Viśvāmitra. She told Gālava the secret of her ever renewable maidenhood; and neither she, nor Gālava, saw anything objectionable in a marriage that led to others without the death of the first husband. It was she who suggested four husbands to father four sons, an idea closely akin to polyandry. Indeed, Sarkar feels that "she was jointly queen to four contemporary and neighbouring kings (viz., Haryaśva of Ayodhyā, Divodāsa of Vārāṇasi, Uśīnara of the North-West, and Viśvāmitra of Kānyakubja)...."[1]; and that the *ṛṣi* Gālava and Garuḍa are mere extenuating superimpositions of a later day. He likens her story to that of Śrī and the Pañcendras discussed earlier, and regards it as an example of plain polyandry.

The *Mahābhārata* also refers to the tradition of Nahuṣa courting Indra's queen Śacī, when he, too, becomes an Indra.[2] Even the gods advise Śacī to accept Nahuṣa as her husband;[3] and the reluctance of the lady protected by Bṛhaspati seems to be a later

[1] Sarkar, *op. cit.*, p. 155.

[2] *Mbh.*, V, chapters 11-15. Cf. V. 11. 15 :
ahamindrosmi devānāṁ lokānāṁ ca tatheśvaraḥ |
āgacchatu śacī mahyaṁ kṣipramadya niveśanaṁ ||

[3] *Ibid.*, V. 12. 13 :
indrādviśiṣṭo nahuṣo devarājo mahādyutiḥ |
vṛṇotviyaṁ varārohā bhartṛtve varavarṇinī ||
There is a still current folk-legend of one Indrāṇī for seven Indras. Cf. Sarkar, *op. cit.*, p. 156, n. 1, where he cites a note from Grierson.

concoction. What is doubtless funny, is the protective role of Bṛhaspati, who is himself brazenly polyandrous.

The Kauravas in the *Mahābhārata* indeed practise *niyoga* of a variety not far removed from polyandry. When Satyavatī calls on Bhīṣma to beget sons with the widows of his younger brother,[1] he refuses to budge from his vow of celibacy, and asks his step-mother to enlist the services of learned brāhmaṇas.[2] He tells her the story of Dīrghatamas, to which we have referred above. Set afloat on the Gangā by his dissatisfied wife, sons and others, the blind seer arrives in the kingdom of Balin, who recognizes and adopts him to give him sons. He is given the freedom of the royal seraglio by Balin, who says: "Please father on my wives sons who know Law and Profit, to continue my line."[3]

Sudeṣṇā, the queen of Balin, finds Dīrghatamas blind, old and unattractive, and, instead of going to him herself, sends her *dāsī* or maid-servant, on whom the seer fathers eleven sons.[4] When Balin claims those sons, Dīrghatamas tells him that they were not the king's but his own, as he begot them with a serf woman. The king then orders his queen Sudeṣṇā to go to the blind but prolific sire that Dīrghatamas is; and the sage "feels" her limbs and tells her that she would have a son of great power, true to his word.[5]

What do we learn from this story? Dīrghatamas begot eleven sons with a serf woman impersonating the queen. The king all along thought that his queen was cohabiting with the man and

[1] *Mbh.*, I. 97. 10.
[2] *Ibid.*, I. 98.
[3] *Ibid.*, I. 98. 23 :
santānārthaṁ mahābhāga bhāryāsu mama mānada /
putrāndharmārthakuśalānutpādayitumarhasi //
[4] *Ibid.*, I. 98. 25-26.
[5] *Ibid.*, I. 98. 31.

producing progeny. So, for our purposes, the maid-servant was as good as the queen. If *niyoga* with one and the same man lasted so long as to enable a woman to secure eleven sons, it was doubtless as good as a permanent union or marriage. Dīrghatamas was as good as a second husband of Balin's wives. This certainly was a state of affairs very close to polyandry. And then, the old man stayed on to sire another son on Sudeṣṇā too.[1]

We are reminded of the story of Śāradaṇḍāyanī told by Pāṇḍu to Kuntī. Instructed by her elders, ritually pure and bathed, this wife of a hero stands at night at the cross-roads, and with a flower chooses an accomplished brāhmaṇa. She offers an apposite oblation to the fire for the birth of a son, completes the rite, and lives with the man, who begets with her three warlike sons, Durjaya and the others.[2] Here, too, we have a union lasting till the woman gets three sons from the man. And we do not know whether they stop living together thereafter. This is a stable relationship; and such a *niyoga*, if the husband lives, is not much different from polyandry.

Satyavatī tells Bhīṣma of her premarital affair with Parāśara resulting in the birth of the illustrious sage Vyāsa, who would, if enjoined by her and Bhīṣma, beget beautiful sons on the fields of Vicitravīrya.[3] Bhīṣma agrees; Vyāsa is called; and Satyavatī

[1] *Ibid.*, I. 98. 32.

[2] *Ibid.*, I. 111. 35:

karmaṇyavasite tasminsā tenaiva sahāvasat |
tatra trīñjanayāmāsa durjayādīnmahārathān ||

Cf. Walker, B., *Hindu World*, vol. I, p. 592.

[3] *Mbh.*, I. 99. 5 ff.; verse 17,...*vicitravīryakṣetreṣu putrānutpādayiṣyati.* The stories of virginity regained by women such as Satyavatī, Kuntī, Mādhavī and Draupadī found in the *Mahābhārata* might, besides betokening later morality, also refer to the popular belief that women were not soiled by sexual relations with more than one man. Cf. *ibid.*, XII. 165, 32, Gita Press Edition, *adūṣyā hi*

thus addresses him:[1] "Just as Bhīṣma is Vicitravīrya's brother on the father's side, so you are his brother on the mother's side... The two wives of your younger brother....lovely in the bloom of their youth, are yearning for sons by the Law. As you are fit for the task, son, beget with them children that are worthy of our family and of continuing our progeny."

Vyāsa, the brother-in-law (*devara*) of the young widows, begets Dhṛtarāṣṭra with Ambikā[2]; and Pāṇḍu with Ambālikā.[3] It is interesting to note that both Bhīṣma and Vyāsa, approached by Satyavatī to beget children with the widows of Vicitravīrya, are the elder brothers of the latter; and that, therefore, the elder brother may also have access to the wife of the younger brother in accordance with Kaurava usages.[4]

---

striyo ratnamāpa ityeva dharmataḥ. "Women, gems and water cannot be polluted". Cf. also Bṛhaspati, *aśaucakāṇḍaṁ*, verse 66:

striyaḥ pavitramatulaṁ naitā duṣyanti karhicit |
māsi māsi rajastāsāṁ duṣkṛtānyapakarṣati. ||

See pp. 167, 362 of *Bṛhaspatismṛti* (Reconstructed) by Aiyangar, K. V. Rangaswami, Baroda, 1941. Endowed as they are with sweet speech and cleanliness, women retain their purity despite the belief that they are enjoyed by the gods before they get married to mortal men; cf. *ibid.*, verse 62 on p. 361:

romodbhede śaśī bhuṅkte gandharvaḥ kucadarśane |
analastur rajo bhuṅkte striyo medhyāstu nānyathā ||

This polyandrous formulation involving the gods with men has also been discussed in the Vedic context in the preceding chapter.

1 *Mbh.*, I. 99. 20ff. Verse 30 has:

yathaiva pitṛto bhīṣmastathā tvamapi mātṛtaḥ |
bhrātā vicitravīryasya yathā vā putra manyase ||

2 *Ibid.*, I. 100. 1 ff. The word *devara,* nowadays denoting only the younger brother-in-law, stands for the elder brother-in-law of a woman as well in the *Mbh.*

3 *Ibid.*, I. 100. 15 ff.

4 The suggestion of Winternitz, in his "Notes on the Mahābhārata", *JRAS*, 1897, p. 721, that Bhīṣma himself sired Dhṛtarāṣṭra and Pāṇḍu, does not appear

Pāṇḍu, elsewhere,[1] speaks of the king Kalmāṣapāda Saudāsa, who requested his wife Madavantī to conceive a child through some other man; whereupon she went to Vasiṣṭha. From him the happy woman obtained a son called Aśmaka, in order to do, like a good wife, a favour to her husband.

Kuntī gets three sons through *niyoga*; but Pāṇḍu, her husband, would like to have more. His second wife Mādrī, too, has two sons through *niyoga*, and still craves for more; but is defeated by Kuntī's determination not to let her have more sons than she has herself.[2] Kuntī's case smacks as much of *niyoga* as of polyandry or cicisbeism, in as much as the *niyogas* are not confined to one person; while Pāṇḍu still lives with his wives without renouncing his conjugal rights over them. Indeed, *niyoga* applied to a wife while the husband is yet alive, not infrequently at his own instance, is quite common and acceptable in the world of the Epic. Its use for widows is doubtless even more common: "A woman who has lost her husband makes the husband's brother her husband."[3]

---

to be correct. Bhīṣma is lauded in song and story as an exemplar of incorruptible moral rectitude, for ever true to his oath of sexual abstinence. That is the reason why he is upbraided by Śiśupāla for so-called dereliction of personal duty in refusing to act himself as the male agent, and consenting to the role of Vyāsa for the purpose of begetting children with the widows of Vicitravīrya. Cf. *Mbh.*, II. 38. 22-24. Vyāsa's status does not glorify a brāhmaṇa by birth, but a brāhmaṇa by deeds. That the later editors of the Epic did not expunge the story of Vyāsa's birth out of wedlock from the womb of a fisherman's daughter, shows the supreme status of a learned ascetic in social estimation notwithstanding the circumstances of his birth, rather than brahmanic impudence at its highest. The whole tenor of Vora's arguments in this instance, in *Evolution of Morals in the Epics*, pp. 86-87, is therefore out of step with reality.

1 *Mbh.*, I. 113.21-22,...*bhartuḥ priyacikīrṣayā*.

2 *Ibid.*, I. 114; 115.

3 *Ibid.*, XIII. 12. 23 (Bombay Edn.), *nārī tu patyabhāve vai devaraṁ kurute patiṁ*.

The *Mahābhārat* makes no attempt to limit the number of offspring that might be raised by a woman through *niyoga*. Kuntī's prescription of 'three' and no more, referred to earlier, is a statement of mere personal opinion by no means binding on others.[1] *Niyoga* thus becomes something similar to polyandry or remarriage in actual practice. Doubt and debate rage around the usage of *niyoga* in the didactic literature, evidenced in later prescriptions to restrict it to the raising of one son only, the birth of girls not counting. Kauṭilya[2], though, allows *niyoga* in its pristine fullness both to widows and to wives whose husbands are physically impaired by disease. Āpastamba[3] questions its spiritual basis by arguing that the spiritual benefit would accrue to the begetter rather than the putative father. Baudhāyana[4] prohibits it only in cases where children are already there. Vasiṣṭha[5] approves of the practice with the condition that it should not be motivated by mere cupidity. Manu[6] recognizes *niyoga* and allows it. Āpastamba's view is controverted by the statement that the field (*kṣetra*) is indeed more important than the seed (*bīja*), and that it is the owner, and not the begetter, who gets the offspring.[7] Manu, however, insists on family authorization for allowing *niyoga* in any case, and recognizes the son thus born as a legal and spiritual heir.[8] Personally,

1 Her own husband is unconvinced.

2 Kauṭilya, III. 5 and 6:

teṣāṁ tu kṛtadārāṇāṁ lupte prajanane sati |
sṛjeyuḥ bāndhavāḥ putrānsteṣāmanśaṁ prakalpayet ||

3 *Āpastamba*, II.6.13.6, asks husbands to guard their wives against *niyoga*, for the spiritual benefit of a child's birth would belong only to the begetter.

4 *Baudhāyana*, II. 4. 9-10.

5 *Vasiṣṭha*, XVII. 65: *rikthalobhānnāsti niyogaḥ.*

6 *Manu*, IX. 57-63.

7 *Ibid.*, IX. 48-51. "Men who have no marital property in women, but sow their seed in the soil of others, benefit the owner of the women; the giver of the seed reaps no benefit." (IX.51).

8 *Ibid.*, IX. 120-121, 145-146, 162-165, 190-191.

though, Manu dislikes *niyoga* and condemns it as a violation of the eternal Law[1]; as unrecognized in the *mantras* of marriage[2]; and as a virtual widow remarriage not mentioned in the rules of marriage.[3] "The learned of the twice-born *varṇas* denounce it as an animal-custom (*paśu-dharma*), which is said to have been current among men only when Vena ruled."[4]

This is blowing hot and cold in the same breath, and the contradiction can be explained only as an example of the revision which the *Mānava-dharmaśāstra* underwent, the prohibition being added to the rules regarding *niyoga* when it fell out of favour. Viṣṇu[5] recognizes the son born of *niyoga*. Nārada[6] accepts it as a lawful custom, but warns against its abuse by calling it illegal if actuated by mere weakness of the flesh; if persisted in after the birth of a son; and if it is not previously sanctioned by the elders of the family. Yājñavalkya[7] also only insists on family authorization, and treats the son raised through *niyoga* as equal to the *aurasa*, the first among all categories of sons.

The custom became comparatively rare, though by no means totally defunct among the twice-born, when Bṛhaspati found it necessary to prohibit it for *kali-yuga* in accordance with the new

1 *Ibid.*, IX.64, *dharmaṁ hanyuḥ sanātanaṁ.*

2 This is indicative only of later morality.

3 *Manu*, IX. 65, *na vivāhavidhau uktaṁ*...

4 *Ibid.*, IX.66:

ayaṁ dvijairhi vidvadbhiḥ paśudharmo vigarhitaḥ |
manuṣyāṇāmapi prokto vene rājyaṁ praśāsati ||

5 *Viṣṇusmṛti*, XV. 3, *niyuktāyāṁ sapiṇḍenottama varṇena votpāditaḥ kṣetrajo dvitīyaḥ.*

6 *Nārada-smṛti*, XII. 80-88.

7 *Yājñavalkya*, II. 127-128:

aputreṇa parakṣetre niyogotpāditaḥ sutaḥ |
ubhayorapyasau rikthī piṇḍadātā ca dharmataḥ ||
auraso dharmapatnījastatsamaḥ putrikāsutaḥ |
kṣetrajaḥ kṣetrajātastu sagotreṇetareṇa vā ||

morality of his epoch. That *niyoga* is unsuitable for the iron age owing to the inferior virtue of its men, is the reason for its interdiction put by Bṛhaspati into the mouth of Manu, who himself did not really say so.[1]

The custom of a husband introducing a brother or kinsman or a stranger to his wife to raise offspring in cases of lack of issue is indeed as ancient as it has been widespread in different parts of the world including India, and is regarded by many as an "attenuated relic of polyandry."[2]

Pāṇḍu tells Kuntī of six kinds of sons who are of the blood and heirs in the eyes of the Law; and of another six who are neither heirs nor of the blood. The first six are:[3] (i) the son born of the husband's own seed (*svayaṁjāta* = *aurasa*); (ii) the son raised on one's wife by the free grace of another man, to whom she is led by the husband (*praṇīta*); (iii) the son raised on one's wife by another man paid for the job (*parikrīta*); (iv) the son of a remarried woman (*paunarbhava*);[4] (v) the son borne by a maiden before

[1] *Bṛhaspati*, 25. 16:
uktvā niyogo manunā niṣiddhaḥ svayameva tu |
yugahrāsādaśakyo 'yaṁ kartuṁ sarvairvidhānataḥ ||

[2] Cf. Briffault, *The Mothers*, Vol. I. pp. 670, 681-82. McLennan also regarded polyandry as a forerunner of levirate, its relic. Cf. *ERE*, VIII, p. 431. Cf. also p. 56 of Ch. II and notes 1, 2, 3. See, too, Gait, E. A., in *Census of India*, 1911, vol. I, "India", Report, p. 247; Crooke, W., *The Tribes and Castes of the North-Western Provinces and Oudh*, vol. I, p. cxc; Winternitz, M., "Notes on the 'Mahābhārata', with special reference to Dahlmann's 'Mahābhārata' ", *JRAS*, 1897, pp. 716 sqq.

[3] *Mbh.*, I. 111. 28:
svayaṁjātaḥ praṇītaśca parikrītaśca yaḥ sutaḥ |
paunarbhavaśca kānīnaḥ svairiṇyāṁ yaśca jāyate ||

[4] According to Baudhāyana, II. 2.3. 27, *punarbhū* means a woman who has given up an impotent husband and taken another. According to Vasiṣṭha, XVII. 19 ff., she signifies a woman whose former husband is impotent, excommunica-

her marriage (kānīna); (vi) and the son conceived by a woman in adultery (*svairiṇyāṁ yaś ca jāyate*).[1] The second category of six consists of:[2] (i) the adopted sons, *datta* or "given away by father and mother", as Nīlakaṇṭha puts it; (ii) the son bought from his parents (*krīta*); (iii) the son brought up as an orphan (*kṛtrima*, 'by artifice'); (iv) the son who comes of his own free will and volition to seek protection (*upagacchet svayaṁ ca yaḥ*); (v) the son of unknown seed, with whom the mother is already pregnant at the time of her wedding (*sahoḍho jātaretas*); (vi) and the son begotten of a woman from a low caste (*hīnayonidhṛta*).[3]

The wife is the husband's *kṣetra* or field; and whatever grows on his field belongs to him, no matter who sows it. The husband's ownership of the children derives from his ownership of the

---

ted from his caste, mad or dead, and who has married another man. She may also be a woman who left her husband, went to live with another man, and then came back again to her husband. According to Viṣṇu, XV. 7 ff., *punarbhū* stands for a woman who is married for the second time as a virgin; or for a woman who has lived with another man before her lawful marriage. Manu, IX. 175, takes her to be one whose husband has left her, or is dead, and who has married again. Yājñavalkya, I. 67, understands by *punarbhū* "one who is, or is not harmed in her maidenhead, and who lets herself be 'dedicated' for the second time." Nārada, XII. 45 ff., lists three kinds of *punarbhū*: (i) the girl who loses her honour, though not her maidenhead, through an earlier taking by the hand; (ii) a woman who runs away from the husband of her youth and goes to another, but later returns to her first husband; (iii) and a woman who is given to a sapiṇḍa of the same caste, because there are no brothers-in-law. The interpretations of the term are by no means exhausted by the variety of opinions cited above, which leave the reader rather baffled, to put it mildly.

1 i.e., *kuṇḍa, gūḍhotpanna, gūḍhaja.*

2 *Mbh.*, I. 111.29:

dattaḥ krītaḥ kṛtrimaśca upagacchetsvayaṁ ca yaḥ |
sahoḍho jātaretaśca hīnayonidhṛtaśca yaḥ ||

3 Cf. Meyer, *Sexual Life in Ancient India*, I, pp. 172-181; Karve, Iravati, *Kinship Organization in India*, p. 74.

mother, and not necessarily from the fact that he may himself be their begetter.[1] The law-books differ from one another regarding the relative ranks of the twelve kinds of sons, as also their division into the two main categories. What is important for our purposes is the placing of the *kṣetraja* next after the son of self by all the law-books except Yājñavalkya, who names before him the son of the inheriting daughter. Another significant pointer is the inclusion of the gūḍhotpanna[2] or the son begotten in adultery by all the important law-givers in group I. Nārada[3] assigns even the *sahoḍha*, the son with whom the mother is already pregnant at the time of her marriage, to the first group, though the others[4]

[1] Meyer, *loc. cit*, pp. 172-73, n. I, cites the old German parallel in the following words: "How little heed was given even by our forefathers, who stood so high in sexual matters, the Old Germans,to the question whether they were actually the father to their children, is shown in detail by Dargun,*Mutterrecht u. Raubehe,* in the third chapter; and on p.45 he gives a valuable passage (which, indeed, sounds rather like a witticism) from the Westphalian peasant laws, according to which the man who was not able to satisfy his amorous wedded wife had to take her himself to another one. Cf. Grimm, *Deutsche Rechtsalterthümer*, ed. by Heusler and Hübner, 1899, vol. I, pp. 613 ff." A law in Sparta required the elderly owner of a young wife to mate her with a lusty youth in the hope of healthy progeny. Cf. Hartland, *op. cit.*, I, p. 322; II, 134. On begetting by proxy among the Greeks, as also among other peoples, cf. Engels, *Ursprung d. Familie*, p. 49; Henne am Rhyn, *Die Frau in der Kulturgesch.*, pp. 193 ff.; Starcke, *Primitive Family*, 1889, p. 124; Schrader, *Die Indogermanen*, p. 93; Meyer, *loc. cit.* "Of the Arabs (pre-Islamic?) we are told there is a form of marriage according to which a man says to his wife when menstruation is over, 'Send a message to such an one, and beg him to have intercourse with you.' And he himself refrains from intercourse with her until it is manifest that she is with child by the man in question. The husband acts this way in order that his offspring may be noble." See Starcke, *loc. cit.*, pp. 123-124. The Chukchi in Siberia get their wives impregnated by others; and some Koryaks made use of the Russian postman as a stud-bull. Cf. Hartland, *loc. cit.*, II, p. 181. For more examples, see Meyer, *loc. cit.*

[2] Cf. *Manu*, IX. 170-81. Literally, the term signifies 'secretly born'.

[3] *Nārada*, XIII. 45.

[4] Cf. *Vasiṣṭha*, XVII. 26; *Viṣṇu*, XV. 15; *Yājñavalkya*, II. 131.

disagree. The unmarried woman's son, too, the *kānīna*, figures in the privileged set of the first six in all except Gautama[1], Baudhāyana[2] and Manu[3], who, however, place him at the top of group II. The *paunarbhava* is included by Vasiṣṭha[4], Yājñavalkya[5], and Viṣṇu[6] among the first six; and it is indeed remarkable that Vasiṣṭha, Nārada, Yājñavalkya and Viṣṇu, all alike assign the first six places in order of precedence to the actual children of the mother, whosoever the physiological father may happen to be. That even illegitimate sons such as the *gūḍhotpanna*, *sahoḍha* and *kānīna* can inherit the property of their mothers' husbands, reflects a certain knowledge of the practices of polyandry and conjoint marriage.[7] A. Mayr[8] sees in the 'secretly born' son (*gūḍhaja*, *gūḍhotpanna*) "a recognition of the right of the other members of the clan upon the married woman", and "one of the most potent proofs of the sometime community of women among the Indian Aryans".[9] And according to Jolly[10], "the well known law (M.9.182 etc.) that the son of one of several brothers may be regarded as the common son of all may refer only to group marriage", if we connect it with polyandry disregarding the interpretation of the later commentators, suggestive only of later morality.

The *Mahābhārata* has more evidence of polyandry than is noticeable at first sight. We hear, for instance, of the *dānava*

1 *Gautama*, XXVIII. 33.
2 *Baudhāyana*, II. 2. 3. 32.
3 *Manu*, IX. 161.
4 *Vasiṣṭha*, XVII. 13 ff.
5 *Yājñavalkya*, II. 128 ff.
6 *Viṣṇu*, XV. 1 ff.
7 For further classification of such sons and their rights, cf. Meyer, *loc. cit.*, pp. 179-180.
8 Mayr, A., *Erbrecht*, p. 113.
9 Cf. Jolly, *Hindu Law and Custom*, p. 105.
10 *Ibid.*, p. 103.

(demon) Dhundhu, who was the son of two brothers, Madhu and Kaiṭabha.[1] Repeated reference to the names of his two fathers[2] is clearly indicative of plain polyandry.

The *Ādi Parva*[3] relates the relevant story of Uttaṅka, a pupil of the seer Veda. Once, when the teacher goes out for some length of time, charging his pupil with the supervision of the settlement, the females of his household come to Uttaṅka and thus address him:[4]

> O Uttaṅka, the wife of your preceptor is in the state (*ṛtu*) in which she might conceive a child. Your teacher is absent, and hence you are requested to stand in his place and do what is required.

Uttaṅka deems the request improper and refuses to oblige. The preceptor returns; hears what happened; and is much pleased. The refusal of Uttaṅka clearly seems to be out of step with current practice; for when the wife of Veda requests him to take the place of her husband and approach her for the sake of 'virtue', she is simply seeking the benefit of a customary latitude allowed to the brāhmaṇa wife amounting to cicisbeism, if not polyandry.[5]

The Epic also refers to the brāhmaṇa Sudarśana, who would not refuse anything to a guest at his door.[6] Dharma calls at

[1] *Mbh.*, III. 193. 16, *madhukaiṭabhayoḥ putro dhundhurnāma sudāruṇaḥ.*

[2] *Ibid.*, III. 195. I. Sarkar, *Some Aspects of the Earliest Social History of India*, p. 146 and n. 11, identifies him with Paurava Sudhanvan Dhundhu, transformed here into an asura adversary.

[3] *Mbh.*, I. 3. 85 ff.

[4] *Ibid.*, 1.3. 89 ff.

[5] A woman would be doing a proper thing by cohabiting with someone else in the husband's absence in order to have a child in her *ṛtu*. It would indeed be sinful to refuse her. Cf. Meyer, *SLAI*, vol. I, 216-218.

[6] *Mbh.*, XIII. 2 (Bombay Edn.)

his house disguised as a brāhmaṇa in his absence, and desires to have sexual intercourse with his wife Oghavatī. While they are yet busy making love, Sudarśana returns, calls his wife, and Dharma tells him from inside the house how she is at the moment engaged. Unruffled, Sudarśana replies: "O best of brāhmaṇas, do whatever you like... My whole life, wealth and wife are dedicated to the service of guests." No doubt, the gratified Dharma blesses the couple. The role of Law Incarnate as a more than willing recipient of this hospitality stamps wife-lending with the seal of approval; and the story seems to hark back to a period when it was by no means uncommon.[1] This is not polyandry, but certainly an ingredient of the social ideology that promotes it.[2]

The *Rāmāyaṇa*, too, clearly attests polyandry. It is doubtless known to the Vānaras, who are not monkeys but members of a totemistic tribe. Vāli and Sugrīva have their wives Tārā and Rumā in common, though they quarrel over them to the point of alternately excluding each other. Rāma tries to justify his killing of Vāli by accusing the latter of appropriating the wife of his younger brother.[3] This shows the younger brother could embrace and enjoy the wife of the elder brother in Rāma's book of ethics; which is what Sugrīva did both before and after the

[1] Cf. Westermarck, *History of Human Marriage*, vol. I, p. 228. The practice is still current in many parts of the world.

[2] Wife-lending was till recently common among the polyandrous Khasas of Jaunsār Bāwar.

[3] *Rāmāyaṇa, Kiṣkindhā*, XVIII. 18-20:
tadetat kāraṇaṁ paśya yadarthaṁ tvaṁ mayā hataḥ |
bhrāturvartasi bhāryāyāṁ tyaktvā dharmaṁ sanātanaṁ || 18
asya tvaṁ dharamāṇasya sugrīvasya mahātmanaḥ |
rumāyāṁ vartase kāmāt snuṣāyāṁ pāpakarmakṛt || 19
tadvyatītasya te dharmāt kāmavṛttasya mahātmanaḥ |
bhrātṛbhāryābhimarśe' smin daṇḍo' yaṁ pratipāditaḥ || 20

death of Vāli. And Rāma finds no fault with his behaviour. On the contrary, he consoles Tārā that she would still be receiving love exactly as before[1]; and we are actually told how happily Sugrīva revels in the delights of sex with his indubitably covetable sister-in-law, as well as wife Rumā, without the faintest suggestion of disapproval.[2] Elsewhere, however, Aṅgada says that Sugrīva is detestable, for he lustfully made his alive elder brother's wife his own, regardless of the fact that she was like a mother to him.[3]

What do we make of it all ? Rāma calls in question the behaviour of Vāli. Aṅgada deplores the deed of Sugrīva. The latter-day moralist does not quite know his ground. The fact of the matter is that the Vānaras were a polyandrous people; and that even Vāli and Sugrīva were begotton by Indra and Sūrya, respectively, with Virajā, the wife of Ṛkṣa.[4]

Vāli's polyandrous predilections are reaffirmed by his willing acceptance of Rāvaṇa's friendly proposal to share everything together including their wives and sons; which, incidentally, also shows the free and easy familiarity of Rāvaṇa and the Rākṣasas with the practice of polyandry.[5] Indeed, as the *Rāmāyaṇa*

[1] *Ibid., Kiṣkindhā*, XXIV. 43, *prītiṁ parāṁ prāpsyasi tāṁ tathaiva...*

[2] *Ibid., Kiṣkindhā*, XXIX. 4 :
svāṁ ca patnīmabhipretāṁ tārāṁ cāpi samīpsitāṁ |
viharantamahorātraṁ kṛtārthaṁ vigatajvaraṁ ||

[3] *Ibid., Kiṣkindhā*, LV, 3 :
bhrāturjyeṣṭhasya yo bhāryāṁ jīvato mahiṣīṁ priyāṁ |
dharmeṇa mātaraṁ yastu svīkaroti jugupsitaḥ ||

[4] Cf. *Brahmāṇḍamahāpurāṇaṁ*, Bombay, 1906, III. 7. 210-216. Also *Mbh.*, III. 147. 25, *sūryaputraṁ ca sugrīvaṁ śakraputraṁ ca vālinaṁ*... Hanumān calls himself the son of Vāyu on the *kṣetra* or field of Kesarī: *ibid.* III. 147. 24; *Rāmāyaṇa, Uttara*, XXXV, 19-20; *Brahmāṇḍamahāpurāṇaṁ*, III. 7. 223-225.

[5] *Rāmāyaṇa, Uttara*, XXXIV. 40-41 :
dārāḥ putrāḥ puraṁ rāṣṭraṁ bhogācchādanabhojanaṁ |
sarvamevāvibhaktaṁ nau bhaviṣyati harīśvara || 41

The *Rāmāyaṇa* no doubt glorifies monogamy and exalts it to ddy heights of feminine fidelity (*pātivratya*) in the touching tale ' Sītā's suffering and self-effacement, and of Rāma's love for but ıe woman. Monogamy is well and truly enthroned as the ideal Āryan India; but other forms of marriage yet remain, as human ature, economy and environment alike lead to the variety of ›nnubial dispensations. The *Rāmāyaṇa* upholds monogamy; ıt knows and tolerates, as it should, polyandry as well as polygyny.

We would perhaps do well to take up here the evidence of the ırly Buddhist and Jaina literature connected with the stories of ıe Epics. The *Kuṇāla Jātaka*[1] speaks of Kaṇhā (Kṛṣṇā Draupadī), "her that has a double parentage[2] and five husbands, nd whose affection was set on a sixth man, a headless, crippled warf."[3] The *Jātaka* versifies it thus:

In ancient story Kaṇhā, it is said,
A single maid to princes five was wed,
Insatiate still she lusted for yet more
And with a hump-backed dwarf played the whore.[4]

Brahmadatta, the king of Kāsī, invades the kingdom of Kosala nd kills its king. He carries off the pregnant queen of Kosala › Banaras, where she gives birth to Kaṇhā. When the girl grows ıto a marriageable maiden, she makes her father (the king of Kāsī) hold a *svayaṁvara* (self-choice) for her. On seeing the five ›ns of Pāṇḍu, Ajjuna, Nakula, Bhīmasena, Yudhiṭṭhila and ahadeva, Kaṇhā falls in love with all the five, and throws a

[1] No. 536, Cowell, *Jātaka*, V, 225 ff.; cf. Malalasekera, G.P., *Dictionary of Pali Proper Names*, Vol. I, p. 503.

[2] *dvepitikā*, having two fathers, i.e., the kings of Kosala and Kāsī, the rea and the putative father.

[3] Cowell, *Jātaka*, V, p. 225.

[4] *Ibid.* Women are indeed called "as insatiate as hell"; cf. p. 226.

tells us, they light a fire, embrace each other and establish a formal bond of brotherhood (*bhrātṛtva*)[1], which makes their polyandrous compact friendly as well as 'fraternal'. All this occurs in the late *Uttara Kāṇḍa*, which does not denigrate the custom, and states the story with unmistakable, if implied, ethical approval.

Talking of the Rākṣasas, Mandodarī, the wife of Rāvaṇa, is thus shared with Vāli; and her relationship with her brother-in-law Vibhīṣaṇa is not innocent of a polyandrous proportion, over and above her later *devṛ*-marriage.[2]

Rāma, on the friendliest of terms with the Vānaras, is certainly familiar with polyandry, fraternal as well as of other kinds. Briffault is, however, wrong in treating the marriages of Rāma and Sītā, Lakṣmaṇa and Ūrmilā, and those of Sītā's two cousins[3] with Bharata and Śatrughna, as an instance of polyandrous group-marriage.[4] The relevant verses in their proper context clearly reveal that the four brothers marry one girl each individually,[5] though one or two *ślokas*, read apart, are somewhat likely to confuse the casual browser.[6]

That polyandry is not an unknown phenomenon, is brought home to us by Virādha's surmise that Sītā is the common wife of Rāma and Lakṣmaṇa, when he sees them together in the forest.

[1] *Ibid.*, verse 42:
tataḥ prajvālayitvāgnim tāvubhau harirākṣasau |
bhrātṛtvamupasaṁpannau pariṣvajya parasparaṁ ||

[2] Cf. Sarkar, *op. cit.*, p. 149.

[3] Māṇḍavī and Śrutakīrti.

[4] Briffault, *op. cit.*, pp. 682-683.

[5] *Rāmāyaṇa*, *Bāla*, LXXI, 21-22; LXXII, 4-6, LXXIII, 25-27, 30-33.

[6] E. g., *ibid.*, *Bāla.*, LXXII. 11:
evaṁ bhavatu bhadraṁ vaḥ kuśadhvaja sute ime |
patnyau bhajetāṁ sahitau śatrughnabharatāvubhau ||

He chides the two young men for roaming around in the garb of ascetics, even though they still carry weapons and enjoy the embraces of a youthful wife.[1] He asks them who they are, and calls them sinful polluters of the order of ascetics.[2]

We must also heed the exchange of words that takes place between Sītā and Lakṣmaṇa, when Rāma goes out to hunt the deer Mārīca. She asks Lakṣmaṇa to go, too, to protect his brother; but he refuses to leave her alone. She then clearly accuses him of designs on her and suspects that he intends to take her as his wife, once Rāma dies or disappears. This is doubtless revealing, and points back to both polyandry and *devṛ*-marriage. Sītā is quite familiar with the practice of a brother-in-law marrying or just taking to his bed the wife of the elder brother in case of his untimely death or disappearance. Hence the fear, and the outburst ![3]

Elsewhere, Rāma himself, doubting Sītā's wifely fidelity during the period of her captivity in Laṅkā, asks her to go and live with

[1] *Ibid., Araṇya*, II. 10. 12:

. . . yuvāṁ jaṭācīradharau sabhāryau kṣīṇajīvitau // 10
praviṣṭau daṇḍakāraṇyaṁ śaracāpāsipāṇinau /
kathaṁ tāpasayorvāṁ ca vāsaḥ pramadayā saha // 11

[2] *Ibid.*, verse 12, *adharmacāriṇau pāpau kau yuvāṁ munidūṣakau*.. Vora, *Evolution of Morals in the Epics*, p. 24, is no doubt mistaken in suggesting that polyandry is repugnant even to a Rākṣasa. It is not, as we have already seen above in the case of the Rākṣasa chief Rāvaṇa. The verses quoted here clearly show that Virādha is not at all castigating the practice of polyandry, though he deems wife and weapons alike incompatible with asceticism. He ridicules and scorns the ascetic masquerade of Rāma and Lakṣmaṇa, and not their 'polyandry'. Vora has probably not cared to examine the original verses, and based her comment only on the statement of Briffault. All the three references to Rāma's, and his brothers' marriages on p. 24 of her book are wrong, and place them in the *Ayodhyā Kāṇḍa* instead of the *Bāla*.

[3] *Rāmāyaṇa, Araṇya*, XLV, 7-8, 20-27.

Lakṣmaṇa or Bharata according to her own sweet will.[1] gives her a free choice between Śatrughna, Sugrīva an Rākṣasa Vibhīṣaṇa, and tells her to go wherever she ma happiness and comfort.[2] Rāma, like Sītā, is quite aware practice of an elder brother's wife also living with his y brothers. That is the reason why Sītā accuses him earlier eve of his banishment of intent to surrender her to Bharata, actor living off the earnings of his wife.[3]

Sarkar[4] surmises that Sītā was the common wife of Rā Lakṣmaṇa in the original earlier tradition; and that th was emended in the *Rāmāyaṇa* in conformity with the dic later morality. But the stories told in the late *Jātaka* c tary, not in the old *Jātaka gāthās*, fail to lend enough creden suggestion. Lüders[5], Jacobi[6], Keith[7], and Winternitz[8] a that the *Jātaka* prose version of the Rāma legend is a la more confused form of the original story.[9]

[1] *Ibid., Yuddha*, CXV. 22:

tadadya vyāhṛtaṁ bhadre mayaitat kṛtabuddhinā /
lakṣmaṇe vātha bharate kuru buddhiṁ yathāsukhaṁ //

[2] *Ibid.*, verse 23 :

śatrughne vātha sugrīve rākṣase vā vibhīṣaṇe /
niveśaya manaḥ sīte yathā vā sukhamātmanā //

[3] *Ibid., Ayodhyā*, XXX. 8-9. Cf. also XXVI. 25-27.

[4] Sarkar, *op. cit.*, pp. 151. Mandodarī might have been a sister or Rāvaṇa; see *Rāmāyaṇa, Yuddha*, CXI, 80-81, where she calls hersel of Sumāli, who was also the maternal grandfather of Rāvaṇa suggestion on p. 149 of his book that Śūrpanakhā might have bee wife of her brothers in a polyandrous set-up during their early is, however, not clearly borne out by the actual text.

[5] Lüders, *NGWG*, 1897, p. 40 ff.

[6] Jacobi, *Das Rāmāyaṇa*, p. 84 ff.

[7] Keith, *JRAS*, 1915, p. 323.

[8] Winternitz, "An Introductory and Critical Note" to Sarkar, *op.*

[9] Cf. Utgikar, N. B., "The Story of the Dasaratha Jātaka a Rāmāyaṇa", *JRAS*, Centenary Supplement, 1924, pp. 203-211

wreathed coil of flowers on the heads of them all. "Dear mother", she says, "I choose these five men." The king, though vexed, gives his daughter as wife to the five. By the great intensity of her passion she wins the affection of all these five princes, and tells everyone of them that she loves him most. But she still sins with a hump-backed slave.

The five brothers are delighted beyond words with their wife,[1] until one day she falls sick, and they gather round her, one chafing her head, and the rest each of them a hand or foot, the hump-backed dwarf sitting at her feet. Ajjuna becomes suspicious of the dwarf, and by questioning him learns the truth. Disgusted, the five brothers retire to a life of asceticism in the Himālayas.[2]

[1] "She is fond of us", they think, "and owing to this the sovereignty will be ours." The marriage is matrilocal. In the *Mahābhārata,* too, the Pāṇḍavas are in exile at the time of their marriage, which is consummated in the bride's own home.

[2] *Jātaka,* V, pp. 226 ff. The story is related by Kuṇāla, who is identified with Ajjuna. This *Jātaka* also refers to brother-sister marriage among the Sākiyas. Cf. also Dialogues, I, 93, 94, where we are told of their ancestors who practised incest to preserve the purity of their blood. According to *Jātaka Commentary* on 465, Pasenadi, the king of Kosala, tried to secure a Sākiya girl as his wife; but the Sākiyas had too much family pride to consent. Cf. Horner, I. B., *Women under Primitive Buddhism*, London, 1930, pp. 178-179. Despite the limitations imposed on marriage by the growing volume of brahmanical injunctions, there are numerous examples of unorthodox marriage listed in the Jaina canonical literature. Marriage with step-mother was allowed in countries like Golla, where the brāhmaṇas (*vippa*) could marry their step-mothers (*māisavitti*); cf. *Āv. Cū.*, II, p. 81; *Nisī. Cū.*, II, p. 715; also *Kathāsaritsāgara*, vol. VII, pp. 116 ff. Sister-marriage was common, according to Jaina mythology, at the time of Usabha, who married his own sister. The *Āvaśyaka Cūrṇi* likewise tells us that the king Pupphaketu permitted his son to marry his own sister; cf. II. p. 178. This kind of marriage was also prevalent in the country of Golla; *ibid.*, p. 81. Cousin-marriages were also known. Cf. Jain, Jagdish Chandra. *Life in Ancient India as depicted in the Jain Canons*, Bombay, 1947, pp. 159-160.

The story of Dovāī or Draupadī also occurs in the Jaina text *Nāyādhammakahāo* (*Jñātādharmakathā*), where her *svayaṁvara* is said to be held in the city of Kampillapura,[1] and the five Pāṇḍavas are chosen by her as her husbands.[2]

If the story of Kaṇhā in the *Jātaka* illustrates fraternal polyandry, that of Pañcapāpā instances its non-fraternal variety.[3] King Baka of Kāsī marries the ugly Pañcapāpā owing to the indescribable softness of her touch, and makes her his chief queen. One day she has a dream suggesting that she should be the chief queen of two kings. She tells the king, who consults his soothsayers. Their prognosis is trouble for him arising from that dream; and the king sets his wife adrift on the river. She drifts down the river, until she comes face to face with king Pāvārika disporting himself in the stream. As soon as he touches her, he is filled with uncontrollable desire, and makes her his chief queen. When Baka hears what happened, he challenges Pāvārika to surrender his wife or give battle. The councillors of the two kings confer and say:

> For the sake of a woman there is
> no need to die. From his being her
> first husband she belongs to Baka,
> but from his having rescued her
> from the ship she belongs to
> Pāvārika. Therefore let her be
> for the space of seven days at a
> time in the house of each of them.

They finally gain over the two kings to this view, and they are

[1] Nāyā., 8, 178; cf. Law, *Some Jaina Canonical Sūtras*, Bombay, 1949, pp. 38-40.
[2] *Nāyā.*, 16.
[3] Cowell, *Jātaka*, V, 236-240.

both exceedingly delighted. Pañcapāpā accepts the position of chief consort to the pair of kings; and they are both, as before, infatuated with her. She now lives for seven days in the house of one, and then crosses over in a ship to that of the other. Bored by the tedium of repeated journeying, she misconducts herself in midstream with the pilot of the ship, a lame and bald old man.

> Wife of Pāvārika and Baka too,
> (Two kings whose lust no pause or limit knew)
> Yet sins with her devoted husband's slave;
> With what vile wretch would she not misbehave ?[1]

The same *Jātaka* tells us later that a woman "may have husbands eight...yet on a ninth she sets her will".[2] I. B. Horner fails to notice the clear example of polyandrous Pañcapāpā, and says of this last statement : "This dictum seems to be employed to emphasize the insatiability of women, rather than the recurrence of polyandry."[3] If that were truly so, the wise Vidhura would have found it quite unnecessary in the *Vidhurapaṇḍita Jātaka* to advise householders against the practice of polyandry.[4] "Let him not have a wife in common with another"[5]..., says the sage; which shows that he is not attacking a non-existent evil, or chasing away a shadow without substance. His own sons seem to share one wife, as only one daughter-in-law is mentioned in relation to sons referred to in plural.[6] Vidhura's wisdom seems to have dawned at home.

[1] *Ibid.*, p. 240.
[2] *Ibid.*, V, p. 243.
[3] Horner, *Women under Primitive Buddhism*, p. 40. She, however, gives a wrong reference to a Ṛgvedic verse that does not exist, to hint at the presence of polyandry.
[4] Cowell, *Jātaka*, VI, pp. 126-141 (no. 545).
[5] *Ibid.*, p. 139.
[6] *Ibid.*, p. 141. Cf. also Sarkar, *op. cit.*, pp. 161-162.

Marriage was a social contract rather than a sacrament in the eyes of the Buddha and his followers. Husband or wife could alike leave home when the spiritual goal beckoned; and though monogamy was often favoured or preferred, Buddhism was perfectly at ease with both polyandry and polygyny in India and Tibet, and with polygyny in China.[1]

Kautilya's counsel would doubtless bear quotation in the present context. "No kind of marriage should be prohibited, provided that it pleases all those who are concerned with it",[2] says the Indian prophet of pragmatism. He also refers to a woman having many male children by many husbands,[3] and to the fairly short periods of time a woman must wait for her husband gone somewhere or lost:

> A young wife who has received the whole amount of *śulka* shall wait for the period of five menses for her absent husband who is not heard of; but if he is heard of, she shall wait for him for the period of ten menses. Then with the permission of judges (*dharmasthairvisṛshṭā*), she may marry one whom she likes; for, neglect of intercourse with wife after her monthly ablution is, in the opinion of Kauṭilya, a violation of one's duty.[4]

> In the case of husbands who have long gone abroad (*dīrgha-pravāsinaḥ*), who have become ascetics, or who have been dead, their wives, having no issue, shall wait for them for

[1] Polygyny was fairly common in China. The evidence of polyandry, though, is not quite clear.

[2] *Kauṭilya*, III. 2. 13, *sarveṣām prītyāropaṇamapratiṣiddham*. Cf. Shamasastry, R., (tr.), *Kauṭilya's Arthaśāstra*, Fifth Edn., Mysore, 1956, p. 172; also Kangle, *The Kauṭilīya Arthaśāstra*, Pt. I, p. 99.

[3] Shamasastry, *loc. cit.*, p. 174.

[4] *Ibid.*, pp. 180-181.

> the period of seven menses; but if they have given birth to children, they shall wait for a year. Then (each of these women) may marry the brother of her husband. If there are a number of brothers to her lost husband, she shall marry such a one of them as is next in age to her former husband, or as is virtuous and is capable of protecting her, or one who is the youngest and unmarried. If there are no brothers to her lost husband, she may marry one who belongs to the same gotra as her husband's or a relative of the same family. If there are many such persons as can be selected in marriage, she shall choose one who is a nearer relation of her lost husband.[1]

What if her husband comes back after she has married one of his brothers or relatives? Kauṭilya is a product of the same epoch in which the Epics assumed much of their present form; and is definitely aware of the presence of fraternal polyandry. The recognition of a sister-in-law's right to marry the brother of her husband gone away from home, not indeed for very long, is certainly a proposition not far removed from polyandry. The long and often unavoidable absence of husbands from their homes is one of the factors conducive to the practice of polyandry.[2]

[1] *Ibid.*, p. 181.

[2] See above, Chapter One.
Cf. the *Āvaśyaka Cūrṇi*, pp. 466-9, where we hear the interesting story of Kayapuṇṇa, a trader of Rāyagiha, who was taken away by a merchant woman to her house from a temple where he was sleeping. The woman had lost her son in a shipwreck; there was no male heir; and the bereaved mother feared that the property might be claimed by the king under the law of escheat. She told her four daughters-in-law that Kayapuṇṇa was their long-lost brother-in-law (*devara*); and the man stayed with them for twelve years, raising children on all the four widows. The right of the *devara* to raise children on his sisters-in-law in the absence of his brother is taken for granted; and none of the ladies objects. This certainly harks back to polyandry.

Talking of undesirable names for girls, Manu says they should not bear the names of stars and constellations. He mentions, for example, the name of Kṛttikā, the object of love of many planets.[1] There is no doubt that this visionary of the later brahmanical social *ideal* does not like anything redolent of polyandry even in the high heavens. And yet, the *Purāṇas*, despite their endless mythification, retain enough sense of the real to include references to polyandry in their tradition. We have hinted at their evidence before, in relation to the Epics, wherever they help us understand the *Mahābhārata* and the *Rāmāyaṇa* a little better. Many of the *Purāṇas* speak of the marriage of Vārkṣī with the ten Pracetasa brothers, one of the examples cited by Yudhiṣṭhira in the great Epic. The *Viṣṇu Purāṇa*[2] tells us the story of the radiant daughter of trees named Māriṣā bestowed on the ten royal ascetics by Soma, who had himself brought her up. She was destined since birth to be their wife (*bhāryā*) and the augmentor of their family (*vaṁśavardhinī*). She would in the fullness of time give birth to the ruler Dakṣa, who would multiply progeny.

When Soma or Brahmā[3] sees nothing wrong in a polyandrous marriage, men cannot afford to be too squeamish about it. The *Matsya*[4], *Brahma*[5] and *Agni*[6] alike refer to Māriṣā; but the last

[1] Cf. Das, R. M., *Women in Manu and his Seven Commentators*, Varanasi, 1962, p. 76.

[2] *Viṣṇu Purāṇa*, I. 15. 5 ff.
ratnabhūtā ca kanyeyaṁ vārkṣeyī varavarṇini |
bhaviṣyajjānatā pūrvaṁ mayā gobhirvivardhitā || 7
māriṣā nāma nāmnaiṣā vṛkṣāṇāmiti nirmitā |
bhāryā vo' stu mahābhāgā dhruvaṁ vaṁśavivardhinī || 8
yuṣmākaṁ tejaso'ddhena mama cārdhena tejasaḥ |
asyāmutpatsyate vidvān dakṣo nāma prajāpatiḥ || 9

[3] Cf. *Śrīmad-Bhāgavatam*, IV. 30. 47-48.

[4] *Matsya*, IV. 47.49.

[5] *Brahma*, II, 33-46.

[6] *Agni*, Chowkhamba Sanskrit Studies, vol. LIV, 1967, p. 84, verses 26-27.

of these *Purāṇas* makes her the daughter of the ascetic Kaṇḍu and the nymph Plamocā.

When the *Matsya* and the other *Purāṇas* tell us that the girl called Āhukī was given in marriage to the Avantis (or Avanti princes), we may perhaps be hearing of a case of polyandry.[1] As it was no longer respectable in the middle country, the references to its practice in the past were purposely obscured, if not altogether deleted.

That polyandry did not disappear from the land, is attested by Bṛhaspati's full familiarity with its fraternal and other varieties. K.V.R. Aiyangar's reconstruction of his *Smṛti* shows Bṛhaspati bewailing its prevalence in all regions or countries, and holding it "up to reprobation" in the words of the editor.[2] He can attack and impugn the propriety of a practice, in as much as he is entitled to his views; but he fails to wish it wholly out of existence.

That polyandry and practices closely akin to it were still in pronounced evidence in certain parts of India, is also borne out by the *Kāmasūtra* of Vātsyāyana. Referring to the *udīcya* or northern division, Vātsyāyana speaks of a custom which the Bāhlīka[3] country has in common with Strī-rājya and the province of Grāmanārī : in all these countries several young men are married

[1] *Matsya*, XLIV, 60-66; *Brahmāṇḍa*, III. 71. 121; 128. Cf. Sarkar, *op. cit.*, p. 153.

[2] *Bṛhaspatismṛti*, Reconstructed by K.V.R. Aiyangar, Gaekwad's Oriental Series, vol. LXXXV, Baroda, 1941, pp. 160, and 286, verse 403:
sujātāś cāpi gṛhṇanti bhrātṛbhāryam sabhartṛkām |
sarvadeśeṣvanācāro rathyātāmbūlacarvaṇam ||
Quoted in *Caturviṁśatimata-saṁgraha*, with the Commentary of Bhaṭṭojī Dīkṣita, Benares, 1907-8, p. 96. Also see above, pp. 82, 83.

[3] The commentator places Bāhlīka in Uttarāpatha:
bāhlīkadeśyā uttarāpathikāḥ. Also see above, p. 80, for the evidence of the *Mahābhārata.*

to a single woman; and their position there is analogous to that of women in harems elsewhere.[1] The commentator explains it as meaning that a number of men had to confine their services to the single lady who was their mistress, and had to attend upon her either singly or in batches.[2] As Chakladar understands it, "this rather unusual custom no doubt refers to a system of polyandry carried to a refined excess".[3] We have remarkable corroboration from other authorities to prove the persistence of polyandry in the north-west and beyond till much later times.[4]

Vātsyāyana's shrewd observation that the wife of a man with many younger brothers may be easily gained,[5] can arise only out of one social situation: the accessibility of a married woman to her brothers-in-law, and the less likelihood, therefore, of her refusal or inability to entertain the thought of loving someone else as well !

Indeed, we hear even of the illustrious king Chandragupta II Vikramāditya[6] marrying his brother's wife. Controversy may continue to rage around the historicity of an imperial Rāma-

[1] *grāmanārīviṣaye strīrājye ca bāhlīke bahavo yuvāno' ntaḥpurasadharmāṇa ekaikasyāḥ parigrahabhūtāḥ.* Cf. *Kāmasūtra*, (ed.) Gosvami, Damodar Shastri, The Kashi Skt. Series no. 29, Benares, 1929, p. 124.

[2] One is immediately reminded of the five sons of Pāṇḍu attending on the sick Kaṇhā, the hump-backed dwarf, too, sitting at her feet, in the *Jātaka* story discussed above.

[3] Chakladar, H. C., *Social Life in Ancient India: Studies in Vātsyāyana's Kāmasūtra*, Calcutta, 1929. pp. 49-50.

[4] Cf. Sachau, E. C., *Alberuni's India*, vol. I,p. 108; Biddulph, J., *Tribes of the Hindoo Koosh*, p. 82.

[5] Cf. Burton, Sir Richard and Arbuthnot, F. F., (tr.) *The Kāma Sūtra of Vātsyāyana*, Edited with foreword and Notes by Muirhead-Gould J., London, 1964, p. 121.

[6] His name should be spelt as Candragupta according to our system of transliteration. But we have retained the popular spelling in the text.

gupta[1], the efforts of whose champions might uncover more evidence to make him somewhat less nebulous than he is at the moment. What is vital for us, however, is the fact that literature[2], belonging to a period when Hindu morality had become fully-fledged and many law-givers had propounded the doctrine of perpetual widowhood, describes Chandragupta II (c. 381-413-14 A. D.)[3] as taking to wife his own sister-in-law without a word of censure or condemnation. That clearly allows a brother-in-law's conjugal interest in his elder brother's wife, dormant if not alive even during the life-time of the latter.

[1] Elder brother of Chandragupta II. Cf. Raychaudhuri, H. C., *Political History of Ancient India*, Fifth Ed., 1950. pp. 553-554. New numismatic evidence has been brought to light by K. D. Bajpai to prove the historicity of Rāmagupta; but no gold coins of this ruler have yet been found.

[2] *Harṣa-Carita*; *Kāvyamīmāṁsā*; *Devī Candraguptaṁ*; Penzer, *Kathā S. S.*, III. 290. Also an epigraph of the ninth century. Cf. Raychaudhuri, *loc. cit.*, p. 553.

[3] *Ibid.*, p. 554.

CHAPTER FOUR

Continuity of the Polyandrous Tradition

There is no doubt that the practice of polyandry ceased to be respectable in the middle country or *madhyadeśa* from the Gupta period onwards. It had its opponents even earlier, whose ethics was loftier than the dictates of often inexorable necessity; and whose idealism was not untainted by an element of male chauvinism. That explains the agonising over the polyandry of Draupadī by the later moralist who mythifies it to explain it away; and the denunciation of regions where it still persisted as dens of wanton indulgence. Life in the plains of the Gangā and Yamunā had become comparatively easier and more assured, as the patient oxen and their industrious masters tilled fertile fields and raised magnificent crops; as commercial growth contributed to common prosperity. With the progressive conquest of the environment, with ever more land being pressed under the plough, the process of cultural refinement proceeded apace, giving birth to a new brand of morality in accord with the needs of the changing socio-economic milieu. The practice of polyandry fell into desuetude where it was no longer required. The stress and strain of migration was now but a remote memory of the past. Constant warfare involving all the able-bodied men of the community was also a mere matter for recollection in the form of ballads and stories. There was no conscription; no obligation to military service; no forced absence from home. The terrain was wide and fruitful, with prospects of unending agricultural and mercantile growth. There were enough women to go round. There was no sense of compulsion to restrict the growth of population. There was no imperative need, either, to keep family property undivided. Migration from one region to another, if at all required, was much easier than before, what with better roads and improved transport. Polyandry became less necessary, and therefore less fashionable.

Notions of the *pativratā* and the *satī* faithful to a single man caught the imagination of the country, even though they were unfair to women and favourable to men, who could contract as many marriages as they desired. The ideal of monogamy, almost as old as the sky above, became supreme. But an ideal is often at variance with reality. Polygyny continued unabated, and even became a symbol of status, affluence and power. Polyandry also lurked here and there in the plains among castes higher as well as lower, owing to the same reasons as had made it much more widespread in times past. But it went under cover, as it was on the defensive and doubtless in full retreat. Elsewhere, though, in parts of India where life was neither so peaceful nor plentiful, it continued as before without any fuss or apology.

The Hūṇas of Central Asia, who invaded Afghanistan and India during the fourth and fifth centuries A. D., were a polyandrous people. The Chinese *Annals of Liang* (VIth century A. D.) clearly refer to their polyandry[1], which is confirmed by R. Girshman who was Head of the French Archaeological Mission in Iran, on the basis of epigraphic evidence discovered by him in Iran and Afghanistan, at Sialk in particular.[2]

[1] Cf. Grénard, F., and Dutreuille de Rhins, J.L., *Le Turkestan et le Tibet, Mission Scientifique dans la Haute Asie,* 1890-95, *IIème Partie.*

[2] Cf. Prince Peter, *op. cit.*, pp. 59-60.

The Hūṇas find mention in Indian inscriptions; in the *Mahābhārata* and the *Purāṇas;* in the *Raghuvaṁśa* and the *Harṣacarita;* in the *Nītivākyāmṛta* and the *Rājataraṅgiṇī*.[1] They left a notable imprint on Indian history, and it is natural to assume that they did not give up their polyandry as soon as they arrived in India. It is equally reasonable to asume that some people in India must have been affected or influenced by their example, since they came as conquerors and certainly intermarried with the local population. They exercised sway over a vast stretch of territory extending from Kabul to Central India, when Mihirakula succeeded in about 515 A. D. to his father Toramāṇa. They shook the great Gupta empire to its very foundations, before Mihirakula was himself defeated by Bālāditya of Magadha and Yaśodharman, and forced to retire about 530 A. D. to Kashmir and the adjoining regions. The influence of the Hūṇas on the local populace, which also influenced them in turn to the point of their total absorption in the Indian community, is clearly brought out by Kalhaṇa in the following passage:

> Brāhmaṇas from Gāndhāra, resembling himself in their habits and verily themselves the lowest of the twice-born, accepted *agrahāras* from him.[2]

The ruler referred to is Mihirakula.[3] Hiuen-Tsang also

[1] Cf. Raychaudhuri, *Political History of Ancient India,* Vth Edn., 1950, p. 578, f.n.1. The *Lalita Vistara* refers to the *Hūṇalipi*, the script of the Hūṇas. Cf. McGovern, W. M., *The Early Empires of Central Asia,* pp. 399 ff., 455 ff., 485 f.; Stein, *Rājataraṅgiṇī*, vol. I, p. 43, note on 289; Fleet in *Ind. Ant.*, XV, pp. 245 ff.; *Corp. Ins. Ind.*, III, pp. 10 sqq.

[2] *Rājataraṅgiṇī*, I. 307; Stein's translation, vol. I, p. 46.

[3] He calls himself Mihirakula or Mihiragula on his coins. The monk Kosmas Indikopleustes refers to him under the name of Gollas. The Hūṇas were finally absorbed into the Indian Rajput population. Cf. Majumdar, R. C. and others, *An Advanced History of India*, Part I, *Ancient India*, London, 1949, p. 154.

refers to his conquest of Gāndhāra[1]; and Kalhaṇa laments his evil impact on the brāhmaṇas of the region. The Calcutta and Paris editions of the *Rājataraṅgiṇī* contain two *ślokas* after this verse, not found by Stein in some of the manuscripts he studied. "They attribute to the descendants of Mlecchas intercourse with their sisters, to the Dāradas illicit relations with their daughters-in-law, and to the Bhāṭṭas sale of their wives and licentiousness of their womenfolk."[2] We may recall the barbed outburst of Karṇa in the *Mahābhārata* against the unorthodox *ācāra* of the inhabitants of the north-west, including Gāndhāra.[3] There was undoubtedly greater laxity in matters of love in the north-west; but much of this deprecation must have arisen out of misunderstanding, misreading and dislike of the ways of polyandry.

Bṛhaspati's fling at the lecherous women of the east[4] can also be similarly explained in terms of his poor or mistaken comprehension of the polyandrous practices of Tibet and Farther India.[5] This, in fact, is the only rational explanation possible. Confusion must have been confounded by garbled versions of both adelphic and non-adelphic polyandry, that obtained there.

We have spoken of *Strī-rājya* before. The *Bṛhat Saṁhitā* of Varāhamihira mentions it as located in north-western India.[6] Numerous, indeed, are the references to it, or to Strī-vāhya or

[1] *Si-yu-ki*, i, p. 171.

[2] Stein's *Rājataraṅgiṇī*, Vol. I, p. 46, n. 307.

[3] Cf. *Mbh.*, VIII. 30.

[4] II. 30; *pūrve vyabhicāraratāḥ striyaḥ* of K. V. R. Aiyangar's Edn., p. 286, verse 402.

[5] Cf. Jolly, *Hindu Law and Custom*, p. 107.

[6] *Bṛhat Saṁhitā*, XIV. 22:

diśi paścimottarasyāṁ māṇḍavyatuṣāratālahalamadrāḥ |
aśmakakulūtahalaḍāḥ strīrājyanṛsiṁhavanakhasthāḥ ||

Cf. The Vizianagram Sanskrit Series, Vol. X (two parts), Benares, 1895-97.

Nārī-viṣaya in ancient Indian literature.[1] We have already noted Vātsyāyana's allusion to their polyandrous practices, which presumably provided somewhat greater social and political weightage for their women than elsewhere. The names of the region might also hark back to its matriarchal past, and to traces thereof.[2]

The Chinese pilgrim Hiuen-Tsang talks of a country in the north of the region around Gaṅgādvāra or modern Haridwār:

> To the north of this country (Brahmapura) and in the Great Snow Mountains, was the Suvarṇa-gotra country...this was called the "Eastern Woman's Country", so called because it was ruled by a succession of women. The husband of the queen was king, but he did not administer the government. The men attended only to the suppression of revolts and the cultivation of the fields. This country reached on the east to T'u-fan (Tibet), on the north to Khoten, and on the west to San-p'o-ha (Malasa).[3]

He is most probably referring to the Kumaon Garhwal region of the Himālayas (and to some territory to the north of it?) where

[1] *Kāmasūtra, op. cit.*; *Śānti Parva*, IV. 7 (Kumbakonam Edn.); *Rājataraṅgiṇī*, IV. 165-185, mentions Strī-rājya as one of the countries conquered by Lalitāditya (first half of 8th century A. D.). Cf. Stein's Translation, Vol. I, pp. 136-138. Kalhaṇa credits Lalitāditya's grandson Jayāpīḍa, too, with the conquest of Strī-rājya; see IV. 587. Strī-vāhya of the *Mārkaṇḍeya Purāṇa*, LVIII. 38, seems to be the same as Strī-rājya of the *Agni Purāṇa*, LV. 17, mentioned as a country in the west of India. Cf. also Chakladar, *op. cit.*, pp. 59-60. For various such realms referred to in Sanskrit literature, and said to be situated in Afghanistan, Orissa, Assam, Nepal, Tibet, etc., see Walker, B., *Hindu World,* II, pp. 432-33.

[2] Cf. Muir, "On the question whether polyandry ever existed in Northern Hindustan", *Ind. Ant.*, vol. VI, p. 315. The Critical Edition of the *Mahābhārata* drops the reference to matriarchal traditions of the northwestern people from Karṇa's statement.

[3] Watters, *Yuan Chwang*, I, p. 330.

polyandry is still practised by brāhmaṇas, kṣatriyas and Ḍoms alike.[1] Life was hard as ever in the high mountainous terrain; and polyandry decidedly helped sibling and family unity, as it ensured the availability of organized labour in the fields, and preserved the houses and scarce agricultural land from the disaster of otherwise inevitable partition. The growth of population was held in check by confining the procreative power of many males to a single female, even as women felt more secure with many husbands in an inhospitable environment. The fine formulations of monogamous morality left them utterly incredulous and cold.

The polyandrous traditions of India, Āryan as well as non-Āryan, are remarkably reflected in the history of the goddess Śrī-Lakṣmī, who originally lived with the asuras, but abandoned them owing to their degradation, in favour of Indra.[2] Her association with elephants[3], too, points to her non-Āryan origin. The *Mahābhārata* repeatedly refers to her association with other gods before she finally chose Viṣṇu. We have already discussed her polyandrous marriage with five Indras reenacted in her role as the wife of the five Pāṇḍavas. Her association with Kubera is no less ancient. If we accept the explanation of the commentator,

[1] Cf. Chakladar, *op. cit.* Cunningham identifies Brahmapura with the districts of Garhwal and Kumaon. Cf. his *Ancient Geography of India*, edited by S. Majumdar Sastri, Calcutta, 1924, pp. 407-408. Eastern Tibet preserves a tradition of female rule in the past, when a woman called Pinchieu ruled over the Nu-wang tribe; and the people in each successive reign chose a woman to be their ruler. Cf. Dey, N. L., *Geographical Dictionary of Ancient and Mediaeval India*, 2nd edn., London, 1927, p. 104.

[2] Cf. *Mbh.* XII. 218; 221. 60 ff.

[3] The *Śrī-Sūkta* describes her delight at the sound of elephants, 3, *hastinādapramodinī*. Her earliest representations, too, such as those at Bharhut, Sānchī, Bodhgayā and Pītalkhorā, depict her in her gajalakṣmī form. Her lasting association with Gaṇeśa is equally significant. Cf. also *Viṣṇu Purāṇa*, I. 9. 102.

the seventh hymn of the *Śrī-sūkta* connects her with Kubera.[1] The *Mahābhārata*[2] and the *Rāmāyaṇa*[3] alike attest her intimacy with the god of wealth, who is explicitly stated to be united with her.[4] Several sculptures of the Kuṣāṇa period provide evidence of her worship with Kubera.[5] A small slab depicts her together with Ardhanārīśvara-Śiva, Viṣṇu and Kubera.[6] She seems to be the common consort of Kubera and Viṣṇu in this little sculpture, as it was only later that she became the consort of Viṣṇu-Nārāyaṇa.[7]

She is also associated with Kārtikeya, whose wife Devasenā is called Lakṣmī.[8] And in the later Hindu art she is frequently depicted in an exceedingly close relationship with Gaṇeśa. Indeed, Śrī-Lakṣmī chooses many, and belongs to many. The post-Gupta images of Lakṣmī associate both Gaṇeśa and Kubera with her. A relief in the Mathurā Museum[9], and another in the State Museum, Lucknow[10], depict the goddess seated in *lalitāsana* pose between Gaṇeśa on the right and Kubera on the left. Does it denote the simultaneous presence of two consorts ?

Another statuette in the Mathurā Museum[11] shows the goddess with only pot-bellied Kubera who holds a bowl in his right hand;

1 *RV.*, *Śrī-sūktaṁ*, 7, *upaitu māṁ devasakhaḥ kīrtiśca maṇinā saha*. The devotee in his prayer requests the goddess to come to him with Devasakhā, i.e., Kubera, Kīrti and Maṇi, i.e., Maṇibhadra, the treasurer of Kubera.

2 *Mbh.*, II. 10. 18.

3 *Rāmāyaṇa*, *Sundara*, IX. 8.

4 *Mbh.*, III. 164. 13; Cf. Hopkins, *Epic Mythology*, p. 143.

5 Cf. Agrawala, *A Catalogue of the Brahmanical Images in Mathura Art*, pp. X, XI, nos. 0.241; C. 30; 2520.

6 *Ibid.*, p. IX, 41, no. 2520.

7 Cf. Jaiswal, Suvira, *The Origin and Development of Vaiṣṇavism*, Delhi, 1967, pp. 100-102.

8 *Mbh.*, III. 218. 47; also see verses 3 and 48.

9 No. 1119.

10 No. 0.251.

11 No. 223.

the left is broken. V. S. Agrawala takes her presence beside Kubera to be a clear indication that she continued to be regarded as his consort till much later.[1]

The *Kriyākramadyoti* by Āghoraśivācārya describes how Lakṣmī-Gaṇapati should be sculptured; while the *Mantramahodadhi* gives one to understand that the fourth arm of Gaṇapati "is intended to hold Lakṣmī in its embrace".[2] The latter text also states that the goddess Lakṣmī, too, should be depicted as embracing Gaṇeśa with one of her arms.[3]

Quite appropriately, therefore, Śrī appeared on the coins of the Kuṇindas as early as the first century B. C.[4] They have been identified by Cunningham and others with the polyandrous Kanets of the Panjab Himālayas.[5] And it looks as though their Śrī was, like her incarnation in the Epic Draupadī, as much the presiding deity of their polyandry, as of their prosperity largely based on the tribal solidarity it fostered.

The muslim scholar-traveller Alberuni confirms the presence of polyandry in India of the 11th century A. D. He is aware of the Hindu theory that "if a stranger has a child by a married woman, the child belongs to her husband, since the wife, being, as it were, the soil in which the child has grown, is the property of the husband, always presupposing that the sowing, i.e the

[1] *JUPHS*, XXII, p. 151. The sculpture belongs to the 7th-8th century A. D.

[2] Cf. Gopinatha Rao, *Hindu Iconography*, I, p. 53.

[3] *Ibid.* Rao has published a plate (XI, fig. I) of Lakṣmī-Gaṇapati in stone from the Viśvanāthasvāmin temple at Teṇkāśi, built in 1446 A. D., by the Pāṇḍya king Arikesari Parākrama Pāṇḍyadeva. Also see p. 64 of his Vol. I.

[4] Cf. Allan, *Catalogue of the Coins of Ancient India in the British Museum*, London, 1936, pp. 159-168.

[5] Cf. *Archaeological Survey of India Reports*, Vol. XIV, pp. 125-135; Joshi, L. D., *The Khasa Family Law*, Allahabad, 1929, p. 17.

cohabitation, takes place with his consent."[1]

He also knows that "the four sons of Pāṇḍu had one wife in common, who stayed one month with each of them alternately."[2] "All these customs", he tells us, "have now been abolished and abrogated."[3] But when he says so, he means the middle country, where monogamy is the ideal, and polygyny synonymous with status. For he himself then informs us that these "unnatural kinds of marriage...still exist in our time, as they also existed in the times of Arab heathendom; for the people inhabiting the mountains stretching from the region of Panchir into the neighbourhood of Kashmir live under the rule that several brothers have one wife in common."[4] Dr. Sachau identifies Panchir with Hindu-Kush, Kafiristan and Chitral.[5]

That polyandry did not disappear from the Panjab, is noted by other Muslim historians, such as Ghulám Básit[6] and Muhammad Kásim Ferishtá.[7] The former refers to the polyandrous tradition of Malíbár, apparently Malābār in south India, and then adds:

1 *Alberuni's India*, ed. with notes and indices by Sachau, E. C., Vol. I, p. 107.

2 *Ibid.*, I, p. 108.

3 *Ibid.*

4 *Ibid.* He refers, too, to marriage of different kinds among the heathen Arabs; such as an Arab sending his wife to someone else in the hope of getting a generous offspring; exchange of wives; and "several men" cohabiting "with one wife". "When, then, she gave birth to a child, she declared who was the father; and if she did not know it, the fortune-tellers had to know it." *Ibid.*, pp. 108-109.

5 *Ibid.*, Vol. II, p. 295. Cf. also Biddulph, *op. cit.*, p. 82.

6 *Tārīkh-i Mamālik-i Hind* of Ghulám Básit, in Elliot's *The History of India as told by its own Historians*, Ed. Dowson, J., Vol. VIII, London, 1877, pp. 202-203.

7 Ferishta, Muhammad Kasim, *History of the Rise of the Mahomedan Power in India*, translated by Briggs, John, Vol. I, p. 184. The Khokhar or Ghakkars are described by Ferishta as savages addicted to polyandry and infanticide. Cf. also *Encyclopaedia Britannica*, Ninth Edn. The article on India, p. 791.

> Originally the infidel Khokhars of the Panjab, before embracing Islam, observed a very curious custom. Among them also polyandry prevailed. When one husband went into the house of the woman, he left something at the door as a signal, so that, if another husband happened to come at the same time, he might upon seeing it return. Besides this, if a daughter was born, she was taken out of the house immediately, and it was proclaimed, "Will any person purchase this girl, or not ?" If there appeared a purchaser, she was given to him; otherwise she was put to death.[1]

The testimony of these Muslim historians indicates that polyandry did not quite die out in the land of the five rivers. One significant reason is perhaps the fact that the Panjab, after the north-west, always bore the brunt of repeated foreign incursions, necessitating inescapable military service by its men with all its concomitants, including prolonged absence from their homes. The military tradition, in fact, continues to this day. "With the Rajputs and Jats in the Sikh regiments of the Indian army, it was, in the middle of the last century, a recognised and common plea for leave of absence that their brothers were away from home and their wife left alone."[2]

Female infanticide, too, regarded as a cause of polyandry,[3] must have owed its incidence at least partially to the insecurity engendered by regularly recurring warfare, often resulting in the successful infiltration of the foreigner. And like the Hūṇas,

[1] *Tārīkh-i Mamālik-i Hind, loc. cit.*

[2] Briffault, *op. cit.*, I, p. 679; Masson, C., *Narrative of Various Journeys in Balochistan, Afghanistan and the Panjab*, Vol. I, p. 435.

[3] Cf. Rivers, *The Todas*, p. 518.

many of these new-comers were also polyandrous,[1] which naturally contributed to the continuance of this form of marriage.

Practices closely akin to polyandry or cicisbeism have been repeatedly reported from parts of northern India both in the nineteenth and twentieth centuries. Thus, in 1881, Sir Denzil Ibbetson was able to quote Delmerick's statement:

> In the Ambala submontane tract from the Jumna to the Satlej, polyandry is very extensively practised. Indeed, a sister-in-law is looked upon as common property, not only by uterine brothers, but by all 'bhai', including first cousins. This is the case among all castes of Hindus.[2]

Traces of polyandry were noticed among the Jāṭs of the Panjab by Ibbetson,[3] Rose,[4] Crooke,[5] Kirkpatrick[6] and Douie.[7] Similar practices were observed among the Gūjars by Crooke[8], Russell[9]

[1] Cf. Specht, E., "Études sur l'Asie centrale d'après les historiens chinois", *Journal Asiatique*, 8e Sèrie, X, pp. 338 ff. (History of Liang), *ibid.*, (History of Wei). *ibid.*, 342, (History of Tcheu), *ibid.*, 346 sq.; (History of Swi). Also see Rémusat, A. de, *Nouveaux mélanges asiatiques*, Vol. I, pp. 240 sq., 245; Briffault, *op. cit.*, pp. 680, 681.

[2] Delmerick, cited by Ibbetson, *Report on the Census of the Panjab*, 1881, Vol. I, p. 365.

[3] *Ibid.*

[4] Rose, H. A., *A Glossary of the Tribes and Castes of the Punjab and North-West Frontier Province*, Vol. II, p. 363, n.

[5] Crooke, W., *Tribes and Castes of the North-Western Provinces and Oudh*, Vol. III, p. 36.

[6] Kirkpatrick, C. S., "Polyandry in the Panjab", *Indian Antiquary*, VII, p. 86.

[7] Douie, Sir J. M., *Gazetteer of the Karnal District*, p. 76.

[8] Crooke, *loc. cit.*, Vol. II, pp. 444 sq.

[9] Russell, R. V., *The Tribes and Castes of the Central Provinces of India*, Vol. III, p. 172.

and Delmerick[1]; among the Ahīrs and Lohārs by Crooke.[2]

In the Panjab Census Report of 1892, MacLagan took note of the "custom" of "polyandry" in the Kulu valley of north Panjab, and in Spiti as well as Lahul.[3]

In the *Census of India of* 1911, Vol. I, E. A. Gait mentioned the polyandry of the Tibetans and Bhotias of the border; of the Kanets and lower castes of the Kulu valley; of the inhabitants of the state of Bashahr; of the Thakkars and Megs of Kashmir; and of the Ghonds of the Central Provinces. He also referred to the polyandry of the Todas and Kurumbas of the Nilgiris in south India; of the Tolkolans of Malabar; of the Ishavans, Kaniyans and Kammalans of Cochin; of the Muduvas of Travancore; of the Western Kallans; and of the Nayars.[4]

In the Census Report of 1931, J. H. Hutton[5] spoke of Jaunsar Bawar in Dehradun district of the United Provinces (now Uttar

1 Cf. Ibbetson, *op. cit.*

2 Crooke, *op. cit.*, Vol. I, p. 58; Vol. III, p. 379. Cf. also Briffault, *op. cit.*, I, 678-680.

3 *Census of India, Punjab*, 1892, p. 224. In the Kulu valley, according to him, the eldest brother was regarded as the father of the first child born in a polyandrous household; while the next eldest brother was considered the father of the second, and so on. In Spiti "polyandry" obtained between the laymen and the monks of the Pin monastery, where celibacy was not the rule. In Lahul all the monks were free to marry, and most of them were co-husbands with their lay-brothers at home.

4 *The Census of India of* 1911, Vol. I, Part I, 1931 Edn. Cf. Prince Peter, *op. cit.*, pp. 81-82. Gait suspected that the Nayars were still polyandrous, though he was not certain; but they assuredly followed *marumakkaṭāyam* or the matriarchal system.

5 *Census of India*, 1931, Vol. I, Part I, 1933 Edn. In his *Caste in India*, Cambridge, 1946, pp. 38, 39, Hutton speaks of "the people of Lahaul and Spiti", "cut off for six months of the year from the Punjab province, of which

Pradesh) as a region where polyandry was extensively practised. Khan Ahmad Hasan Khan[1] was struck by the figures of married men exceeding those of married women in the area comprising the districts and states of Ambala, Bashahr, Sirmoor, Kalsia, Ludhiana, Maler Kotla, Ferozepur, Faridkot and Amritsar; and attributed the dispartity to the incidence of polyandry.

Thus, from Tibet in the north down to Ceylon in the south, from the Hindu-Kush in the west upto Sikkim and Bhutan in the east, different parts of the Indian sub-continent inhabited by Āryan as well as non-Āryan races are reported to have known, or to be still practising, polyandry or practices closely akin to it.[2]

---

these are outlying domains, by heavy snow, and the poverty of their country.. has assisted in perpetuating... a social system... of fraternal polyandry..." They are Buddhists; while the Kanets of the Kulu valley are Hindus, and "perhaps still have a somewhat similar practice by which brothers might share one wife or more than one."

In his other well-known book *The Angami Nagas*, Oxford University Press, Second Edn., Bombay, 1969, pp. 398-400, Hutton points out the possibility of a matriarchate amongst the Nagas in the past, and relates a Sema legend of the origin of exogamous clans. Nikhoga, the first man, had six sons. He was able to find a wife only for the eldest, with the result that the other five were always intriguing with their brother's wife. Nikhoga, on that account, drove them out to establish separate families and eventually exogamous clans. The story might indicate some period of polyandry in the past.

J. P. Mills, in his book *The Lhota Nagas*, London, 1922, p. 154, n. 1, tells us that the Rengmas practise something very close to polyandry. "A younger brother who has a fancy to his elder brother's wife by no means necessarily waits for his brother's absence, nor does the elder brother necessarily object to his younger brother's having intercourse with his (the elder) wife. I have known the elder brother acquiesce in this even when the younger was married to a wife of his own. This last it was who objected."

1 *Census of India*, 1931, Vol. XVII, *Punjab Part I*, 1933 Edn., p. 178.

2 For example, the inhabitants of Coorg, a small wooded region of the Western

When we talk of the Āryans, it might be worthwhile recalling what Max Müller said about them:

> There is no Aryan race. Aryan is in scientific language utterly inapplicable to race. It means a language, and

---

Ghats in south India, have been repeatedly reported to be polyandrous. In 1784, Tipu Sultan of Mysore thus harangued the people of Coorg in order to quell their refractory intent:

> If six brothers dwell together in one house, and the elder brother marries, his wife becomes equally the wife of the other five, and the intercourse, so far from being disgraceful, is familiarly considered as a national rite; not a man in the country knows his father, and the ascendancy of women, and bastardy of children, is your common attribute....You have rebelled seven times...I forgive you once more, but if rebellion be ever repeated, ...I will make (you) aliens in your own home, and establish (you) in a distant land, and thus at once extinguish rebellion, and plurality of husbands, and initiate (you) in the more honourable practices of Islam.

From Wilks, Mark, *Historical Sketches of the South of India in an attempt to trace the History of Mysoor*, (Two Volumes), Mysore, 1930-32, Vol. II, pp. 280-81. Of the "national rite" referred to above, Wilks says in a footnote, "Perfectly true."

In *A Study of Polyandry*, published in 1963, Prince Peter of Greece and Denmark listed the Tibetans, the inhabitants of Sirmoor, Tehri-Garhwal and Jaunsar Bawar, the Dards of Dah in Kashmir, the Sikkimese Bhotias and the Bhutanese of Tibetan extraction, all in the north, as polyandrous. Those polyandrous in the south included the Todas of the Nilgiris, the Thandans, Kammalans and the allied artisan castes of Kerala, and the Kandyans of Ceylon. Those practising cicisbeism included the Tibetans, Rengma divisions of the Lhota Nagas, Todas of the Nilgiris, Kotas of the Nilgiris, Nayars of Kerala, Sikhs and Jats of the Panjab, Lepchas of Bengal, Sikkim and W. Bhutan, Irulas, Kurumbas, Canarese-speaking Mysoreans, Tamils, Telugus and Badagas of the Nilgiris. Cf. p. 507. He cited instances of cicisbeism from France and the U. S. A. of the 20th century, as well as elsewhere. He also confirmed the existence of polyandry in some other parts of the world, including Indo-China. Swinging and wife-swapping in the western world with organized clubs and advertisements in papers constitute a new phenomenon.

> nothing but a language...I have declared again and again that if I say 'Aryan' I mean neither blood, nor bone, or hair or skull. I mean simply those who speak an Aryan language. To me an ethnologist who speaks of Aryan race, Aryan blood, Aryan eyes and hair, is as great a sinner as a linguist who speaks of a dolicocephalic dictionary or a brachycephalic grammar. It is worse than a Babylonian confusion of tongues."[1]

It is clearly beyond the scope of a book confining itself to the quest of polyandry's past in India to make more than a passing reference to the polyandrous practices of the present. The Khasas, though, deserve special attention on account of their undoubted Āryan affinities[2] and the notice they attract in the sacred and

[1] Max Müller, F., *Biographies of Words and the Home of the Aryas*, pp. 89, 90, 120.

[2] Cf. Grierson, Sir G. A., *Linguistic Survey of India*, IX, Part IV, pp. 7, 8, 373; Ibbeston, Sir D., *Punjab Census Report* (1883), Vol. I, p. 268. According to Atkinson, the "Khasas of Kumaon are in physiognomy and form as purely an Aryan race as any in the plains of northern India." Cf. Atkinson's *Gazetteer*, p. 379; Oakley, E. S., *Holy Himalaya*, p. 87. The Kanets of Kangra and Kulu alike belong to the Khasa race, and are identified with the Kulindas or Kuṇindas of classical antiquity. Cf. Cunningham, *ASI Reports*, Vol. XIV, pp. 125-135. Sir Athelstaine Baines says of them: "There seems reason to think that they belong to a very early wave of northern immigration, possibly Aryan, but not of the Vedic branch, which has received an infusion of other northern blood since its settlement in the Himalaya." Cf. his *Ethnography* (*Castes and Tribes*), 1912, p. 49. For the Khasas in general, see Joshi, L. D., *The Khasa Family Law*, Allahabad, 1929, pp. 24, 31. D. N. Majumdar says that despite some intermixture with the Mongoloids of the upper Himalayas or with the Doms of the lower region, the Khasas are clearly distinguishable from the proto-Australoids or Mongoloids, who form the bulk of the tribal peoples. He draws attention to their "true Mediterranean features." Cf. his *Races and Cultures of India*, Fourth Edn., Bombay, 1973, Chapter VIII; "Some Aspects of the Cultural Life of the Khasas of the cis-Himalayan Region", *Journal and Proceedings of the Royal Asiatic Society of Bengal*, Third Series, Vol VI, 1940, pp. 1 ff. According to this article,

secular texts of ancient India. The *Mahābhārata* credits them with great courage, and calls them "unyielding and obstinate in battle."[1] They are included among those who bring presents to King Yudhiṣṭhira on the occasion of his *rājasūya* sacrifice.[2] And the *Droṇa Parva* describes them as "arrived from diverse realms."[3] Karṇa castigates them for their unorthodox 'immorality' together with the Bāhlikas, Madras and Gāndhāras.[4]

Manu,[5] for the same reason, refers to them as vrātya-kṣatṛiyas, or those members of the warrior-class who do not live up to their sacred obligations. The *Mārkaṇḍeya*[6], *Vāyu*[7], *Viṣṇu*[8] and the *Bhāgavata*[9] *Purāṇas* speak of them; and the *Bṛhat Saṁhitā*[10] places them in the north-western region. Kalhaṇa[11], the historian

---

polyandry enabled the Khasas of Jaunsar Bawar to retain their racial purity. Cf. also Saksena, R. N., *Social Economy of a Polyandrous People*, Agra University Series, No. 1, 1956; Parmar, Y. S., *Polyandry in the Himalayas*, Delhi, 1975.

1 *Mbh.*, VIII. 20. 10-11 (Calcutta Edn.).

2 *Ibid.*, II. 48. 3-5 (Critical Edn.) mention both Khaśas and Kuṇindas. The Khaśas brought honey and gold from Himavat, which points towards the Khasiyas of Garhwal. Cf. Joshi, *op. cit.*, p. 14; Atkinson, *op. cit.*, XI, pp. 245, 543, for gold dust and honey of Garhwal.

3 *Mbh.*, VII. 11. 17-18 (Calcutta Edn.); VII. 10. 18, n. 18 on p. 59, Critical Edn.

4 *Ibid.*, VIII. 44; 45. (Calcutta Edn.). VIII, 30. 47, n. 47 on pp. 264-265 of the Critical Edn., where the Khasas are thus mentioned: ...*prasthalā madragāndhārā ārattā nāmataḥ khaśaḥ.*

5 *Manu*, X. 22.

6 *Mārkaṇḍeya*, LVIII. 7, 12 and 51 tell us that the Khasas were also living in the *madhyadeśa*. Pargiter's *Mārkaṇḍeya Purāṇa*, 1904, Canto LVII, 56, p. 345.

7 *Wilson's Works*, Vol. VIII, 1800, p. 292.

8 Wilson, *Viṣṇu Purāṇa*, 1840, p. 195, n. 157.

9 *Bhāgavata Purāṇa*, II. 4. 18, refers to the Khasas as an outcast tribe, that attained salvation by adopting the religion of Kṛṣṇa.

10 *Bṛhat Saṁhitā*, XIV. 29-31. They are also mentioned in X. 12, and XIV. 6.

11 *Rājataraṅgiṇī*, I. 317; see Stein's note on pp. 47-48 of Vol. I. Khasas are referred to in VII. 979, 1271, 1276 sqq.; VIII. 887, 1466, 1868, 1895.

of Kashmir, mentions them as exciting the ire of the Hūṇa chief Mihirakula.

They "spoke a language closely allied to Sanskrit, but with a vocabulary partly agreeing with that of the Iranian Avesta..."[1] Always known as a powerful race, they came at a very early period from Central Asia, and probably left their trail in such names as Kashgar, Kashkara, the Hindu-Kush, Kashmir, and in places bearing similar root-names in the entire mountainous region extending from Kashmir to Nepal.[2] Thus, "the great mass of the Aryan speaking population of the lower Himalaya from Kashmir to Darjeeling is inhabited by tribes descended from the ancient Khasas of the *Mahābhārata*."[3] The Khakhas of the Jhelam valley, the Kanets of the hill country between Kangra and Garhwal, and the Khasas of Jaunsar Bawar, are all children of common ancestors. A representative Khasiya tract, Jaunsar Bawar "forms a very important link between the almost Hinduised Khasiyas of Kumaon and their brethren converts to Islam on the ethnical frontier in the mountains of the Hindu-Kush, and apparently gives customs and practices of the Khasiya race in full force at the present day which distinguished them a thousand years ago."[4]

"A fossil of the *Mahābhārata* age," as they are called,[5] the Khasas of Jaunsar Bawar include Brāhmaṇas and Rājpūts[6] who

[1] Grierson, *LSI*, IX, Part IV, p. 7.

[2] Cf. Saksena, R. N. , *op. cit.*, p. 9.

[3] Grierson, *loc. cit.*, p. 8. The earliest Aryan speaking inhabitants who used and developed the Western Pahāṛī dialect, were the Khasas. Cf. *ibid.*, p. 373.

[4] Atkinson, *Gazetteer of the Himalayan Districts of the North Western Provinces*, Vol. XII, p. 353.

[5] K. M. Munshi's *Foreword* to Saksena, *op. cit.*

[6] Tod tells us that polyandry was an integral element of the social organization

freely intermarry, and are alike polyandrous. Agricultural land being limited, property is held in common by a household consisting of a patrilocal and patrilineal family. Brothers collectively own the children borne by their polyandrous wife. If they share more than one wife in common, as some of them do, it becomes a case of conjoint or group-marriage. It is normally only the eldest brother who is expressly given the status of a husband at the marriage ceremony; but all his younger brothers, too, are thereby automatically married to the woman, and are therefore called her husbands (*khwand*). If a younger brother desires some other woman, he either persuades his eldest brother to marry her as well, and then allot her to him in particular; or else, with his eldest brother's permission, he marries her on his own. In the first case, his other brothers have a theoretical and often actual right to cohabit with the new wife; but in the latter he contracts a monogamous marriage, while theoretically retaining his sexual rights in the common spouse. We may thus have polyandry, polygyny and monogamy coexisting in intimate proximity in the same Khasa household,[1] which forcefully reminds us of the close Pāṇḍava parallel.

The eldest brother is the head of the Khasa household, and its external representative. Children are occasionally allotted to different fathers within the family, though this nominal arrangement is confined only to the collective group. If one of the men decides to leave the group and set up a household of his own, he is not allowed to take any of the collective children away with him. And when he dies, his share of the ancestral property reverts

common to the Rajputs and to the peoples of the Hindu-Kush and Chitral. Cf. his *Annals and Antiquities of Rajasthan*, Vol. I, p. 23. Cf. also Biddulph, *op. cit.;* Alberuni, *op. cit.*

[1] Cf. Peter, *op. cit.*, pp. 84-85; and the works of Majumdar, Saksena and Parmar already cited.

to his children by the common wife; and his offspring by his new monogamous wife inherit only what he is able to earn or acquire after his separation from the family fold.[1]

Increasing contact with the non-polyandrous society of the plains is making serious inroads into their distinctive family organization; and their polyandry is perhaps on the way to comparative obsolescence. The environment, however, dictates its own terms; and customs grow out of necessity and human invention. There is no doubt that the Khasa family law is based on traditions older than Manu, representing an early stage of the Indo-Āryan society in evolution. The north and north-western regions of India were the home of some Āryan communities, which did not care to keep pace with the cultural changes that took place in the *madhya-deśa,* and were for that reason subjected to censure by the authors of later brahmanical morality.[2]

[1] Peter, *op. cit.*, pp. 84-85. Parmar, *Polyandry in the Himalayas*, pp. 80-81, tells us that though usually only own brothers share a common wife, first-cousins and uterine brothers and occasionally even strangers may share a wife in common in certain tracts on the Tibetan border. Group marriages, too, take place in Kanawar. On p. 84, we are told that all the sons in the polyandrous families of subordinate land-holders receive equal shares of their fathers' holdings; but in practice they hardly ever divide, and live with wife, land, house and cattle all held in common. They value their unity, which would be impossible to maintain with a number of sisters-in-law under the same roof. Prince Peter, *op. cit.*, p. 562, speaks of an Ansari informant in Kerala (south India), whose vindication of polyandry was rather picturesquely couched: "Where four breasts cannot agree, two heads can." Men could get on without quarrelling; but women could not.

[2] Cf. Kapadia, K. M., *Marriage and Family in India*, Third Edn., p. 75. It has indeed been customary to speak of marriage usages differing from those established in one's own part of the world as 'immoral' or 'barbarous'. For example, the Jews regarded the marriage of Christians as wholly invalid, so that if a Jew made love to a Christian's wife, he was not considered guilty of adultery. Cf. Eisenmenger, J. A., *Endecktes Judenthum*, Vol. I., p. 433; Briffault, *op. cit.*, I, pp. 611-612.

"Immemorial usage is transcendent law", said the great Manu.[1] The usages of the Khasas, too, derive their validity from hoary antiquity, in as much as "the highland regions of the Himalaya are but a residual cultural island which preserves social customs that had once a far more extensive distribution. The institutions which are found surviving there were common throughout the greater part of Central Asia."[2] Both polyandry and widespread levirate are, from our point of view, the most striking of those customs.[3]

[1] *Manu*, I. 108, 110.

[2] Briffault, *op. cit.*, I, p. 671. The Khasas hold festivals in honour of the Pāṇḍavas, who are their favourite deities. Many important spots in the Jaunsar Bawar area are supposed to have associations with the Pāṇḍavas. They have temples dedicated to the Pāṇḍavas, called Pāṇḍavon-kī-chaurī. The courtyard of the temple is called Pāṇḍavon kā āṅgan. The central feature of their festivals is the Pāṇḍava dance. It has been suggested that Śataśriṇga of the *Mahābhārata*, where Pāṇḍu lived in retirement according to the story, was around the same region. K. M. Munshi, *op. cit.*, identifies the place where the Pāṇḍavas were born, with Pāṇḍukeśvara on the way to Badrīnāth. Also see Kapadia, *op. cit.*, pp. 75-76.

[3] Majumdar, D. N., *Himalayan Polyandry*, Bombay, 1962, p. 18, gives census figures from 1881 to 1951, to show the shortage of females in Jaunsar Bawar. They were during this period about 20% less than the number of males. Parmar, *op. cit.*, attributes the polyandry of Himachal Pradesh to the same cause. That is, indeed, only one of the causes, as we have seen before. See Chapter One above.

Khasa polyandry and levirate are alike illustrated by some of their proverbs, one of which runs thus: *kai rāṇḍā divara bhauj ni suvava.* "What accursed woman would not go to bed with her brother-in-law ?" Even in those areas where polyandry is no more practised, the younger brothers of the married man are more than familiar with his wife; and marriage with the brother's widow is a common Khasa custom. They also have what they call *ṭekwās* "raising issue on the widow of a deceased person, children of such unions being affiliated to the deceased..." Cf. Joshi, *Khasa Family Law*, p. 107. The custom of a brother taking to wife his brother's widow is more of a right than an obligation on the part of the brother-in-law. And there is no taboo on the elder brother. Cf. *ibid.*, pp. 104-107. The

Despite the unquestionably illustrative quality of the Khasa practices, the picture of polyandry's past in India is not as rich in details as one would like it to be. We have already gone into some of the reasons that contributed to its decay and disreputability in areas which became the cradle of orthodox brahmanical culture with its elaborate caste hierarchy and code of ethics, subjected to a ceaseless and sometimes senseless exercise in classificatory formulations through the ages. The operation of varying economic and political factors apart, the disappearance of polyandry from large parts of India can be partly explained in terms of the caste and individual exclusiveness that Brahmanism promoted, and that militated against the clannish proclivity of polyandrous households. That clannish or tribal feeling was, however, kept alive by caste; and even polyandry could not be totally uprooted.

---

question naturally arises whether polyandry was once much more widespread in these parts than it is now; and whether levirate here is a survival of polyandry. "It is obvious", said McLennan, "that it could more easily be feigned that the children belonged to the brother deceased, if already, at a prior stage, the children of the brotherhood had been accounted the children of the eldest brother, i.e., if we suppose the obligation to be a relic of polyandry." Cf. his *Studies in Ancient History*, 1886, p. 113. The fact that adultery with a brother's wife even in parts where polyandry has ceased to be fashionable is considered quite pardonable, clearly shows that levirate is a survival, and cannot be explained away by insisting that men have property rights over women in Khasa law. Cf. Joshi, *op. cit.*, pp. 108-110. According to the old Hindu law, too, wives are heritable property. *Gautama*, XXVIII, 47, tells us that women shall not be partitioned; which clearly points to a time when they were regarded as family property. Cf. *CHI*, I, p. 134: "Women were excluded from the inheritance. A woman had no property of her own; if her husband died, she passed to the family with the inheritance like the Attic epikleros; her earnings, if any, were the property of husband or father." Polyandry is not a primitive institution, and itself depends upon a pre-existing sense of family property. The right of ownership over women is alike conducive to polyandry and levirate, which are in the case of Khasas, as even Joshi, p. 110, concedes, closely interrelated.

Many practices of the *Mahābhārata* age would raise not only eyebrows today, but hostile resentment and even the long arm of the law. That is but an index of the mutability of human affairs. There can, however, be no doubt that the Āryans were fully familiar with polyandry. Though even the caste system has been traced in its embryonic form to pre-Āryan usages,[1] as are the prohibitions relating to marriage within certain degrees of kinship[2], it would be entirely erroneous to presume that the Āryans were either ignorant or innocent of polyandry prior to their contact with the Indian non-Āryan races. They were already a mixed race before they arrived.[3] And their children, speaking Āryan languages, still harbour polyandry or practices akin to it, overtly or covertly, depending on the attitudes of the people around them. Polyandry presupposes a developed sense of private and family property; and though recessive, it is by no means a primitive cultural trait. The rich and the poor alike practise it in regions where it prevails. Ceylonese history attests the polyandry of reigning kings; as does that of Ladakh too.[4]

The mythology of a people doubtless reflects practices with which they are, or were, familiar. This is true as much of the Hindū myths as of the supernatural tales of the Todas.[5] The

[1] Cf. Basham, *The Wonder that was India,* the section on caste.

[2] Cf. Chatterji, S. K., in *The Vedic Age,* p. 167.

[3] Cf. Chattopadhyay, K. P., *Ancient Indian Culture Contacts and Migrations,* Calcutta, 1970.

[4] Cf. Prince Peter, *op. cit.,* p. 515.

[5] According to the Todas, two of their gods, Podzövördjen and Pödjörj, were polyandrous. They were sons of the goddess Terkish and her mortal husband Püth. Both of them married Notirsh, who gave birth to Kwoten, the legendary man-god. This was a case of fraternal polyandry in the divine sphere. Cf. *Ibid.* Prince Peter also speaks of the Kathakali dances he attended, in which scenes from the *Mahābhārata* were depicted, including the story of a twin Aśvin sharing his wife Sūryā with his brother. *Ibid,* p. 58.

ancient Indian texts largely refer to the polyandry only of the brāhmaṇas and kṣatriyas, who naturally attract more attention than the others. Indeed, the brāhmaṇas practise it even today, side by side with the Rājpūts in the holy Himālayas,[1] whence flow the rivers Gangā and Yamunā to fertilize, as to purify, the plains that lie at their feet below.

[1] Higher up in the Himālayas, the Tibetans have delightful phrases to denote their polyandry, such as *ku-tra dre-pa*, i.e., "semen-blood extend"; and *sa-sum-pa*, i.e., "the three who eat together". Cf. *Ibid.*, p. 415.

The compelling logic of necessity often brings cicisbeism, if not polyandry, to the fore. According to Risley, fraternal polyandry was practised by the Venetian nobility of the eighteenth century. Cf. his *The People of India*, Second Edn., Delhi, 1969, p. 133. Linton reports cicisbeism from 20th century U. S. A., where "the secondary husband is usually known as a boarder." Cf. his *The Study of Man*, New York, 1936, pp. 182-3. Prince Peter reports "near-polyandry" practised by the Polish coal-miners in modern France. Cf. Peter, *op. cit.*, p. 62. And now, we hear of a polyandrous proposition from modern Japan: "Wanted: 1000 brides for 8,000 grooms. Young women must be willing to work hard in house and fields. Daily cooking. Also husband's bath preparation. Desire for many children imperative. Must be respectful and obedient to in-laws. Taste for long winters away from town preferable. One-way air-fare provided. Fluent Japanese required. Apply Hokkaido Farmland Bride Liaison Bureau." The *New York Times* reports that there simply are not enough women in the countryside to go around. In a society based on the extended family where each member has his or her assigned duties, many young women are deciding not to have a family, at least not on a farm. They are heading for the big cities. And the single male farmers left behind face the prospect of a family-less life void of heirs and free help.

The flight of girls from the gruelling country routine of work at home and in the fields has posed a painful problem, which the organizations of rural Japan are seeking to solve through 'want' advertisements, posters, pamphlets and group tours. That is how the merry-go-round of life goes on, without being dull for one moment! This information is based on a report published under the caption "Signs of the Times" in *The Pioneer*, Lucknow, March 22, 1978.

Bibliography

A. Sanskrit Texts

Agni Purāṇa of Maharṣi Vedavyāsa. Ed. UPADHYAYA, BALADEVA, *The Kashi Sanskrit Series*, no. 174, Varanasi, 1966.

Aitareya Āraṇyaka. Ed. KEITH, A. B., Oxford, 1909.

Aitareya Brāhmaṇa. Ed. AUFRECHT, THEODOR, Bonn, 1879.

The Aitareya and Kauṣītaki Brāhmaṇas of the Ṛigveda. Tr. KEITH, A. B., *HOS*, vol. 25, Cambridge, Mass,. 1920.

Āpastamba Dharma Sūtra. Ed. SASTRI, A. MAHADEVA, Mysore, 1898.

Āpastamba and Gautama.

The Sacred Laws of the Āryas. Pt. I. Tr. BÜHLER, G., *SBE*, vol. II, Oxford, 1879.

Āpastamba Gṛhya Sūtra.

Grihya-Sūtras. Tr. OLDENBERG, H., *SBE*, vol. XXX, Oxford, 1892.

Āśvalāyana Gṛhya Sūtra. Ed. APTE, V. G., Poona, 1937.
Tr. OLDENBERG, H., *SBE*, vol. XXIX, Oxford, 1886.

Atharva Veda.

Atharva Veda Sanhitā. Herausgegeben von ROTH, R., und WHITNEY, W. D.,... zwelte verbesserte Auflage besorgt von DR. MAX LINDENAU, Berlin, 1924.
Tr. with a Critical Commentary by WHITNEY, W. D. .... revised and...

edited by LANMAN, C. R., *HOS*, vols. 7 and 8, Cambridge, Mass., 1905.

The Hymns of the Atharva Veda. Tr. GRIFFITH, R. T. H., 2 vols., Benares, 1916-17.

Baudhāyana Dharma Sūtra, with the Commentary of Govindasvamī. Ed. SASTRI, A. CHINNASWAMI, *Kashi Sanskrit Series*, no. 104, Varanasi, Saṁ. 1991.
Tr. BÜHLER, G., *SBE*, vol. XIV, Oxford, 1882.

Baudhāyana Gṛhya-Sūtra. Ed. SHAMASASTRI, R., Mysore, 1920.

Bhāgavata Purāṇa. Nirnayasagar Press, Bombay, 1905.

Brahmāṇḍamahāpurāṇaṁ. Sanskrit Text, Bombay, 1906.

Brahma Purāṇaṁ. Ānandāśrama Skt. Series, 28, Poona, 1895.

Bṛhad-devatā, attributed to Śaunaka, A Summary of the Deities and Myths of the Rig-Veda. Parts I and II. Tr. MACDONELL, A. A., *HOS.* vols. 5 and 6, Second Issue, Delhi, 1965.

Bṛhaspatismṛti. Reconstructed by AIYANGAR, K. V. R., *Gaekwad's Oriental Series*, vol. LXXXV, Baroda, 1941.

The Minor Law Books. (Nārada, Bṛhaspati) Part I. Tr. JOLLY, J., *SBE*, vol. XXXIII, Oxford, 1889.

Bṛhat Saṁhitā of Varāhamihira.

Brihat Samhita, with the Commentary of Bhaṭṭotpala. Ed. DVIVEDI, M. M. SUDHAKARA, *The Vizianagram Sanskrit Series*, vol. X, Two Parts., Benares, 1895, 1897.

Caturviṁśatimata-saṁgraha, with the Commentary of Bhaṭṭojī Dīkṣita. Benares, 1907-8.

Chāndogya Upaniṣad. *Ānandāśrama Skt. Series*, vol. 14, Poona, 1902.

Daśakumāracarita of Daṇḍin. — Skt. Text. Ed. GODABOLE, N. B., and PARABA, K. P., Bombay, 1883.

Gautama Dharma Sūtra, with Maskari bhāṣya. — Ed. SRINIVASACHARYA, L., *Government Oriental Library Series*, Mysore, 1917. Tr. BÜHLER, G., *SBE*, II, Oxford, 1879.

Harṣacarita.

The Harshacarita of Bāṇabhaṭṭa, with Exhaustive Notes. — Ed. KANE, P. V., 2nd Edn., Delhi, 1965.

Kāmasūtra.

The Kāmasūtra by Śrī Vātsyāyana Muni, with the Commentary... of Yaśodhara. — Ed. SHASTRI, SRI GOSVAMI DAMODAR, *The Kashi Sanskrit Series*, no. 29, Benares, 1929. Tr. by BURTON, SIR RICHARD, and ARBUTHNOT, F. F., Ed. MUIRHEAD-GOULD, J., London, 1964.

Kathā Sarit Sāgara.

The Ocean of Story, being C. H. Tawney's Translation of Somadeva's Kathā Sarit Sāgara. — Ed. PENZER, N. M. Ten volumes. London, 1924-1928.

Kāṭhaka Saṁhitā.

Kāṭhakaṁ. — Herausgegeben von LEOPOLD VON SCHROEDER. 3 Bde. und Wort-Index von RICHARD SIMON, Leipzig, 1900-1912.

Kauṭilīya Arthaśāstra.

The Kauṭilīya Arthaśāstra. — Sanskrit Text, Ed. KANGLE, R. P., with English Introduction and Translation, First Edn., Bombay, 1960-65; Second Edn., 1969.

Kauṭilya's Arthaśāstra. — Ed. SHAMASASTRI, R., Revised Edn., Mysore, 1924.

	Tr. SHAMASASTRY, R., Fifth Edn., Mysore, 1956.
Kūrma Purāṇa.	Ed. MUKHOPADHYAYA, NILAMANI, *Bibliotheca Indica*, Calcutta, 1913.
Lalitavistara.	Ed. LEFMANN, S., 2 vols., Halle, 1902-08. Tr. MITRA, R. L., *Bibliotheca Indica*, Calcutta, 1886.
Mahābhārata.	For the first time critically edited by SUKTHANKAR, V. S., and others.
The Ādi Parvan.	Ed. SUKTHANKAR, V. S., Poona, 1933.
The Sabhā Parvan.	Ed. EDGERTON, F., Poona, 1944.
The Āraṇyaka Parvan.	Ed. SUKTHANKAR, V. S., Poona, 1942.
The Virāṭa Parvan.	Ed. RAGHUVIRA, Poona, 1936.
The Udyoga Parvan.	Ed. DE, S. K., Poona, 1940.
The Bhīṣma Parvan.	Ed. BELVALKAR, S. K., Poona, 1947.
The Droṇa Parvan.	Ed. DE, S. K., Poona, 1953-58.
The Karṇa Parvan.	Ed. VAIDYA, P. L., Poona, 1954.
The Śalya Parvan.	Ed. DANDEKAR, R. N., Poona, 1961.
The Sauptika and Strī Parvans.	Ed. VELANKAR and PARANJPE, Poona, 1956.
The Śānti Parvan.	Ed. BELVALKAR, S. K., Poona, 1949-1966.
The Anuśāsana Parvan.	Ed. DANDEKAR, R. N., 1963-1966.
The Āśvamedhika Parvan.	Ed. KARMARKAR, R. D., Poona, 1960.
The Āśramavāsika Parvan	Ed. BELVALKAR, S. K., Poona, 1959.
The Mausala Parvan.	Ed. BELVALKAR, S. K., Poona, 1959.
The Mahāprasthānika Parvan.	Ed. BELVALKAR, S. K., Poona, 1959.
The Svargārohaṇa Parvan.	Ed. BELVALKAR, S. K., Poona, 1959.

(All the references in our text, unless otherwise stated, are to this *Critical Edition* of the *Mahābhārata*.)

Mahābhārata.	Bombay Edn., published by KRISHNAJI, G., Bombay, Śaka 1799.

Śrī Mahābhāratam. Ed. ROY, P. C., 3rd Edn., Calcutta, Śaka 1809.

Mahābhārata. Text and trn. by ŚĀSTRĪ, R. N., PĀṆḌEYA, 6 vols., Gita Press, Gorakhpur, Saṁ. 2017-2023.

Mahābhārata. Nirnayasagar Press. Ed. MADHAV Vilas Book Depot, Kumbhakonam, Madras, 1931.

The Mahābhārata The Book of the Beginning. Tr. BUITENEN, J. A. B. VAN, Second Impression, Chicago, 1975.

Maitrāyaṇī Saṁhitā. Herausgegeben von DR. VON SCHROEDER, LEOPOLD, 4 vols., Leipzig, 1881-1886.

Manusmṛti. Ed. JOLLY, J., London, 1887.

The Laws of Manu. Tr. BÜHLER, G., with extracts from seven commentaries, *SBE,* vol. XXV, Oxford, 1886.

Mārkaṇḍeya Purāṇa. Skt. Text. Ed. BANERJEA, K. M., *Bibliotheca Indica,* Calcutta, 1862.

Tr. PARGITER, F. E., *Bibliotheca Indica,* Calcutta, 1888-1904.

Matsya Purāṇam. Skt. Text. Ed. BHATTACHARYA, J. VIDYASAGARA, Calcutta, 1876.

Matsya Purāṇa. *Ānandāśrama Sanskrit Series,* 54, Poona, 1907.

Nārada-Smṛti.

The Minor Law-Books, Part I, Nārada, Brihaspati. Tr. JOLLY, J., *SBE,* vol. XXXIII, Oxford, 1889.

Nirukta of Yāska.

The Nighaṇṭu and the Nirukta. Ed. and tr. SARUP, LAKSHMAN, Delhi, 1967.

The Nirukta of Yāska Muni. Ed. JHA, PT. MUKUND, First Edn., Nirnayasagar Press, Bombay, 1930.

Parāśara-Smṛti. Ed. TARKALANKARA, M. M. CHANDRAKANTA, Sanskrit text, 3 vols., *Bibliotheca*

Indica, Calcutta, 1889.

The Institutes of Parāśara. Tr. BHATTACHARYYA, KRISHNAKAMAL, *Bibliotheca Indica,* Calcutta, 1887.

Pāraskara Gṛhya Sūtra. Tr. OLDENBERG, H., *SBE,* vol. XXIX, Oxford, 1886.

Rājataraṅgiṇī of Kalhaṇa.

Kalhaṇa's Rājataraṅgiṇī, A Chronicle of the Kings of Kashmir. Tr. STEIN, M. A., 2 vols., Westminster, 1900.

Rāmāyaṇa.

Śrīmadvālmīkīya Rāmāyaṇa. 2 vols., 3rd Edn., Gita Press, Gorakhpur, Saṁ. 2033.

Ṛgveda Saṁhitā. Ed. ŚRĪPĀDA ŚARMĀ DĀMODARA SĀTAVALEKAR, Oundh, 1940.

Der Rig-Veda. Aus dem Sanskrit ins Deutsche übersetzt und mit einem laufenden Kommentar versehen von GELDNER, K. F., *HOS,* vols. 33, 34, 35. Cambridge, Mass., 1951.

The Hymns of the Rigveda. Tr. GRIFFITH, R. T. H., with a popular commentary, 2nd Edn., Benares, 1896-97.

(The versified English translations of Ṛgvedic passages in our text have been borrowed from Griffith, with emendations wherever necessary.)

Samayamātṛkā. Ed. PRASAD, DURGA, and PARAB, KASHINATH PANDURANG, Skt. Text. 2nd Edn., Kāvyamāla 10, Bombay, 1925.
Tr. MATHERS, E. P., *Eastern love,* vol. II, 1927.

Śāṅkhāyana Āraṇyaka. Ed. KEITH, A. B., *Anecdota Oxoniensia,* Aryan Series, Part IX, Oxford, 1909.

Tr. KEITH, A. B., *Oriental Translation Fund, New Series*, vol. XVIII, London, 1908.

Śatapatha Brāhmaṇa. Ed. WEBER, A., Berlin-London, 1855.

The Śatapatha Brāhmaṇa according to the text of the Mādhyandina School. Tr. EGGELING. J., 5 vols., *SBE*, vols. XII, XXVI, XLI, XLIII, XLIV, Oxford, 1882-1900.

Smṛticandrikā. Mysore, 1914.

Taittirīya Āraṇyaka. *Ānandāśrama Sanskrit Series,* no. 36, 2 vols., Poona, 1898.

Taittirīya Brāhmaṇa. *Ānandāśrama Sanskrit Series,* no. 37, 3 vols., Poona, 1898.

Taittirīya Saṁhitā.

The Sanhitā of the Black Yajurveda with the Commentary of Mādhava Ācārya. Ed. ROER, E., and COWELL, E. B., vol. I; vol. II, ed. COWELL, E. B.; vols. III, IV, V, ed. NYĀYARATNA, MAHEŚACANDRA; vol. VI, ed. SĀMAŚRAMI, S., *Bibliotheca Indica,* Calcutta, 1860-1899.

Tantravārtika of Kumārilabhaṭṭa. Tr. JHA, G. N., 2 vols., *Bibliotheca Indica,* Calcutta, 1924.

Upaniṣads.

The Principal Upaniṣads. Ed. and tr. RADHAKRISHNAN, S., London, 1953.

Vājasaneyi Saṁhitā Ed. SATAVALEKAR, S. S. D., Oundh, Vikrama Saṁ. 2003.

The Texts of the White Yajurveda... Tr. GRIFFITH, R. T. H., IInd Edn., Benares, 1927.

Varāha Purāṇa Ed. ŚĀSTRĪ, HṚSHĪKEŚA, Skt. Text, *Bibliotheca Indica*, Calcutta, 1893.

Vasiṣṭha Dharma Sūtra. Tr. BÜHLER, G., *SBE*, vol. XIV, Oxford, 1882.

Vāyu Purāṇa. *Ānandāśrama Skt. Series*, 49, Poona, 1905.

Viṣṇu Purāṇa.

Vishṇu Purāṇa, with the Commentary of Śrīdharaswamī. Skt. Text. Ed. VIDYASAGARA, J., Calcutta, 1882.

Vishṇu Purāṇa. Tr. WILSON, H. H., London, 1840. Tr. WILSON, H. H., ed. HALL, F., 5 vols., London, 1864-77.

Śrī Viṣṇu Purāṇa. Text and trn. by GUPTA, M. L., Sixth Edn., Gorakhpur, Saṁ. 2024.

Viṣṇu-Smṛti. Skt. Text, ed. KRISHNAMACHARYA, PT. V., The Adyar Library Series, vol. 93, Madras, 1964. Ed. JOLLY, J., *Bibliotheca Indica*, Calcutta, 1881.

The Institutes of Vishṇu. Tr. JOLLY, J., *SBE*, vol. VII, Oxford, 1880.

Vyākaraṇa-Mahābhāṣya of Patañjali.

Patañjali's Vyākaraṇa-Mahābhāṣya... Skt. Text, ed. JOSHI, S. D., and ROODBERGEN, Poona, 1968.

Yājñavalkya-Smṛti, with the Mitākṣarā Commentary. Bombay, 1909. Tr. BASU, S. C., 1909.

B. Pāli and Prākrit Texts

Āvassaya Cuṇṇi.

Āvaśyaka Cūrṇi. Ascribed to JINADĀSAGAṆI, RUTLAM, 1928.

Dīgha Nikāya. Ed. RHYS DAVIDS, T. W., and CARPENTER, J. E., 3 vols., *PTS*, London, 1890-1911.

Dialogues of the Buddha. Tr. RHYS DAVIDS, T. W., and C. A. F., 3 vols., *PTS*, London, 1899-1921.

Jātaka. Ed. FAUSBÖLL, V., 6 vols., and index, London, 1877-97.

Tr. by various hands, ed. COWELL, E. B., 6 vols. and index, Cambridge, 1895-1907.

Nāyādhammakahāo. Critically ed. VAIDYA, N.V., Poona, 1940.

Nisīha Cuṇṇi.

Nisītha Cūrṇi. Ascribed to Jinadāsagaṇi. Ed. SŪRĪŚVARA, VIJAYA PREMA, Cyclostyled Copy, V. S., 1995.
Mss. from Patan Jain Bhandar.

C. Miscellaneous Sources

Aeschylus.

Aeschyli septem quae supersunt tragoediae. Recensuit MURRAY, G., Editio altera. *Scriptorum Classicorum Bibliotheca Oxoniensis*, Oxford, 1955.

Aeschylus. With an English trn. by SMYTH, H. W., *The Loeb Classical Library*, 2 vols. Cambridge, Mass. and London, 1922-57.

CAESAR, C. JULIUS *Commentarii de bello Gallico.* Ed. LONG, G., London, 1853.

HERODOTUS Ed. PAGE, T. E., and others , *Loeb Edition*, 4 vols. London, 1928.

McCRINDLE, J. W. (Trn.) *Ancient India as described in Classical Literature.* Westminster, 1901.
Ancient India as described by Megasthenes and Arrian (A Translation of the Fragments of the Indika of Megasthenes collected by DR. SCHWANBECK, and of the First Part of the *Indika* of Arrian), London, 1877.

MIGNE, J. P. *Patrologiae Cursus Completus, Series Latina,* 221 vols., Parisiis, 1844-55.

Series Greaeca, 162 vols., Parisiis, 1856-66.

PLATO — *The Republic.* With an English trn. by SHOREY, P., *The Loeb Classical Library*, vols. 11 and 12, London, 1930-35.
Republic. Tr., with an Introduction by LINDSAY, A. D., N. Y., 1950.

PLUTARCH — *Plutarch's Lives.* With an English Trn. by PERRIN, B., *The Loeb Classical Library*, 11 vols., London, 1916-51.

POLYBIUS — *The Histories*, Loeb Edn., London, 1922.

SOPHOCLES — *Sophocles.* With an English trn. by STORR, F., *The Loeb Classical Library*, 2 vols., London, 1924-32.

STRABO — *Strabonis Geographica* (Greek). Recognovit MEINEKE, A., 3 vols. in I, Leipzig, 1866.
Strabonis rerum geographicarum libri XVII...2 vols., Oxonii, 1807.
The Geography of Strabo. With an English trn. by JONES, H. L., The Loeb Classical Library, 8 vols., London, 1917-32.

THEOPOMPOS — *Deipnosophistarum libri quindecim.* CASAUBON J., recens, 2 vols., Lugduni, 1657-64.

WEST, E. W. — *Pahlavi Texts*, Part II, *The Dādistānī-Dīnik and the Epistles of* Mānuskīhar, *SBE*, vol. XVIII, Oxford, 1882.

XENOPHON — *Quae extant*, Ed. SCHNEIDER, I. G., 6 vols., Leipzig, 1821-38.
The Respublica Lacedaemoniorum ascribed to Xenophon..., ed. CHRIMES, afterwards ATKINSON, K. M. T. Manchester, 1948.

XIPHILINUS, JOHANNIS — *Epitome Dionis Cassii.* Ed. REIMARI, Hamburgi, 1752.

D. Reference Books, etc.

Archaeological Survey of India. — *Annual Reports*, Calcutta and Delhi.

BALFOUR, E. — *The Cyclopaedia of India and of Eastern and Southern Asia*, 3 vols., Third Edn., London, 1885.

BÖHTLINCK, O., AND ROTH, R. — *Sanskrit Wörterbuch.* 7 vols., St. Petersburg, 1855-75.

Census of India — Reports.

Encyclopaedia Britannica — 1974.

ROBINSON, VICTOR, (ED.) — *Encylopaedia Sexualis*, 1935.

GRIERSON, SIR G. A. — *Linguistic Survey of India.* 1916.

HASTINGS, J., (ED.) — *Encyclopaedia of Religion and Ethics*, 12 vols., Edinburgh, 1908-26.

MACDONELL, A. A. AND KEITH, A. B. — *Vedic Index of Names and Subjects*, 2 vols., London, 1912.

MALALASEKERA, G. P. — *Dictionary of Pali Proper Names*, 2 vols., London, 1974.

MONIER WILLIAMS, SIR M. — *Sanskrit-English Dictionary*, New Edn., Oxford, 1960.

Royal Anthropological Institute. — *Notes and Queries on Anthropology*, 6th edn., 1951, reprinted 1954.

SÖRENSEN, S. — *An Index to the Names in the Mahābhārata with short Explanations*... London, 1904.

WALKER, B. — Hindu World, 2 vols., London, 1968.

E. Monographs and Articles

ADAMS, M. S., AND NEEL, J. V. — "Children of Incest", *Pediatrics*, 1967, vol. 40, pp. 55-62.

AGRAWALA, V. S. *A Catalogue of the Brahmanical Images in Mathura Art, UPHS*, Lucknow, 1951.

AIYAPPAN, A. "Fraternal Polyandry in Malabar", *Man in India*, vol. XV, II, 1935.
"Nayar Polyandry", *Man*, vol. 32, no. 99, 1932.

ALLAN, J. *Catalogue of the Coins of Ancient India* (in the British Museum), London, 1936.

ALTEKAR, A. S. *The Position of Women in Hindu Civilization*, 2nd Edn., Delhi, 1973.

APTE, V. M. *Social and Religious life in the Grihya Sūtras*, Reset Edn., Bombay, 1954.

ATKINSON, E. T. *The Himalayan Gazetteer*, Allahabad, 1882.
N. W. P. Gazetteers, vols. X, XI, XII, 1884.

BACHOFEN, J. J. *Das Mutterrecht: Eine Untersuchung über die Gynaikikritie der alten Welt nach ihrer religiosen und rechtlichen Natur*, Stuttgart, 1861.

BAINES, SIR J. ATHELSTAINE *Ethnography (Castes and Tribes)...* Strassburg, 1912.

BASHAM, A. L. *The Wonder that was India*, London, 1961.
(Ed.) *A Cultural History of India*, Oxford, 1975.

BÁSIT, GHULÁM "Tárikh-i Mamálik-i Hind", in ELLIOT'S *The History of India as told by its own Historians*, vol. VIII, London, 1877.

BIDDULPH, J. *Tribes of the Hindoo Koosh*, Calcutta, 1880.

BRIFFAULT, R. *The Mothers*, 3 vols., London, 1927.

BURROW, T. "The Proto-Indo-Aryans", *JRAS*, 1973, pp. 123-140.

CALAND, W. *Altindischer Ahnencult*, Leiden, 1893.

CHAKLADAR, H. C. *Social Life in Ancient India: Studies in Vātsyāyana's Kāmasūtra*, Greater India Society Publication no. 3, Calcutta, 1929.

CHATTERJI, S. K. "Polyglottism in Indo-Aryan", *Seventh Oriental Conference*, pp. 177-189. "Non-Aryan Elements in Indo-Aryan, *Journal of the Greater India Society*, Calcutta, vol. III.

CHATTOPADHYAY, K. P. "On Polyandry", *Journal of the Asiatic Society of Bengal, Science*, vol. XXII, no. 2, 1957.

Ancient Indian Culture Contacts and Migrations, Calcutta, 1970.

CHAUCER, GEOFFREY *The Works of Geoffrey Chaucer*, ed. ROBINSON, F. N., Second Edn., Oxford, 1974.

COSER, R. L. (ED.) *The Family : Its Structure and Functions*, New York, 1964.

CROOKE, W. *Tribes and Castes of the North-Western Provinces and Oudh*, 4 vols., Calcutta, 1896.

CUNNINGHAM, A. *Cunningham's Ancient Geography of India*, ed. MAJUMDAR, SASTRI, S., Calcutta, 1924.

Ladak, London, 1854.

DANDEKAR, R. N. "Vṛtrahā Indra", *ABORI*, vol. 31, 1950, pp. 1-55.

DAS, R. M. *Women in Manu and his seven Commentators*, Varanasi, 1962.

DAS, S. C. *A Journey to Lhasa and Central Tibet*, London, 1904.

"The Marriage Customs of Tibet",

JASB, vol. LXII, Part II, Calcutta, 1893.

DELBRÜCK, BERTHOLD — "Die indogermanischen Verwandtschaftsnamen", *Abhandlungen der Königlichen Sächsischen Gesellschaft der Wissenschaften*, vol. XXV, Leipzig, 1890.

DEY, N. L. — *Geographical Dictionary of Ancient and Mediaeval India*, 2nd Edn., London, 1927.

DIAKONOV, I. M. — *Istoriya Midii*, Moscow, 1956.

DOUIE, SIR J. M. (ED.) — *Gazetteer of the Karnal District*, Lahore, 1892.

DÜBEN, G. VON. — *Om Lappland och Lapparne*, Stockholm, 1873.

EBELING, E. — *Bruchstücke einer mittelassyrischen Vorschriftensammlung für die Akklimatisierung und Trainierung von Wagenpferden*, Berlin, 1951.

EISENMENGER, J. A. — *Entdecktes Judenthum*, 2 vols., Frankfurt, 1700.

ELLIOT, H. M. — *The History of India as told by its own Historians*, ed. Dowson, J., 8 vols., London, 1867-1877.

ENGELS, F. — *The Origin of the Family, Private Property and the State*, London, 1884.

FERISHTA, MUHAMMAD KASIM — *History of the Rise of the Mahomedan Power in India*, Tr. BRIGGS, JOHN, 4 vols., London, 1829.

FIELDING, WILLIAM J. — *Strange Customs of Courtship and Marriage*, London, 1961.

FISCHER, H. TH. — "Polyandry", *International Archives for Ethnography*, vol. XLVI, Leiden, 1952.

FLEET, J. F. — *Corpus Inscriptionum Indicarum*, vol. III, Varanasi, 1970.

FORTUNE, R. F. "Incest", in Coser, R. L. (ed.), *The Family : Its Structure and Functions*, New York, 1964, pp. 70-74.

FOX, J. R. "Sibling Incest", *British Journal of Sociology*, 1962, 13, pp. 128-150.

FREUD, SIGMUND *Totem and Taboo*, in *The Basic Writings of Sigmund Freud*, ed. BRILL, A. A., New York, 1938, pp. 807-930.

Moses and Monotheism, New York, 1955.

FROMM, E. *The Art of Loving*, New York, 1963.

FÜRER-HAIMENDROF, C. VON *The Sherpas of Nepal*, London, 1964.

(Ed.) *Caste and Kin in Nepal, India and Ceylon*, Bombay, 1966.

GIERKE, O. VON *Der Humor in deutschen Recht*, Berlin, 1871.

GJERSET, K. *History of the Norwegian Peoples*, 2 vols., New York, 1915.

GOGUET, A. Y. *The Origin of Laws, Arts and Sciences*, 3 vols., Edinburgh, 1761.

GOPAL, RAM *India of the Vedic Kalpasūtras*, Delhi, 1959.

GOUGH, KATHLEEN E. "The Nayars and the Definition of Marriage", *Journal of the Royal Anthropological Institute*, vol. 89, pt. I, 1959.

GRÉNARD, F., AND DETREUILLE DE RHINS, J. L. *Mission Scientifique dans la Haute Asie 1890-95. IIème Partie : le Turkestan et le Tibet*, Paris, 1898.

GRIERSON, SIR G. A. Review of T. BAILEY's *The Languages of the Northern Himalayas, being Studies in the Grammar of twentysix Himalayan Dialects*, in *JRAS*, 1909, pp. 184 sqq.

GRIMM, J. L. C. *Deutsche Rechtsalterthümer*, Göttingen, 1828.

GRISWOLD, H. D. *The Religion of the Ṛgveda*, London, 1923.

HARTLAND, E. S. *Primitive Paternity*, 2 vols., London, 1909-10.

HAYS, H. R. *From Ape to Angel, An Informal History of Social Anthropology*, New York, 1960.

HENNINGER, J. "Polyandrie in Vor-Islamische Arabien", *Anthropos*, 1954.

HILLEBRANDT, ALFRED *Vedische Mythologie*, 3 vols., Breslau, 1891-1902.

HOBHOUSE, L. T., WHEELER, G. C., AND GINSBERG, M. *The Material Culture and Social Institutions of the Simpler Peoples*, London, 1917.

HOPKINS, E W. "The Social and Military Position of the Ruling Caste in Ancient India as represented by the Sanskrit Epic", *JAOS*, 13, 1889, pp. 57-329.

Religions of India, London, 1895.

Epic Mythology, Delhi, 1972.

Ethics of India, New Haven, 1924.

HORNER, I. B. *Women under Primitive Buddhism*, London, 1930.

HUPPÉ, BERNARD F. *A Reading of Canterbury Tales*, New York, 1964.

HUTTON, J. H. *Census of India*, 1931, Vol. I, Part I, 1933 Edn.

Caste in India, Cambridge, 1946.

The Angami Nagas, Second Edn., Bombay, 1969.

IBBETSON, SIR DENZIL C. J. *Report on the Census of the Punjab*... 1881, 3 vols., Calcutta, 1883.

IYER, L. K., ANANTHA KRISHNA "Nayar Polyandry," *Man*, vol. 32, 1932, no. 320.

The Cochin Tribes and Castes, vols. I and II, Madras, 1909.

Travancore Castes and Tribes, Trivandrum, 1937.

JAIN, JAGDISH CHANDRA *Life in Ancient India as depicted in the Jain Canons*, Bombay, 1947.

JAISWAL, SUVIRA *The Origin and Development of Vaiṣṇavism*, Delhi, 1967.

JAYAL, S. *The Status of Women in the Epics*, Delhi, 1966.

JOLLY, J. "Recht und Sitte", in *Grundriss der Indo-Arischen Philologie*, Strassburg, 1896.

Hindu Law and Custom, Calcutta, 1928.

JOSHI, L. D. *The Khasa Family Law in the Himalayan Districts of the United Provinces, India*, Allahabad, 1929.

KANE, P. V. *History of Dharmaśāstra*, 5 vols., 2nd Edn., 1968-1977.

KAPADIA, K. M. *Marriage and Family in India*, Third Edn., Bombay, 1966.

KARVE, IRAVATI *Kinship Organization in India*, 2nd Edn., Bombay, 1965.

KHAN, AHMAD HASAN KHAN *Census of India*, 1931, vol. XVII, Punjab, Part I, 1933 Edn.

KIRKPATRICK C. S. "Polyandry in the Panjab", *Ind. Ant.* VII, Bombay, 1878.

KONOW, STEN "The Aryan gods of the Mitanni People", *Kristiania Etnografiske Museums Skrifter* Bind 3 Hefte I; Kristiania, 1921.

KRONASSER, H. "Indisches in den Nuzi Texten", *Wiener Zeitschrift für die Kunde des Morgenlandes*, vol. LIII, 1957, pp. 181 ff.

LAW, B. C. *Some Jaina Canonical Sūtras*, Bombay

Branch of the Royal Asiatic Society Monograph no. 2, Bombay, 1949.

LEACH, E. R. "Polyandry, Inheritance and the Definition of Marriage with particular reference to Sinhalese Customary Law", *Man*, vol. 55, no. 199, 1955.

LÉVI-STRAUSS, CLAUDE "Reciprocity the Essence of Social Life," in COSER, R. L. (ed.). *The Family : Its Structure and Functions*, New York, 1964.

The Elementary Structures of Kinship, Revised Edn., translated from the French by BELL, J. H., STURMER, J. R. VON, and NEEDHAM, R., Editor, Boston, 1969.

LINTON, RALPH *The Study of Man*, New York, 1936.

LIPPERT, JULIUS *Kulturgeschichte der Menschheit*, 2 vols. Stuttgart, 1886-87.

LUBBOCK, SIR J. *The Origin of Civilization and the Primitive Condition of Man*, 5th Edn., New York, 1892.

MCCULLOCH, J. A. *The Religion of the Ancient Celts*, Edinburgh, 1911.

MCGOVERN, WILLIAM MONTGOMERY *The Early Empires of Central Asia*... Chapel Hill, North Carolina, 1939.

MACLAGAN, E. D. "The Punjab and its Feudatories", *Census of India*, 1891, vol. XIX, Calcutta, 1892.

MCLENNAN, J. F. *Primitive Marriage, An Inquiry into the Origin of the Form of Capture in Marriage Ceremonies* (originally published in Edinburgh, 1865), ed. Rivière, P., Chicago, 1970.

Studies in Ancient History, London, 1886;

The Second Series, London and New York, 1896.

MAINE, H. J. S. — *Ancient Law*, London, 1861.

MAJUMDAR, D. N. — "Some Aspects of the Cultural Life of the Khasas of the cis-Himalayan Region", *Journal and Proceedings of the Royal Asiatic Society of Bengal*, Third Series, vol. VI, 1940, pp. I ff.

The Matrix of Indian Culture, Lucknow, 1947.

Himalayan Polyandry, Bombay, 1962.

Races and Cultures of India, Fourth Revised and Enlarged Edn., Bombay, 1973.

MAJUMDAR, R. C. (ed.) — *The Vedic Age*, Fourth Impression, Bombay, 1965.

MAJUMDAR, R. C., RAYCHAUDHURI, H. C., and DATTA, K. K. — *An Advanced History of India*, London, 1948.

Ancient India, Part I of the above, London, 1949.

MALINOWSKI, B. — *Sex and Repression in Savage Society*, London, 1927.

The Sexual Life of Savages, London, 1932.

Sex, Culture and Myth, London, 1963.

"Parenthood, the Basis of Social Structure", in COSER, R. L. (ed.), *The Family : Its Structure and Functions*, New York, 1964.

MANDELBAUM, D. G. — "Polyandry in Kota Society", *American Anthropologist*, vol. 40, no. 4, 1938.

MAURER, G. L. von — *Geschichte der Dorfverfassung in Deutschland*, 2 vols., Erlangen, 1865-66.

MAYR, A. — *Das indische Erbrecht*, Wien, 1873.

MAYRHOFER, M. — *Die Indo-Arier im alten Vorderasien*, Wiesbaden, 1966.

MEISSNER, BRUNO — *Babylonien und Assyrien*, 2 vols., Heidelberg, 1920-25.

MEYER, J. J. — *Sexual Life in Ancient India.........*, 2 vols., London, 1930.

MIDDLETON, R. — "Brother-sister and Father-daughter Marriage in Ancient Egypt", *American Sociological Review*, 1926, 27, pp. 603-611.

MILLS, J. P. — *The Lhota Nagas*, London, 1922.

MONIER-WILLIAMS, SIR M. — *Indian Epic Poetry*, London, 1873.

MORGAN, L. H. — *Ancient Society, or Researches in the Lives of Human Progress from Savagery, through Barbarism to Civilization*, New York, 1877.

MORRIS, D. — *The Naked Ape*, London, 1968.

MUIR, J. — "On the Question whether Polyandry ever existed in Northern Hindustan" *Ind. Ant.*, VI, pp. 315 sq.

MÜLLER, F. MAX — *Biographies of Words and the Home of the Aryas*, London, 1888.

MURDOCK, G. P. — *Social Structure*, New York, 1949.

MURSTEIN, B. I. — *Love, Sex and Marriage through the Ages*, New York, 1974.

NAKANE, CHIE — "A Plural Society in Sikkim: A study of the Interrelations of the Lepchas, Bhotias and Nepalis", in Fürer-Haimendorf (ed.), *Caste and Kin in Nepal, India and Ceylon*, Bombay, 1966.

PANIKKAR, K. M. — "Some Aspects of Nayar Life", *JRAI*, vol. XLVIII.

PARMAR, Y. S. — *Polyandry in the Himalayas*, Delhi, 1975.

PELLISON, M. — *Roman Life in Pliny's Time*, (trans.), Meadville, Pennsylvania, 1897.

PETER, PRINCE OF Greece and Denmark — *A Study of Polyandry*, The Hague, 1963.

PIDDINGTON, RALPH — *An Introduction to Social Anthropology,* vol. I, 1950.

PINKHAM, M. W. — *Woman in the Sacred Scriptures of Hinduism,* New York, 1941.

PISCHEL, R., and GELDNER, K. F. — *Vedische Studien,* 3 vols., Stuttgart, 1888-91.

PRZYLUSKI, J. — "Emprunts anaryens en Indo-aryes", *Le Monde Oriental,* vol. 28, 1934, pp, 140 ff. "Hippokoura et Satakarni", *JRAS,* 1929, pp. 273 ff.

"Satvant, Sātvata and Nāsatya", *IHQ.* IX, 1933, pp. 88-91.

"Asses, Horses and Gandharvas", *Indian Culture,* vol. 3, 1936-37, pp. 613-620.

RADCLIFFE-BROWN, A. R. — "The Study of Kinship Systems", *JRAI,* vol. LXXXI, 1941.

RAO, T. A. GOPINATHA — *Elements of Hindu Iconography,* vol. I, Madras, 1914; vol. II (two parts), Madras, 1916.

RAPSON, E. J. (ed.) — *Cambridge History of India,* vol. 1, Cambridge, 1922.

RAYCHAUDHURI, H. C. — *Materials for the Study of the Early History of the Vaiṣṇava Sect,* Calcutta, 1936.

Political History of Ancient India, Vth Edn., Calcutta, 1950.

RÉMUSAT, J. P. A. — *Nouveaux mélanges asiatiques,* 2 vols., Paris, 1830.

RISLEY, Sir H. H. — *The People of India,* Second Edn., Delhi. 1969.

RIVERS, W. H. R. — *The Todas,* London, 1906.

Social Organization, New York, 1924.

ROSE, H. A. — *A Glossary of the Tribes and Castes of the Punjab and North-West Frontier Province,* 3 vols., Lahore, 1911-19.

RUSSELL, R. V. *The Tribes and Castes of the Central Provinces of India*, 4 vols., London, 1916.

SACHAU, E. C. (ed.) *Alberuni's India,* Two vols. in one, Delhi, 1964.

SAKSENA, R. N. *Social Economy of a Polyandrous People,* Agra University Studies Series, No. 1, Agra, 1956.

SARKAR, S. C. *Some Aspects of the Earliest Social History of India (Pre-Buddhist Ages),* London, 1928.

SCHRADER, OTTO. *Prehistoric Antiquities of the Aryan Peoples...* tr. JEVONS, F. B.,.... from the second edn., with the cooperation of the author. London, 1890.

SCHULL, W. J., and NEEL, J. V. *The Effects of Inbreeding on Japanese Children,* New York, 1965.

SINGH, SARVA DAMAN *Ancient Indian Warfare with Special Reference to the Vedic Period,* Leiden, 1965.

SLATER, M. K. "Ecological Factors in the Origin of Incest", *American Anthropologist,* 1959, vol. 61, pp. 1042-1059.

SLOTKIN, J. S. "On a possible Lack of Incest Regulations in Old Iran", *American Anthropologist,* 1947, vol. 49, pp. 612-615.

SMITH, W. ROBERTSON *Kinship and Marriage in Early Arabia,* New Edn., London, 1903.

SPECHT, E. "Étude sur l'Asi centrale d' après les historiens chinois", *Journal Asiatique,* 8e Sèrie, X, pp. 338 ff., Paris, 1883.

SPENCER, H. *The Principles of Sociology,* 3 vols., 3rd Edn., New York, 1921.

STARCKE, C. N. *The Primitive Family in its Origin and Development,* London, 1889.

STOKES, WHITLEY — "On the death of Some Irish Heroes", *Revue Celtique,* XXIII, Paris, 1902.

SUMNER, WILLIAM GRAHAM. — *Folkways,* Boston, 1940.

SUMNER, W. G., and KELLER, A. G. — *The Science of Society,* 4 vols., New Haven, 1927.

SYKES, SIR P. — *A History of Persia,* 2 vols., London, 1921.

TAMBIAH, S. J. — "Polyandry in Ceylon with Special Reference to the Laggala Region", in Fürer-Haimendorf (ed.), *Caste and Kin in Nepal, India and Ceylon,* Bombay, 1966.

THIEME, PAUL — "The 'Aryan' gods of the Mitanni Treaties", *JAOS*, 80, 1960, pp. 301 ff.

THOMAS, P. — *Indian Women through the Ages,* London, 1964.

THURNEYSEN, R. — *Die irische Helden-und Königsage biss zum siebzichten Jahrhundert,* Halle, 1921.

TOD, J. — *Annals and Antiquities of Rajasthan, or the Central and Western Rajpoot States of India,* 2 vols., London, 1829.

UPADHYAYA, B. S. — *Women in the Ṛgveda,* 3rd Edn., Delhi, 1974.

UTGIKAR, N. B. — "The Story of the Dasaratha Jātaka and of the Rāmāyaṇa", *JRAS, Centenary Supplement,* 1924, pp. 203-211.

VINOGRADOFF SIR P. — *Outlines of Historical Jurisprudence,* 2 vols., New York, 1920.

VON SCHROEDER — *Indiens Literatur und Cultur in historischer Entwicklung*.....Leipzig, 1887.

VORA, D. P. — *Evolution of Morals in the Epics,* Bombay, 1959.

WATTERS, THOMAS — *On Yuan Chwang's Travels in India,* Ed. RHYS DAVIDS, T. W., and BUSHELL,

S.W., with two Maps and an Itinerary by SMITH, V. A., Two vols., Second Indian Edn., Delhi, 1973.

WEBER, A. — *Indische Studien,* V, Berlin, 1861; IX, Leipzig, 1865; X, Leipzig, 1868.

WEINHOLD, K. — *Altnordisches Leben,* Berlin, 1856.

WESTERMARCK, E. — *The History of Human Marriage,* Third Edn., London, 1901.

The History of Human Marriage, 3 vols., London, 1921.

WILKS, MARK. — *Historical Sketches of the South of India in an attempt to trace the History of Mysoor: from the origin of the Hindoo Government of that state to the Extinction of the Mohammedan Dynasty in* 1799......., 2 vols., Mysore, 1930-32.

WINDISCH, W. O. E. — *Irische Texte mit Wörterbuch,* 4 Series, Leipzig, 1880-1909.

WINTERNITZ, M. — *Die Frau in den indischen Religionen....I Teil : Die Frau im Brahmanismus,* Leipzig, 1920.

"Notes on the 'Mahābhārata', with special Reference to Dahlmann's 'Mahābhārata'," *JRAS,* 1897, pp. 716 ff.

ZIMMER, H. — *Altindisches Leben,* Berlin, 1879.

Index